AN ALGEBRA OF SOVIET POWER

Soviet and East European Studies

Series list continues on p. 180

AN ALGEBRA OF SOVIET POWER

Elite circulation in the Belorussian Republic 1966–86

MICHAEL E. URBAN

Professor of Political Science
Auburn University

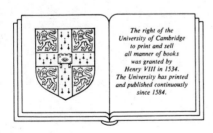

The right of the
University of Cambridge
to print and sell
all manner of books
was granted by
Henry VIII in 1534.
The University has printed
and published continuously
since 1584.

CAMBRIDGE UNIVERSITY PRESS

Cambridge
New York   Port Chester   Melbourne   Sydney

Published by the Press Syndicate of the University of Cambridge
The Pitt Building, Trumpington Street, Cambridge CB2 1RP
40 West 20th Street, New York, NY 10011, USA
10 Stamford Road, Oakleigh, Melbourne 3166, Australia

© Cambridge University Press 1989

First published 1989

Printed and bound in Great Britain by
Redwood Burn Limited, Trowbridge, Wiltshire

British Library cataloguing in publication data
Urban, Michael E.
An algebra of Soviet power: elite circulation in the
Belorussian Republic, 1966–86 – (Soviet and East European
studies; 67)
1. Soviet Union. Political elites
I. Title   II. Series
322.4′3′0947

Library of Congress cataloguing in publication data
Urban, Michael E., 1947–
An algebra of Soviet power: elite circulation in the
Belorussian Republic, 1966–86/Michael E. Urban
        p.   cm. – (Soviet and East European studies: 67)
Bibliography.
Includes index.
ISBN 0-521-37256-9
1. Belorussian S.S.R. – Officials and employees.
2. Elite (Social sciences) – Belorussian S.S.R.
3. Social mobility – Belorussian S.S.R.
4. Belorussian S.S.R. – Politics and government.
I. Title.   II. Series.
JN6646.Z1U74 1989
305.5′2′094785 – dc20   89-1038 CIP

ISBN 0 521 37256 9

CE

To Veronica, Emily and George

Contents

Figures and tables

FIGURES

TABLES

Preface

This book probably got started in Moscow some eight years ago. Its immediate occasion was yet another bout of insomnia, induced this time not by one of the usual offenders – heartaches, backaches and financial woes – but by the insistence of a single nagging question which I found myself helpless to avoid: How does this system work? Moments on the street, in the office, in the cafeteria taught me what I had learned and not learned through years in the classroom and the library, namely, that, although I might know a number of things about the Soviet Union, when it came to its basic 'laws of motion' I was drawing a blank. I simply had not developed concepts that could make sense of the confusing variety of experiences that I was undergoing. I lacked a method that was adequate to the task.

While this book is by no means an attempt to address in full the fundamentals of the Soviet order, it does have a few ambitions along these lines. Accordingly, one of its aims is to take method seriously. By 'method' I have in mind no more than a particular way of looking at the world that specifies *ex ante* how we might compose what would otherwise be a welter of discordant perceptions into a comprehensible system of ideas and facts. By this measure, of course, we are always relying on method, whether we are reading a newspaper or writing a book on Soviet elites. My point is simply to acknowledge this reliance and, in so doing, to take it, again, seriously.

In my view, such an orientation toward method neither implies that the object of analysis disappears behind abstractions, nor that it represents a mere vessel to be fashioned and refashioned in order to accommodate some purely methodological exercise. If anything, the reverse is true. Method might be regarded as the vessel and its utility consists precisely in its capacity to contain the object of our interest. Further, we can no more divorce the object from the method which constitutes it than we can the perception from the perceiver. Method functions in such a way as to link the object of our interest to our interest in the object. Through it, we organize our data according to the categories that we provide for them. Method is our eyes.

This book undertakes a structural study of elite circulation in the Belorussian Republic of the USSR over the years 1966–86. The idea of structure as used here should not be confused with that of formal organizational relations, although the two at times may coincide. Instead, the concept of structure represents an analytic orientation away from viewing the fundamental features of the social world as reducible to individuals and toward a perspective in which the relations among them, ordered or 'structured' in particular ways, become the primary focus of attention. As such, this study, while looking at the Belorussian political elite, is little concerned to describe those individuals who have held power. For good or ill, the reader will not find presented here the sort of data – namely, the personal attributes of individual officeholders – ordinarily encountered in studies of Soviet elites. Stranger still, this is a book about an elite in one of the national republics of the USSR that includes no data on the respective nationalities of the elite's members. The reason for these omissions is simple enough. Rather than a description of the personnel who have held power, the purpose of this study is to describe the personnel system itself as a set of power relations and to inquire into the matter of how it is structured. As a consequence, the candidates for the role of structuring factors which have been identified in more conventional works on Soviet elites – central control, regional influences, and patronage relations – appear in a rather unconventional light. They are not regarded as operating directly on individual actors but on the set of relations that bind the actors into a system.

The narrative is designed to move from the macro- to the micro-level. It thereby introduces individual actors, who appear more and more frequently as the discussion proceeds, in the context of those relations in which their actions are embedded. Chapter 1 sets out in some detail the methodology which the book follows and develops a model for elite analysis congruent with this orientation by contrasting it to the model that has been commonly employed in the field. Appended to the end of this chapter is a brief description of this study's site, the Belorussian Republic, which outlines the salient historical factors bearing upon the analysis of the Belorussian elite in the contemporary period.

Chapter 2 is an exercise in elite stratification. Here, the idea of relations is used to construct a hierarchy of offices in the Republic required for subsequent stages of analysis. Specifically, the relations among offices is translated as the mobility of the actors who move among them. The offices themselves are then ranked according to their respective distances from an uppermost stratum of positions, with 'distance' measured by the mobility patterns of their incumbents. When a specified probability exists that the holder of a given office can enter some position ranked in a stratum somewhere above him, then the office which he occupies is ranked at one remove from (one stratum below) the stratum which he has a certain probability of reaching.

With a hierarchical ranking of offices in place, ensuing chapters take up the heart of the empirical analysis, viz., the influences of centralization, regionalism and patronage on the circulation of elites in the system. Chapter 3, which tests for the centralizing effect, introduces into Soviet elite studies the method of vacancy chain analysis. This method abstracts from individuals, their attributes and the jobs that they hold at a particular time in order to determine, in this instance, whether the mobility patterns of the actors are systematically shaped by the influence of the centralized *nomenklatura*. In the same way that the foregoing chapter distinguishes between the nominal rank of an office and its rank as determined by the probability for upward mobility empirically associated with it, this approach distinguishes between nominal (the formal appointments mechanism) and effective centralization and finds that the latter is of remarkably little consequence in shaping the circulation process.

Chapter 4 replaces the framework of hierarchically ordered strata of positions with the category of region and repeats the analysis. It finds that a regionally based model of mobility is able to predict the movement of personnel in the system with a considerable degree of accuracy. Certain characteristics of the system when viewed in regional terms, however, cannot be explained without recourse to the stratified model of positions and the personal connections among the actors that link them together into patronage groups.

Patronage is the topic of Chapter 5. With the results of the foregoing vacancy chain analyses of macro-level characteristics of the personnel system as a frame of reference, the discussion shifts at this point toward the micro-level and focuses the vacancy approach on individual actors whose mobility patterns evince mutual linkages that suggest the presence of patronage ties. The data are subjected to two techniques for discerning patronage affiliations and the patronage groupings thereby identified become categories for carrying the investigation further along the route of micro-level analysis in the chapters that follow.

Chapter 6 examines the influence of patronage ties on three sets of events within the system. It seeks to determine, first, whether affiliation with a given patronage group accounts for differential rates of mobility in the system for those entering through various recruitment channels. Secondly, it inquires into the career chances of a particular sub-group of actors, women, in order to determine whether these are affected by the respective patronage groups with which various female politicians have been associated. Finally, it takes up the matter of what might be called 'negative sanctions' – officially voiced criticism, reprimands and publicly announced dismissals from office – and asks whether patronage ties account for the rates at which negative sanctions have been deployed and the effects which they have had.

Chapter 7 discusses the political succession that took place in Belorussia over the latter years of this study. Here, the factional affiliations based on patronage ties are found to be the salient factor in structuring the competition for office and in shaping the eventual outcome. Moreover, since the succession in Belorussia began some two years before the Brezhnev succession in Moscow, this episode in many respects appears as a diminutive forerunner of the events that subsequently transpired in the Soviet capital. Although the Brezhnev succession ultimately determined certain aspects of the succession in Belorussia, the analysis here shows that the personnel system in the Republic cannot accurately be regarded as a collection of mere effects which issue from some primary cause located in the Kremlin. Rather, the process of elite circulation in Belorussia, taken in this case as leadership replacement, has its own structure and moves largely according to its own rhythms. In the end, these indigenous factors have proven to be the decisive ones in accounting for the transfer of power from one group to another. Or so it would seem, at least, when we follow a method that privileges the forest over the tree, that enables us to see actors in their relational aspect and to study these relations in their own right.

Acknowledgements

It has been my good fortune throughout the period that I have worked on this book to have received much valuable criticism, advice and encouragement from a number of very capable people. The conception of the project benefited from discussions with Dave Willer, Bob Antonio, Jerry Hough, Harrison White and Dan Nelson. I owe a particular debt of gratitude to those who read and commented on my work as it progressed. In particular, I would like to thank Ron Hill, Stephen White, Joel Moses, George Breslauer, David Lane, Alastair McAuley, Gene Huskey, Nick Lampert, Larry O'Toole, John Heilman and Rachel Walker.

Assistance of another sort came from a second group of individuals. Bruce Reed supplied not only some very creative computer programming for the vacancy chain analysis but an understanding ear and some sound advice on many aspects of the project. Vlad Toumanoff, Lee Sigelman and Michael Holdsworth lent their encouragement to me at times when it mattered most. Vitaut and Zora Kipel made available to me their knowledge of both Belorussia and Belorussian materials. Virginia Prickett typed successive drafts of the manuscript with the skill familiar to those who know her.

I am grateful for the funding provided to this project by the National Council for Soviet and East European Research and the National Science Foundation under Grant SES–8618055. I wish to thank Gerald Johnson and Robert Montjoy, each of whom as my Department Head at Auburn University slew bureaucratic monsters on my behalf. For permission to reprint portions of my work that have previously been published elsewhere, my appreciation goes to Edward Elgar and the editors of *Slavic Review* and *British Journal of Political Science*. The works in question are: 'Elite Stratification and Mobility in a Soviet Republic', David Lane (ed.) *Elites and Political Power in the USSR* (Aldershot:

Edward Elgar, 1988); 'Regionalism in a Systems Perspective: Explaining Elite Circulation in a Soviet Republic', *Slavic Review*, Vol. 48 (Fall, 1989); 'Centralization and Elite Circulation in a Soviet Republic', *British Journal of Political Science*, Vol. 19 (Jan. 1989).

1 Method, model and historical background

This chapter aims to locate the method, model and object of this study within the field of research devoted to the analysis of Soviet political elites. The first section examines the matter of setting or context with a basic theoretical question in mind; namely, how might we conceptualize the set of sociopolitical relations extant in the USSR which both defines the system's elite(s) and structures their activity? Here, our concern is to probe the characteristics of the Soviet form of organization and, in so doing, to highlight some of the issues associated with elite analysis in the Soviet case.

The second section covers much the same ground from a methodological perspective. It presents an outline of the method and model heretofore employed in Soviet elite studies, and argues that the conventional approach, which focuses on individual actors and their attributes, is hampered by some important limitations on the questions that it can pose and the conclusions that it can reasonably draw. In order to overcome these shortcomings, a method is introduced which directly incorporates into the analysis the relations among actors in the system as they circulate through the array of elite positions. This method, vacancy chain analysis, and a revised model for the study of Soviet elites are then explicated in some detail.

Finally, the third section places the object of our study, political elites in the Belorussian Soviet Socialist Republic (BSSR), in an historical perspective. It takes up those national, socioeconomic and political features of Belorussia's development which bear upon the empirical analysis of elites in the contemporary BSSR.

Bureaucracy, personnel and the Soviet form of organization

Bureaucracy, as Max Weber appreciated so well, is a highly refined and singularly effective system of power. In contrast to the

1

tendency in much contemporary scholarship to interpret the concept of bureaucratic power narrowly, as the enlarged influence displayed by formal organizations in the political life of this or that nation state, Weber's concern was to understand bureaucracy itself as a form of life whose logic worked in the direction of rationalized social control through an impersonal mechanism that represented the last word in both task accomplishment and human domination.[1] The adjective 'impersonal' is of particular importance to the issue of bureaucratic power as Weber saw it. On the one hand, the empirical characteristics of modern bureaucracy – the location of authority in offices rather than in individuals, the organization and gradation of such authority according to written rules and so forth – emerged out of deep changes in the structure of social relations which accompanied the passing of traditional society.[2] Foremost among these was the introduction of commodity relations endemic to the capitalist market economy.[3] As Marx understood, relations of this type are in fact social relations which appear as relations among mere things.[4] But it was Weber who pursued the implications that this insight held for human organizations in the modern world. In modern bureaucracy, in which individual action transpires through the medium of an impersonalized, rule-bound structure of authority, he discovered the human embodiment of thing-like relations. Individuals operating within the bureaucratic mode of organization find that their activity always reduces to something outside themselves – the job description, the work schedule – epitomized in the balance sheet of the capitalist firm and its celebrated 'bottom line'. Relations of this sort enable the thinking parts of bureaucracy to think in characteristically bureaucratic fashion, calculating costs and benefits for the organization (rather than for the individuals who comprise it) and improving its performance (but not necessarily the performance of individuals *qua* individuals) by means of an ongoing rationalization of the extant set of relations and routines within it.[5]

On the other hand, this impersonal form of power ensures at least the appearance that the power to command, and the content of the commands themselves, are not the product of some individual(s) will(s), made, and susceptible to being unmade, by the action of individuals. Rather, power and the commands which mediate it brook no (rational) argument; they appear to flow out of the objective logic of the situation. And well they might. The point, however, is that the 'objective logic of the situation' is itself constructed upon a power relationship, one that functions all the more effectively because it presents itself in impersonal, naturalized forms that are beyond the control of the individuals who occupy roles within it.[6] Through the control mechanisms inherent in modern bureaucracy – each actor's potential for upward mobility in the hierarchy of offices, the role of letters of recommendation in transfers to other organizations, the promise of pension benefits on retirement, and so on – individual motivations are brought into agreement with organizational objectives, producing thereby a relationship of domination in which, at its apogee, a command of the dominators is received by the dominated as if the latter 'had made the content of the command the maxim of their conduct for its own sake'.[7]

Couching the concept of bureaucracy in terms of a Weberian ideal-type and specifying its social basis enables us to draw some important distinctions with respect to Soviet organizations on an abstract level. These, in turn, find their utility in framing the more concrete categories by means of which we study these organizations empirically. It is perhaps too often the case that the word 'bureaucracy' has been employed by Western analysts of the Soviet system in a rather indiscriminate fashion, oriented to the appearance or outer shell of Soviet organizations – which, after all, share certain of the characteristics of modern bureaucracy (Soviet organizations, appear to be ordered hierarchically, to operate on the basis of written regulations, and so forth) – without tapping their internal structure and dynamics. When the latter is our concern, however, we notice the absence of a number of elements which are central to the bureaucratic phenomenon in capitalist states. The calculability and rationality for which bureaucracy is known depend upon the commodity forms (especially, monetization) of a market economy and either appear in truncated fashion or disappear altogether in the Soviet context.[8] Accordingly, as Jerry Hough's well-known work showed some 20 years ago, Soviet organizations do not evince a legal-rational basis for the organization of authority such as we find in bureaucracies in advanced capitalist systems.[9] Soviet officialdom, too, seems to be organized around certain non-bureaucratic or even anti-bureaucratic norms[10] and displays orientations, such as a tendency toward the personal appropriation of public office,[11] that are at odds with modern bureaucratic practice as we know it. With such things in mind, some scholars have preferred to think of Soviet organizations as variants of Weber's (pre-modern) patrimonial bureaucracy.[12] Terminological questions are, however, of less interest to us here than is the matter of how Soviet organizations structure the action of their members.

In an earlier study, I have drawn the conclusion that the Soviet pattern of organization rests on 'weak structures' which, relatively speaking, are ill-suited to sustain domination in Weber's sense of the term. In sharp contrast to the impersonal relations of a bureaucratic order, the ensemble of personalized relations extant in the Soviet form of organization tends to structure the action of officials around immediate and commonly identified incentives that have little if any connection to honouring the commands issuing from nominal superiors.[13] In the language of contemporary sociology, we can distinguish the strong (impersonal) structures and weak (personal) ties[14] associated with bureaucracy in advanced capitalist states from the weak structures and attendant strong ties found in Soviet organizations. These inject a powerfully *personal* element into Soviet personnel systems and lead to two important considerations for their study.

First, the relative weakness of formal Soviet organizational structures in shaping the concrete activity of those within them cautions us against making assumptions about the relations among actors who occupy various organizational roles. Unlike our experience with Western bureaucratic systems in which such roles tend to be reasonably well defined and are related one to another in specific ways, those who enter Soviet organizations do not step into ready-made relations of a bureaucratic type. Rather, the roles and relations among them are infused with a largely personal element that sets the stage for a considerable amount of negotiation among the parties concerned as to the content of the roles themselves and how relations among them are to be organized.[15] The student of Soviet organizations, then, is above all a student of the personnel who comprise them, for it is at this level, rather than at the level of formal organizational design, that so much of the basic determinants of organized activity are set in motion.

Secondly, the student of personnel is necessarily engaged in a project that goes beyond the issues associated with personnel administration in a bureaucratic setting; personnel studies in the Soviet context spill over into the area of power relations far more so than would be true, *ceteris paribus*, for advanced capitalist systems. When we consider the question of how power is organizationally deployed in the USSR, how the policy mechanism functions (or fails) to ensure that subordinates implement the decisions of superiors, it becomes apparent that the main gear in this mechanism is the placement of personnel. Unable to offer positive inducements such as substantial salary increases, stock options, the promise of a partnership and so forth, and lacking as well anything resembling the major negative sanction found in capitalist countries, the threat of unemployment, those who head Soviet organizations must rely primarily on the exchange of appointments and promotions in return for compliance with their substantive directives. In studying elite mobility in the Soviet context, then, we are at the same time studying the concrete operation of this singularly important mechanism of power.

Thirdly, the design of our study should benefit by taking these points into account. A survey of the literature on Soviet elite studies would point up the influence of certain background assumptions rooted in the bureaucratic experience which seem largely out of place in the Soviet milieu. The methodology that informs the present study can be explicated by contrasting it to (a) the basic model which has underpinned the great bulk of Western studies in this area and (b) the specific methodology which they have employed.

Models and methods

The basic model relied upon by Western analysts of Soviet elites[16] might be described as the 'turnover model'. It utilizes individual level data, considers one-to-one turnover in jobs (i.e., the number of individual jobs that changed hands, often for specific time periods) and employs such variables for incumbents and recruits as age, education, nationality, sex, career history and so forth.[17] The turnover model of mobility is designed to tell us (1) the rate at which jobs change hands, (2) the characteristics of incumbents as an aggregate profile, and (3) those attributes among recruits which are likely to be selected for as replacement occurs. Studies of this type have produced a series of pictures that change over time, enabling analysts to make certain empirical statements about elite composition and to forecast trends by extrapolating from changes in elite composition. However, as Bohdan Harasymiw has pointed out, 'we still have not explained the phenomenon epitomized by the classic theorists' notion of the "circulation of elites" . . . namely, "how do they circulate?"'[18]

The reason for this persistent lacuna in studies of the Soviet leadership is simple enough; in the turnover model there is neither a concept of, nor an empirical referent for, circulation. The turnover model in fact does not concern itself with elite circulation as a process but deals instead with the personal attributes of officeholders. These are two quite different things. By establishing turnover as the focus of attention and treating the attributes of individuals as the primary concern, analysts employing this model tend to frame their basic research questions in a way which is not especially conducive to asking what seems to me to be the basic question: What does elite circulation tell us about political power in the USSR? Rather, the research interests associated with the turnover model[19] lead to asking the questions set out abstractly in Figure 1.1.[20] This approach treats the personal attributes of individuals who have risen to high office in the Soviet Union as factors defining the elite in a given instance. That is, the elite is considered from the perspective of how its members 'score' on the variable of personal attributes. These scores, which in longitudinal studies change over time, are in turn regarded as indicators of change in the policy orientations of the ruling elites or, relatedly, as indicators of change in the Soviet political system. Here the tacit influence of the 'bureaucratic' model is apparent. Whether elite attributes are used as surrogates for policy orientations or leadership statements on policy are employed,[21] the analysis treats such orientations as meaningful in themselves, assumedly because the Soviet 'bureaucracy' can or will translate them into practice.

As to the second of the distinctions that we are drawing here, Valerie Bunce is correct to point out that the field of Soviet elite studies has relied exclusively on 'methodological individualism' as the principle governing empirical analysis.[22] As we have seen in our discussion of the turnover model, this approach regards individuals and their attributes as the basic unit of analysis and attempts to correlate these with mobility in order to analyse policy or systems change. The logic in this method involves a certain leap from aggregated individual characteristics to the characteristics of the system under consideration. Absent, here, is a method oriented to the level of the system itself (however we might define it in a given instance), one in which the *relations* among individuals, rather than the skin-bound individuals themselves, appear as the unit of analysis. Whereas the perspective implicit in methodological individualism cannot but apprehend elite circulation as the product of aggregated individual choices or intentions,[23] a method that gives primacy to the bundle of relations that constitute a system would view it as the result of an interactive set of opportunities and constraints to which individuals, *qua* individuals, react but which they do not control.[24]

It goes without saying that conventional studies of elite mobility have greatly expanded our knowledge of the individuals who at one time or another constitute the elite(s) in the USSR. Moreover, the changing profile of elite characteristics is not without implication for elite behaviour. The life experiences that shape the outlook of a given

Figure 1.1 The basic model underlying Western analyses of Soviet elites

generation and the rising educational level of those holding public office in the Soviet Union, for instance, are important factors in specifying the dimensions of leadership change in the Soviet system today. But as much as a focus on individuals might tell us about the orientations of the members of the elite at some point(s) in time, it remains ill-suited to the tasks of examining the set of relations which order the activity of these individuals and of answering the question of how these relations might themselves be changing. In this respect, the foregoing exegesis and critique of the field's conventions have been intended to call attention to certain gaps in our knowledge which issue from gaps in our methods. We can fill some of these by correcting the bias implicit in methodological individualism, by recognizing, that is, that individuals are neither the only nor necessarily the most appropriate unit of analysis that we might adopt. Since we intend to analyse the relations among individuals that structure their concrete activity, we require a method that incorporates the concept of relations into its basic design. Proceeding in this way, we are also led to a reformulation of the conceptual model which frames our empirical analyses of Soviet elites.

Vacancy chain analysis, a method developed by Harrison C. White,[25] seems particularly well-suited to our purpose. It begins by abstracting from individuals and focusing instead on positions, particularly on those that have fallen vacant. Once a vacancy has appeared in some position, it can circulate within the system of offices and form a chain in the process of doing so. That is, when a vacancy occurs and is then filled by some incumbent in the system, another vacancy has been created in the job which this incumbent has just left. This vacancy, in turn, might be filled by another incumbent, creating thereby another vacancy until the chain formed by the movement of vacancies has passed outside the system (recruitment of a non-incumbent). Alternatively, this process might be regarded as a replacement chain composed of the actors (replacements) whose movement in the system flows in a direction opposite to the flow of

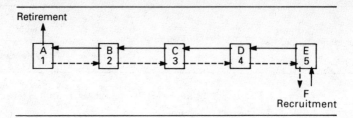

Figure 1.2 A vacancy chain encompassing five positions

* Letters indicate actors, numbers indicate positions. Solid lines
  denote the movement of actors, broken lines, the movement of
  vacancies

vacancies. Figure 1.2 illustrates this process by means of a hypo-
thetical example. In this instance, a vacancy has appeared in Position 1, with the retirement of Actor A. Since B then fills the opening in
Position 1, the vacancy moves to Position 2 which B has just left. It
continues to circulate until a non-incumbent (Actor F) is recruited to
fill Position 5, at which point the vacancy has passed outside the
system and the chain terminates.

In subsequent chapters we shall have occasion to develop some of
the conceptual and mathematical aspects of the vacancy model as we
apply it to the analysis of our data. Here we are concerned with the
methodological advantages which it holds for the study of Soviet
elites.[26] First, it repairs the deficiency that we noted in the turnover
model with respect to the issue of circulation. The vacancy model
analytically includes the concept of circulation and offers an immediate empirical interpretation for it: vacancies circulate in chains.
Secondly, the circulation of vacancies is cast within a relational
framework, their circulation in chains reports events within the
system that are themselves empirically linked. This is illustrated in
Figure 1.2 in which Actor F, for instance, enters the system because of
an opportunity which resulted from events having little if anything to
do with his/her own intentions or decisions. In the first instance, F's
entry into the system is occasioned by E's movement out of Position 5
and into Position 4. Similarly, E's movement is brought about by the
opportunity to move to Position 4, an event conditioned by the
movement of D and the resulting vacancy in his previous job.
Carrying forward this logic, it becomes clear that A's retirement and
F's recruitment are in fact related. This relationship, however, would
not be noticed were our focus on individuals and their attributes.

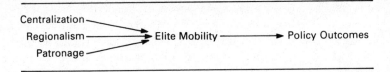

Figure 1.3 Revised model for Soviet elite analysis

Viewing the process of elite circulation in this way allows us also to make some revisions in the conventional model that underlies Soviet elite studies. The model adopted here, as set out in Figure 1.3, links elite mobility to the question of policy outcomes in the context of those variables thought to influence the circulation process:[27] centralization, regionalism and patronage. Although a direct analysis of policy outcomes in the Belorussian Republic is beyond the scope of this study, this model highlights the fact that in analysing elite mobility we are simultaneously examining the relative weights of the factors which shape such outcomes. In consonance with our discussion of 'bureaucracy' in the Soviet context, we can regard the presence of effective centralization in the process of elite circulation in Belorussia as an indication of structural strength in the deployment of political power. In this respect, the political centre, whether at the all-union or republic level, would be seen as directly effecting the mobility of elites and thereby controlling inducements (jobs, promotions) which it can exchange for performance. Conversely, regionalism and patronage would influence elite circulation in the opposite direction, contributing to the personalization of relations within Belorussia's formal organizations, fragmenting control over the personnel process and, by implication, over the policy process as well.

Finally, the method employed in this study allows for both a diachronic and a synchronic approach to the category of time and the related phenomenon of the mobility of the actors within the system. Mobility has conventionally been grasped in a diachronic fashion. It concerns those snapshots taken at various points in time which, when compared one to another, reveal certain changes in elite composition that have resulted from changing patterns of mobility. A diachronic approach to mobility is essential when the question of change is under consideration and, accordingly, it is often employed in this study. However, in the same way that vacancy chain analysis enables us to see the links among what might otherwise be perceived as discrete events within the system, it also opens another vista on the category of time which conduces to a synchronic appreciation of mobility and its effects. From this vantage, we view events as if they were occurring all at once. Mobility, when placed in synchronic perspective, can then be used in novel ways in order to specify characteristics of the system itself. In the following chapters, a synchronic concept of mobility is employed to determine the hierarchical structure of the system, and the influence of centralization, regionalism and patronage on the circulation of elites within it. Before turning to an empirical analysis of the relative effects of these factors on the circulation of elites in the BSSR, however, a word by way of background on the particular site of this study is in order.

Historical sketch

In discussing the history of any of the East European peoples, one's narrative invariably inclines toward the semantic pole marked out by terms such as 'difficult', 'troubled' and 'tragic'. This is particularly true of Belorussia. The name itself, 'White Russia' ('Belarus'' in the native tongue), provides an illustration of this. It first appeared as a political-administrative designation referring to Russian lands outside the zone of taxation during the period of the Tartar yoke. Its official usage in documents dates from 1667 when it was applied by the Russian government to the western lands annexed from the Lithuanian–Polish state. The name, however, did not enter the local vernacular until the nineteenth century, at which time it was simultaneously banned from official administrative language due to the nationalist or separatist nuances which it was believed to carry.[28] Belorussia has historically designated a 'land between' and connotated, correspondingly, a relatively 'backward' place governed and exploited by contiguous nationalities.

The long epoch of serfdom in Belorussia was especially cruel, retarding and even reversing the development of the broad masses of the population. The burdens borne by those bound to the land in Belorussia were made the heavier by the fact that more than economic and social differences set masters apart from serfs. The pattern of foreign landowning in which Poles and Russians appeared as masters of the land added national, linguistic and religious differences as well, with the result that enserfed Belorussians experienced conditions of bondage that eclipsed feudalism's paternalistic face and enhanced in equal measure its capacity for brutal exploitation. Some indication of how this particular form of feudalism glaciated the development of the Belorussian people can be taken from the fact that pagan traditions and superstitions, similar to those described in Russia by Moshe Lewin,[29] endured longer in Belorussia than they did anywhere else in the Slavic world.[30]

Those economic and demographic changes which signal the advent of what we have come to call 'modern society' arrived later in Belorussia than they did in the other European parts of the Russian Empire. And when they did come they generally excluded the Belorussians themselves. For the Russian Empire as a whole in 1897, industrial workers accounted for some 1.43 per cent of the total population. In Belorussia, this same statistic was only 0.5 per cent, and a sizeable portion of this figure was composed of individuals who had come from other parts of the Empire[31] to find employment in the new industrial enterprises, themselves the offspring of 'foreign' (i.e., Polish and Russian) capital.[32]

The development of a national consciousness among the various peoples of East Europe seems to have been predicated on a certain sequence or pattern of social and demographic changes. This sequence begins with the concentration of a critical mass of the indigenous population in towns whose social and occupational differentiation is sufficient to support the emergence of a native intelligentsia which in turn generates a particular idea of the nation. This idea, communicated through the medium of a national literature, incorporates the broader masses of the population into a national identity as literacy spreads throughout the society.[33] All of these conditions were missing in the case of Belorussia. According to the census of 1897, for instance, only a small minority (7.3 per cent) of those residing in Belorussia's larger towns spoke the Belorussian language.[34] Overwhelmingly, the population centres were dominated by Poles, Russians, Lithuanians and Jews, and it was these groups who made up the professional and business classes. Urban-dwelling speakers of Belorussian were primarily employed as labourers and servants.[35] The masses of the Belorussian people, as we have seen, remained on the land and were largely isolated from those influences which all around them pointed toward the awakening of a national identity among the peoples of East Europe. Not only did Belorussia evince the lowest level of literacy in the European part of the Russian Empire, even its oral tradition of folklore was devoid of any national idea and centred instead on an undifferentiated concept of man and his (unhappy) lot.[36] Absent, then, were both the orally transmitted concept of nation, common among other East European peoples, and an emerging national intelligentsia which might appropriate it as raw material to be fashioned into the poetry, prose and drama which compose nationalism's cultural dimension in the modern period. Indeed, the first literature to appear in the Belorussian vernacular was written not by Belorussians but by Poles, Russians and Lithuanians and it was often characterized by ridicule of, rather than reverence for, a Belorussian national identity.[37]

Against this considerable set of adverse circumstances, a Belorussian national literature did begin to emerge by the end of the nineteenth century. Paradoxically, however, the political expression of a national consciousness in this same period seems to have taken on an intentionally *Russian* cast, designed to link Belorussian nationalists with the major movement of the time, the anticipated Russian revolution.[38] Given what we have seen with respect to the less-than-propitious conditions for the development of a national consciousness in Belorussia, it is hardly surprising to find that the nationalist movement which emerged at the beginning of this century remained small and of marginal import in the events that shook and ultimately overthrew the Empire.[39]

From out of the Russian Revolution, Civil War and Russo-Polish War, emerged the first Belorussian state, the Belorussian Soviet Socialist Republic (BSSR). The Treaty of Riga (1921) established a western boundary for the BSSR which detached from it and incorporated into Poland some 38,600 square miles of land and some 3,460,900 Belorussians.[40] During the interwar period, then, Belorussia was bifurcated into the 'western territories' under Polish sovereignty and a BSSR which by 1926 included the provinces of Mogilev and Vitebsk, the Gomel' and Rechitsa districts, and the capital, Minsk, with its surrounding districts, amounting in all to a population of some 5 million.

During the twenties, Soviet policy emphasized the recovery and development of national cultures. This brief period, with its literacy campaigns, support for native literature and cultural forms and reliance on national elites in government and administration, is without parallel in the development of the bases of nationhood in the BSSR.[41] By the end of the twenties, however, such policies were reversed, nationally oriented elites in and out of the Communist Party became targets for repression in the BSSR, as they were throughout the Soviet Union, and the development of a Belorussian national consciousness received severe setbacks. In the western territories, the situation was, if anything, worse. There the Polish authorities undertook by 1927 an intensive campaign of Polonization that consciously sought the eradication of all Belorussian cultural, religious and educational institutions. Ironically, the most active expression of indigenous Belorussian nationalism in the western territories during the thirties came from the underground Communist Party of Belorussia (KPB) whose presence in what was then Polish territory grew in proportion to the oppression displayed by the Polish authorities.

In the BSSR itself, national development took the slower route of laying the perhaps necessary but by no means sufficient conditions for its further progress, namely, industrialization, urbanization and their attendant responses in the fields of education and culture. Even as the outward expressions of Belorussian nationalism were becoming more and more truncated, its social, economic and, ultimately, cultural foundations were being expanded as never before.[42] The profile of Belorussian industry was altered and enormously enlarged in the thirties with the construction of machine-building, metal-working, and textile plants.[43] New construction in the urban centres, of course, drew in workers from the countryside. The urban sector of the population increased by some 50 per cent over this period and by 1940 accounted for over one-fifth of the total population of the BSSR.[44]

The Second World War devastated Belorussia, laying waste her land, demolishing her cities and claiming the lives of a quarter of her people.[45] During the German occupation, civil society and state authority collapsed outside the larger cities. Belorussians on the land turned inward for defence against both the occupiers and the assorted and fluid array of bandit gangs who roamed the countryside, reviving thereby the ancient institution of the *mir* and returning to subsistence agriculture.[46] Resistance was organized by the Soviets from the first days of the German invasion,[47] but the Soviet sponsored partisan movement did not become a massed-based resistance against the Germans until the latter, through prodigious applications of terror, succeeded in driving large numbers of people into the sanctuaries of Belorussia's ample forests where they would join up with partisan units.[48]

Two aspects of the partisan movement are of particular concern to our study of Belorussian politics. First, the future political leaders of Belorussia were tempered in the crucible of partisan resistance. Operating behind enemy lines and in infrequent communication with Soviet authorities, the partisans enjoyed considerable autonomy in all aspects of their activity and organization.[49] Out of the shared experience of wartime resistance and governmental administration in those areas liberated by the partisans, emerged a tightly knit cadre whose members rapidly ascended the political ladder in the postwar years and found their way into leading party and governmental posts in the

BSSR by the mid fifties.[50] The putative leader of this political faction, Kyril T. Mazurov, became First Deputy Chair of the Council of Ministers of the USSR and a full member of the Soviet Politburo in 1965. He appears to have been instrumental in bringing other Belorussian partisans to high office in Moscow, thereby turning this Belorussian faction into an important political grouping on the national scene.[51] In subsequent chapters we shall often have occasion to examine the place occupied by the Partisan faction within the constellation of contemporary Belorussian politics,[52] using the upper case to designate this postwar political grouping.

Secondly, during the early postwar years, a period in which expressions of political nationalism were acutely circumscribed in the USSR, the Belorussian Partisans succeeded in constructing a particular national myth[53] which situated the ideals of a heroic Belorussian *national* resistance movement within the larger framework of the heroic sacrifices of the *Soviet* people. Accordingly, the liberation of Belorussia was regarded as having been brought about by the combined efforts of the Belorussian partisans and the Soviet Army,[54] and the official rites and monuments that commemorate this achievement today highlight the idea of a joint undertaking. We have, in this respect, the emergence of a uniquely national symbology appropriate to Soviet circumstances, one which could, as such, openly propagate a distinct Belorussian identity in a manner not overtly antagonistic to things Soviet. The form of this myth, then, insured against irritating Moscow's sensitivities on the national question. The political symbology of the partisan myth was both appropriate to the context in which this group acted and apparently quite instrumental in conveying to its members and to others a certain 'worthiness' (we will stop short of using the word 'legitimacy') for the members of this group to serve as national leaders in the postwar years. The struggles and sacrifices of the Partisans for and with the people during the German occupation marked them as fit to lead. As communicated in the national myth, this marking resulted from the long trial by fire that they endured and the enormous difficulties that they overcame in the fight for liberation. Hence, both their sacrifices and their abilities speak to the worthiness of this group to lead the nation.[55] To be sure, the question of worthiness was never put to an open vote and its acceptance by the population, therefore, was always open to doubt.[56] Nonetheless, under Soviet circumstances, it represented an acceptable form of national expression, a symbology in the service of advancing the political aspirations of its members, and an articulation of shared experience that delineated a group identity and promoted the group's cohesion.

The experience of the Partisan group should remind us of an obvious fact that too frequently receives less than the attention it warrants in the study of Soviet elites, namely, the role of indigenous and often 'faceless' forces in shaping the context in which elites emerge, organize and carry on political activity. In the same way that wartime resistance produced a political group that established itself as the Belorussian leadership some twelve years after the war's end, other political factions who came to vie for power with the Partisans developed their own bases and structures of organization and these, too, cannot be adequately understood without reference to the extensive changes that have occurred in postwar Belorussia. Industrialization might be mentioned first. Minsk, the capital, is also the centre of industry in the BSSR and Minsk's industry is primarily a product of the postwar period. The expansion of machine-building, metal-working and precision instruments production after the Second World War, combined with the addition of large new firms such as the Minsk Tractor Factory and Minsk Automatic Lines, have made Minsk into one of the Soviet Union's leading industrial cities, accounting for some 25 per cent of total industrial production in the BSSR.[57] Elsewhere, large metal-working and machine-building industries have been established.[58] These, in turn, feed their product into the manufacture of automobiles,[59] heavy trucks[60] and agricultural machinery,[61] while integrated potassium mining and chemical fertilizer production (amounting to 50 per cent of the USSR's total)[62] represent important inputs into the agricultural sector. Belorussian industry has also expanded its production of artificial fibres,[63] textiles,[64] and other consumer durables.[65]

The industrialization of Belorussia has fundamentally changed its demographic structure. Whereas only about one-third of the BSSR's population lived in urban centres as recently as 1970,[66] some 62 per cent, out of a population which has now reached 10 million, were urban residents by the end of 1985.[67] These changes appear most immediately in the political sphere in the growth and occupational composition of the Communist Party of Belorussia (KPB). Between 1945 and 1978, for example, KPB membership (excluding candidates) rose from 19,787 to 520,283, while the percentage of members who had been recruited from working-class occupations in those same years changed from 11.6 to 57.1 per cent.[68] As Soviet authors themselves point out, the increase in working-class recruitment reflected a national policy, established in 1965, that aimed to attract more workers into the CPSU.[69] But in the Belorussian case, at least, the impact of this policy can only be interpreted as helping to accelerate a process already underway.[70]

In subsequent chapters we shall observe a political expression of Belorussia's postwar industrialization in the form of a political group which emerged out of the industrial organizations in the capital. Its members rose from the skilled sector of the working class to top positions in enterprises, party and trade union organizations, then to the elite jobs in the capital's party and governmental machinery and, ultimately, to leading posts at the republic and all-union levels. What is more, we shall see how the internal organization of this group, in consonance with its members' occupational backgrounds and professional roles, differed markedly from that of the Partisans whom they replaced. Finally, the socioeconomic changes taking place in postwar Belorussia in many respects appear to have weakened the bases of national identity. Correspondingly, the rather muted sense of nationalism associated with the political faction that emerged from Minsk's industrial enterprises contrasts rather sharply with the symbology employed by their Partisan predecessors.

Offering any generalizations regarding the eclipse of nationalist sentiment within the Soviet context is particularly hazardous. A number of studies, however, have reached such a conclusion for contemporary Belorussia. The use of the Belorussian tongue, for instance, declined considerably during the years between the 1959 and 1970 censuses,[71] and among native speakers of minority languages in the USSR, Belorussians in 1970 registered the lowest percentage still regarding their own language as the one of primary use. Correspondingly, the BSSR contains the highest percentage of native speakers who are also fluent in Russian.[72] These figures, no doubt, reflect the decline of Belorussian language, and the concomitant increase in Russian language, publications in the BSSR,[73] a trend that has elicited spirited public protest from prominent members of Belorussia's cultural elite.[74] But they may also have resulted from the less visible process of cultural assimilation that has accompanied the postwar industrialization and urbanization of the BSSR. The longstanding situation of non-Belorussian dominance in the urban areas of Belorussia is epitomized today by the fact that the capital, Minsk, is the most Russianized city in the BSSR.[75] Upwardly mobile, second-generation, urban residents would seem to have experienced the centripetal pull of the Russian language and culture as they entered into higher education and professional careers in a manner analogous to that of, say, black elites in the United States today who tend to exchange sub-cultural dialect for the conventional language structure of white society as they move into mainstream careers. The relatively weak sense of nationalism present in the contemporary BSSR, however, offers us a certain advantage in the study of Soviet political elites in as much as elite circulation in the Republic would less likely be affected by the issue of indigenous nationalism or reactive cadres policies coming from Moscow. Hence, the results of this study of Belorussia might suggest something about elite circulation in the RSFSR or in the other republics were nationalism somehow factored out, and would serve as a point of departure for gauging the relative influence of nationalism on the personnel systems of other republics by comparing them to the Belorussian case.

2 Hierarchy, mobility and a stratified model

The rather modest purpose of this chapter – the construction of a stratified model of offices for the Belorussian Republic which can be used to analyse elite circulation in the chapters that follow – immediately confronts a thicket of complications raised by our discussion of the Soviet form of organization. Taking, first, the question of intra-organizational hierarchies, it would appear that the relative absence of a bureaucratic pattern of organization in the USSR would raise serious questions about the utility of relying simply upon the nominal designations of the various offices in order to arrive at an adequate conception of how power and authority are actually distributed among them. If, for instance, communications among these offices do not consistently conform to bureaucratic rules whereby orders are passed along an explicit chain of command, but instead involve numerous cases in which middle-level offices are bypassed in the course of direct communications between 'top' and 'bottom',[1] we cannot safely infer that the formal standing of offices in Soviet organizations is coincident with their operational or practical significance. Consequently, formal rank emerges as a rather imprecise index of the gradations in power and authority that may in fact prevail in Soviet organizations. In what follows, we find that this is also true for the mobility of actors within formal organizational hierarchies.

Secondly, there is the matter of what may be regarded as multiple hierarchies in the Soviet system – the array of party jobs, state jobs, and jobs in mass organizations or soviets – all of which intersect in various committees and bureaux at various levels. Since the careers of actors commonly span a number of these, the student of Soviet elites must be something of a juggler, keeping a number of such balls in motion simultaneously in order to chart promotions, demotions and simple transfers. This issue of multiple hierarchies compounds, and is in turn compounded by, the problems associated with determining

18

rank within organizations considered individually. If the names of positions do not necessarily represent a reliable guide to their actual standing within the system of offices, how might we compare positions in one organization with those in another and determine thereby which jobs are above, below or on a par with others?[2]

Finally, the specific mechanism for filling positions in the Soviet system, the *nomenklatura*, introduces yet another set of difficulties. We know that elite mobility occurs through the medium of the *nomenklatura* system of appointments. One gets a position, a promotion and so on on the basis of one's name being entered on these appointments' lists.[3] We also know that the *nomenklatura* system enables one organization, the party, to 'interfere' with the staffing of other organizations, such that moves across hierarchies – from, say, a party to a soviet office or vice versa – may in fact be moves within a single *nomenklatura*.[4] Moreover, appointment powers are staggered in this system such that the top official in a given organization will likely appoint some of his staff but not his immediate subordinates. Consequently, officials are often beholden to others outside their respective organizations for their positions and career opportunities.[5] The fact that appointments in many cases are made by units at one administrative level on the basis of nominations and/or recommendations issuing from their counterparts at lower levels or from other units attached to different administrative hierarchies produces a situation in which we are at a loss to know who in fact appointed whom and, as a result, where the actual lines of responsibility among officials lie.[6]

Previous attempts at mapping out an explicit hierarchy of positions in the Soviet system have in my view given too little attention to these peculiar features of Soviet organization. Tacitly, the assumption seems to have been that there is a hierarchy 'out there' which the analyst can locate.[7] Location, in turn, has been largely nominal; a position's name and the duties, authority, or importance known or thought to be associated with it would place it above, below, or on par with some other position.[8] As a consequence, analysts have tended to focus on the characteristics of this job or that – its formal rank, whether it is represented on central committees, the size of the organization in which it exists, the 'importance' of the unit in the economy, and so on – and the drawing of comparisons between these characteristics and those of other jobs. This method would likely encounter few if any difficulties were we dealing with hierarchies in advanced capitalist systems. But when applied to organizations of the Soviet type it produces results that are difficult if not impossible to validate.

While retaining the same objective – the specification of a hierarchy of positions in order to gauge elite mobility – this study departs from the nominal method of ranking conventionally employed. Rather than treating hierarchy and mobility as two separate phenomena, which is the common approach, we shall conjoin them. In so doing it becomes possible (a) to see each as a function of the other and (b) to reverse their order of determination. If we wish to specify a hierarchy in order to study mobility, might we not study mobility in order to specify a hierarchy? This is the tack taken here. The hierarchy of positions in our Belorussian sample will be determined by the probabilities displayed by incumbents in a given set of jobs for reaching positions grouped into strata above them. The hierarchy of positions generated by this method avoids the problems associated with nominal ranking by allowing empirical patterns of mobility to designate which jobs occupy which ranks.

Before going further, we might underline some of the assumptions and implications associated with this method of ranking. First, we are bracketing the notion of an objective hierarchy based on the names of offices. In this approach there is no *a priori* reason to assume that jobs with the same name also share the same rank, nor is there reason to designate jobs as above or below one another simply on the basis of their respective appellations. As we shall see in what follows the assigning of jobs to strata in accordance with their probabilities of transition to higher strata yields results that are often at odds with nominalist assumptions regarding both the equivalence and the gradation of positions.

Secondly, the hierarchy of job stratification produced by the method employed here is specific to time and place. It cannot claim to be 'the' hierarchy of positions in Belorussia; even less should it be taken as a ready-made hierarchy applicable to other republics in the USSR. Its status is restricted to the Belorussian Republic over the period, 1966–86. This characteristic of the method follows from the purpose for which the method was devised, namely, to analyse elite mobility in this republic over this period of time. Hence, what is generalizable is not the specific results derived from the method (these belong to time and place) but the method itself. That is, those analysing Soviet elites at any level might use this method for delineating elite stratification in the context of their own data and research interests.

Data and method

In order to employ the principal method adopted in this study for the analysis of elite circulation in the BSSR, the method of vacancy chain analysis, a more or less complete inventory of positions and incumbents in the Belorussian Republic is required. This consideration rules out the time-saving device of using data sets that have been prepared by organizations such as Radio Free Europe/Radio Liberty or the CIA, or of consulting the biographical sketches which appear in Soviet publications. Although these sources might assist in the task of compiling a full inventory of positions and incumbents, they are nonetheless themselves insufficient for our purposes. The reason for this insufficiency is straightforward enough: the data compiled by these agencies are organized around individual actors rather than positions. Consequently, these sources may tell us which jobs a particular actor held over the span of his career, but they do not tell us whom the actor replaced when he assumed a given position nor who replaced him when he left a certain job. Complete career histories for a set of actors do not, that is, translate into what our method of analysis requires as a data base – a complete set of *positions* and the actors who filled them at one time or another.

In order to generate the requisite data base, it was necessary to follow personnel changes in the Belorussian elite by systematically reading a number of Soviet newspapers and journals.[9] In the course of doing so, a file was opened for each officeholder whose name appeared in these publications. (Military offices constitute a distinct personnel system and, as such, were not recorded as part of the data set.) Alongside the individual's name in each file were entered the initial position listed for him plus all subsequent jobs which he held as these were reported in the data sources. Once these files for the period, January, 1966–June, 1986, were complete, a computerized data set was constructed wherein each actor appeared as a 'case,' and to each 'case' was appended a code that designated the position held by the actor in specified years. This yielded a matrix of 3,127 rows (officeholders) and 21 columns (each a one-year interval over the period, 1966–86) into which the 2,034 jobs which appeared in the sample were entered.

To accommodate the purpose of tracking the mobility of actors, a range of hierarchically ordered positions is called for. Consequently, the scope of data collection was designed to include incumbents in factory-level jobs at (assumedly) the lower end of the hierarchy and those occupying certain all-union jobs at the upper end. The array of positions spanned the following hierarchies: Communist Party of Belorussia (KPB), governmental positions in the Belorussian Republic (ministeries, state committees and soviets), Komsomol, trade union, cultural and educational posts. The vertical range extended from republic-level positions in these hierarchies through *oblast'* (and, for party and soviet positions, *raion*) level jobs, and to the positions of directors (and in some cases deputy directors) and the secretaries of primary party organizations and trade union presidents in large enterprises. Additionally, 24 jobs at the all-union level known to have been taken by former officeholders in Belorussia were included.

The matrix of officeholders/years (1966–86) with offices as the entries was then transformed into a matrix of offices/years (1966–86) wherein the entries were the officeholders.[10] This matrix of 2,034 rows (each representing a job) and 21 columns (each designating a year) is illustrated in Table 2.1. Each actor who held a given position at the end of a particular year would then occupy that cell in the matrix designated by the intersection of the corresponding row (position) and column (year). Row entries change with mobility into and out of the positions which designate the row. This is illustrated in row 3 of Table 2.1 by the replacement of D. F. Filimonov by V. F. Mitskevich as Secretary of the Central Committee of the KPB in charge of agriculture in 1968.

With this position/year matrix for the data set in place, the next step in generating a hierarchy on the basis of transition probabilities to higher strata was to select the top stratum itself. A number of considerations bear upon this choice. This stratum functions as the ultimate 'destination' of all those holding jobs in the Belorussian Republic. Since jobs are to be ranked in accordance with the probabilities which their incumbents have for reaching higher positions, and since this first stratum will therefore define a second stratum which will, in turn, define a third and so on, it is clear that the first stratum should be limited to top jobs but at the same time be large enough to accommodate the purpose of generating a second stratum which is itself sufficiently large to generate a third, etc., such that the hierarchy thereby derived will contain a number of strata suited to the purpose for which the model was devised.

With these considerations in mind, two sets of positions were selected for the top stratum. The first set is composed of those jobs whose incumbents regularly held positions on the Buro of the Central Committee of the KPB (i.e., those to whom a seat on the Buro was awarded at at least four of the five congress of the KPB held during the time frame of the study). There is no reason to believe that these jobs are all equal in their importance. They probably are not. The point is only that regular membership on the Buro, the highest decision-

Table 2.1. *Sample position matrix for Belorussian Republic, 1966–86*

	1966	1967	1968	...	1986
1. First Secretary of KPB	P. M. Masherov	P. M. Masherov	P. M. Masherov	...	N. N. Slyun'kov
2. Second Secretary of KPB	F. A. Surganov	F. A. Surganov	F. A. Surganov	...	G. G. Bartoshevich
3. Secretary of KPB (Agriculture)	D. F. Filimonov	D. F. Filimonov	V. F. Mitskevich	...	N. I. Dementei

.
.
.

2,034

making organ in the Republic, defines a particular set of jobs which are set apart from all others by virtue of their incumbents' membership on a body that can be regarded the uppermost layer of the Republic's elite.

A second set of jobs selected for the top stratum is composed of national positions to which Belorussian officeholders moved during the course of their careers. The inclusion of this group follows again from the purpose for generating the positions hierarchy, namely, in order to study elite circulation and mobility in Belorussia. Here, the assumption is that moving into one of these all-union positions is equivalent to moving into one of the jobs regularly represented on the Buro of the KPB. In either case, a promotion to the top stratum has occurred. Stratum 1 jobs at the all-union level were defined as executive positions, whether in the party or state apparatuses, at the level of deputy minister of, or, for the party, deputy head of a department of the Secretariat of the Central Committee or those with formal rankings above these (first deputy, minister, etc.).[11] The two sets of jobs yielded a top stratum numbering 25 positions, 13 of which were regularly represented on the Buro of the KPB, 12 of which were executive jobs at the national level.

Having assigned these two sets of positions to Stratum 1, it became clear that such a ranking would not serve the purpose of generating a sizeable second stratum for the hierarchy. That is, there is a relatively high frequency of circulation among those holding jobs in the top stratum and a rather low degree of mobility into this stratum. Moreover, if regular Buro membership and executive jobs at the national level were the criteria for inclusion into Stratum 1, might not consistency suggest that irregular Buro membership and subexecutive jobs at the all-union level constitute the criteria for membership in Stratum 2? This was the approach adopted. To all those jobs that would appear in Stratum 2 by virtue of their transition probabilities to jobs in Stratum 1 were added at the onset 15 positions, nine of which were heads of either ministerial departments or sectors of the CPSU Secretariat, six of which were infrequently represented on the Buro of the KPB or were regularly candidate members of that body.

Once the positions comprising Stratum 1 had been specified and those comprising Stratum 2 had been partially specified, a computer program was designed to create succeeding strata for the remainder of the jobs in the data set and to assign individual jobs to individual strata on the basis of the formula:[12]

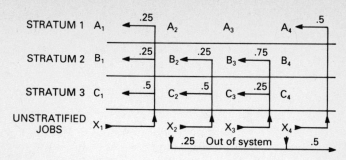

Figure 2.1 Representation of ranking procedure for jobs in sample

$$S_c = P_{i-a} + P_{i-b}$$

where S_c represents the stratum to which a given job is assigned, P designates the level of probability (at this point, not yet fixed) that an incumbent in a given job will move into one of the positions in S_b (i.e., the stratum above S_c), and the subscripts, $i-a$, $i-b$, denote movement from i (initial, unstratified position) into jobs in hierarchically ordered strata (a, b) above S_c. If the computed probabilities that the holder of a given position can move to jobs in, say, the first and second strata are summed, and if this sum equals or exceeds the probability level set for inclusion into the third stratum, then the job will be ranked in that third stratum. Succeeding strata are created and composed in the same way.

Which level of probability should serve as the cutoff point for the inclusion of jobs into their respective strata? Obviously, the answer to this question turns on the purpose for which this hierarchical ranking is generated. In order to employ the stratified ranking of jobs to study mobility, we should prefer a cutoff point neither too high (in which case too few jobs would be grouped into too many strata) nor too low (which would produce the opposite result of too many jobs in too few strata). Consequently, some experimentation was in order. The cutoff point was set first at a probability of 0.5, but this proved to be too restrictive as the computer program was able to create only two additional strata and rank only 40 jobs (not counting those specifically assigned to the first and second strata) under this criterion. Relaxing the cutoff point by setting it at 0.4 yielded more promising results; some 168 jobs were ranked in six strata. This procedure is illustrated in Figure 2.1. The subscripted jobs A, B and C belong to Strata 1 through

3, respectively. The group of jobs at the bottom of the figure (X_1, X_2 etc.) are ranked by the frequency of transition of their incumbents to jobs in the three strata depicted here. So, job X_1, whose summed probabilities for transition to Strata 1 and 2 exceeds the 0.4 criterion (0.25 + 0.25) is ranked in Stratum 3; job X_2 has no transition to Stratum 1, only 0.25 to Stratum 2 and 0.5 to Stratum 3, ranking it therefore in Stratum 4; accordingly, X_3 is ranked in Stratum 3 and X_4 in Stratum 2.

As the ranking progressed a snag in the procedure became evident, viz., the great majority of positions in the data set could not be assigned to strata on the basis of this (unmodified) method in as much as a majority of positions with nominally high rank have no transition probabilities at all. That is, if incumbents in such jobs as, say, Minister of Agriculture or first secretary of a given obkom never moved from these jobs to others in the data set, then these 'transitionless' jobs could not be ranked by this method. Accordingly, those positions which the incumbents left in order to become Minister of Agriculture or obkom first secretary would also go unranked since these transitions were to unranked jobs. This same problem, the absence of transitions to other jobs, was also apparent in the case of many positions thought to be of middle rank (deputy ministers, gorkom secretaries, and so forth) and as such prevented the ranking of those positions which were vacated when incumbents moved to these middle-level jobs. Clearly, if the general procedure for creating and filling strata on the basis of the probability of movement to higher strata was to succeed, some modifications were required in order to deal with the positions lacking transition probabilities.

Two modifications were introduced. First, unranked positions nominally equivalent to ranked positions were assigned to the same stratum in which a decisive majority of the ranked positions had been ordered. In the first such iteration, this involved assigning all unranked ministers to Stratum 3 (where all ministers who had been ranked by the first computer run were located) and all unranked heads of departments of the Secretariat of the KPB to Stratum 4 (where the majority of ranked department heads were to be found). Subsequent runs of the computer program yielded similar ranking patterns for other nominally equivalent positions and transitionless jobs were assigned to strata accordingly. In those cases in which patterns were unclear, other criteria became important. The first secretaries of raikoms were a case in point. Those with transition probabilities to other jobs were ranked in a number of different strata with the greatest concentrations falling in Stratum 7 and Stratum 8. By consulting the size of the party membership in their respective raions,[13] it became clear that those in Stratum 8 were also those with small party memberships (under 2,000). Hence, unranked first secretaries of raikoms were assigned to Stratum 7 unless the party membership in their respective raions fell below 2,000, in which case they were included in Stratum 8.

The second modification involved a pooling of jobs of nominally equivalent rank in the same organization. Examples of such job pools are: inspectors or instructors in a department of the Secretariat of the KPB, department heads in a ministry, and secretaries of gorkoms (but not the first secretary). Once pooled, all jobs in the pool were included in a single stratum on the basis of the sum of the probabilities for transition into other strata (in accordance with the formula set out, above) divided by the total number of such transitions for all jobs in the pool. To illustrate, take the case of heads of sectors in the Propaganda Department of the Central Committee of the KPB. The five positions of sector head in the data set were treated as one pool. Taking together those who held the top position in a sector, we observe that transitions occurred for the heads of two sectors on two occasions, that for another sector head one transition took place, and that for the remaining two positions of head of a sector there is no record of any transition. Hence, for the pool of five sector heads, five transitions occurred. On three occasions a sector head's next job was Deputy Head of the Propaganda Department, in one instance his next job was First Deputy Head of the Central Committee's Department of Culture, and in the fifth case, the next job was First Deputy Chair of the Belorussian State Committee for Publications. All five of these jobs to which the sector heads moved were ranked in Stratum 5. Consequently, the computer program ranked the entire pool of sector heads in Stratum 6.

The two modifications just discussed, assigning unranked jobs to the stratum in which their nominally equivalent counterparts had been ranked and (where possible) creating pools of jobs in order to stratify those in the pool that had no transitions to other positions, were undertaken simultaneously, but the first modification was introduced in series from the top downward. That is, the first computer run which ranked 168 jobs in six strata became the basis for ranking by nominally equivalent position another 87 jobs. With these inserted into the hierarchy, the program was run again and produced a ranking for 727 jobs in ten strata. This made possible the assignment by nominally equivalent position of another 196 jobs for which there were no records of transitions. Repeating this procedure, the computer program now ranked 1,413 jobs in ten strata. With these rankings in place, the remaining 621 transitionless jobs could be assigned to strata on the basis of the rank of nominally equivalent positions.

Two minor adjustments were made in the hierarchy at this point. First, those pooled jobs that ranked markedly below their nominally equivalent counterparts were examined. In a few cases it was evident that their ranking on the basis of transition probabilities to other strata yielded misleading results. For instance the two gorkom secretaries in Soligorsk were ranked in the bottom stratum, and this because their respective pool had only one transition to another job, that of secretary of the primary party organization at the Belarusskali mining works at Soligorsk, a position ranked in Stratum 9. Consequently, it was decided that nominally equivalent ranking would yield a more accurate result in this case and both gorkom secretaries were re-assigned to Stratum 7 where the majority of gorkom secretaries had been ranked by the computer program.

A second adjustment was made for jobs that might be considered to be sinecures. A transitionless position such as Director of the Institute of Party History seemed to serve as a final destination for certain politicians whose careers had led to high ranking positions but not to jobs in the top strata. Two individuals who served as Director had previously risen to Stratum 3 jobs (Second Secretary of the Minsk Obkom, Head of the Department of Scientific and Educational Institutions of the Central Committee of the KPB). Hence, it was decided to treat positions such as Director of the Institute of Party History as sinecures and to rank them one stratum *below* that from which their incumbents had arrived.

The stratified model and its implications for the question of hierarchy in Soviet organizations

The jobs in the data set and their respective rankings in the ten strata of the hierarchy are set out in Appendix A. The shape of the hierarchy generated on the basis of transition probabilities to jobs in the various strata is non-pyramidal, and this aspect reflects both the nature of the data and the method used to order them. It will be noticed, however, that the top four strata do resemble a pyramid (especially if we subtract the all-union jobs from Strata 1 and 2), Stratum 5 enlarges the base of this pyramid considerably, the number of jobs per stratum then peaks at Stratum 6, tapers off at Strata 7 and 8 and declines in the last two strata. A major reason for the bulge in membership in the two largest strata results from the inclusion – both via the method of assigning transitionless positions to the stratum of nominally equivalent jobs and that of creating job pools which ranks all jobs in the pool according to the pool's transition probability – of sub-ministerial positions in these strata. In Stratum 5 we find 58 deputy minister positions, in Stratum 6, the heads of 135 departments of ministries. These two sub-groups of positions form something of a special case. As the relative absence of transitions here might suggest, we are likely dealing with positions in which adjectives such as 'professional-managerial' have more salience than is true for other types of jobs in the system, and access to them is largely concentrated within the hierarchies of their respective organizations.[14] These positions are very rarely (in the data set) entered from outside their organizational hierarchies and the number of cases in which their incumbents leave for positions in other organizations is equally negligible. Were we to take this aspect into account and subtract as special cases these sub-groups from the data set, the mobility-based hierarchy which we have generated would much more resemble a pyramid. Additionally, if we keep in mind the fact that a major reason for the relative paucity of membership in the bottom two strata is the method of data collection (job holders in Strata 9 and 10 appear in print far less often than do those in higher strata), then we can enlarge these strata to pyramidal proportions in our mind's eye by adding in all the other, say, raiispolkom department heads, whom we know to be in the world but whose names did not appear in the data sources.

With these qualifications in mind, the hierarchy of positions generated here seems well-suited to the purpose of analysing elite circulation in the Belorussian Republic. It distributes the 2,034 jobs in the sample across ten strata, thereby providing us with ample range to chart the mobility of the actors in the system. It keeps intact the idea of a 'top elite' by confining Stratum 1 positions to those regularly represented on the Buro of the KPB and to executive positions at the all-union level, while at the same time populating each stratum with a number of jobs that is large enough to record frequent movements into and out of each hierarchical rank. The stratified ranking of positions is used in subsequent chapters for the purpose of investigating the determinants of elite circulation in the BSSR. Here, we might consider some of the implications which this exercise in position stratification has for the question of hierarchy in Soviet organizations.

Table 2.2. *Representation* of positions on the Central Committee of KPB by stratum (in percentages; N=93)*

Stratum 1	100 (n=13)	Stratum 6	1	(n=5)
Stratum 2	94 (n=16)	Stratum 7	1	(n=2)
Stratum 3	49 (n=33)	Stratum 8	0	(n=0)
Stratum 4	17 (n=16)	Stratum 9	0	(n=0)
Stratum 5	3 (n=7)	Stratum 10	0.6	(n=1)

* 'Representation' is defined as election to the Central Committee at 3 or more of the 5 congresses of the KPB, 1966–86.

First, let us take up the issue of central committee membership, an indicator commonly used in the field to designate the relative standing of positions (i.e., those positions whose incumbents regularly appear on a central committee are commonly regarded as having greater standing than those, perhaps nominally equivalent, positions whose members do not). If we examine the percentage figures in Table 2.2, there seem to be strong grounds for accepting the utility of this indicator, evinced by the close correlation between regular representation of positions on the Central Committee of the KPB and the stratified ranking of positions on the basis of their transition probabilities. The size of the percentages diminishes as one moves down the hierarchy, except for a single case in Stratum 10 which we take up below. From this perspective, regular representation of positions on the Central Committee would appear to be a reasonably accurate indicator of the status of positions.

Were we to focus on the *number* of regularly represented positions instead of their relative frequency of appearance by stratum, however, serious questions would arise regarding the utility of this indicator of status.[15] First, if regular Central Committee representation marks a given position for inclusion in the elite strata of the hierarchy, it is then difficult to account for the appearance of such 'elite' positions in Stratum 5 and Stratum 6. Secondly, three raikom first secretary positions are regularly represented on the Central Committee of the KPB. These – the Molodechno, Grodno and Orsha raikoms – are all agricultural districts that adjoin sizeable urban centres. They might therefore be considered as particularly important raions which provide foodstuffs to the proximate urban populations. But this consideration would only raise the more insistent question of their assumedly more important counterparts, say Minsk and Gomel' raions, whose raikom first secretaries are not regularly represented on

Table 2.3. *Position transitions for department heads, sector heads and inspectors in the Organization-Party Work Department of KPB*

Positions Next career moves of incumbents	Stratum
Deputy department heads:	
First Deputy Head, Org.-Party Work Dept., KPB	4
First Deputy Head, General Dept., KPB	5
First Deputy Head, Agriculture Dept., KPB	5
Asst. to First Secretary of KPB	4
Deputy Chair, People's Control Committee, BSSR	4
out of system (two)	
Sector Heads:	
Head, Dept. of Administration of Affairs, KPB	4
Second Secretary, Minsk Obkom	3
First Deputy Head, Org.-Party Work Dept., KPB	4
First Deputy Head, General Dept., KPB	5
Second Secretary, Grodno Obkom	4
Asst. to First Secretary of KPB	4
Deputy Chair, People's Control Committee, BSSR	4
out of system (three)	
Inspectors:	
First Deputy President, Minsk Oblispolkom	4
Deputy Dept. Head, Org.-Party Work Dept., KPB (two)	5
Second Secretary, Vitebsk Obkom	4
Second Secretary, Gomel' Obkom (two)	4
First Deputy Dept. Head. Org.-Party Work Dept.	4
Instructor, Org.-Party Work Dept., KPB	7
First Deputy Chair, People's Control Committee, BSSR	4
Chair, Minsk Oblast People's Control Committee	7
out of system (three)	

the Central Committee. It may be in fact that Central Committee membership in these cases has more to do with the first secretaries themselves than with the importance of the positions they hold. In the case of the First Secretary of the Grodno Raikom this seems to be true as membership on the Central Committee is coterminous only with the tenure of A. I. Belyakova. In both the Molodechno and Orsha raikoms, however, Central Committee membership was awarded to more than one first secretary. The absence of a clear pattern makes it difficult to see how these three cases conform to a single rule, whether it be the bestowing of Central Committee membership on individuals or whether it accrues to them on the basis of the positions they occupy. In short, we cannot be sure in these cases what this 'indicator' (Central Committee membership) is in fact indicating.

This confusion is compounded when we examine other cases. The Editor of the daily, *Zvyazda*, is regularly represented on the Central Committee of the KPB. Accordingly, *Zvyazda*'s Editor, M. I. Delets, was on the Central Committee in 1971, but on receiving what appears to have been a promotion to Chair of the State Committee for Publications he was demoted to candidate membership in 1976 and 1981. Then, while still Chair, he was dropped from the Central Committee altogether in 1986. A similar pattern is evident in the careers of other individuals. V. V. Matveev held a spot on the Central Committee while Editor of *Sel'skaya gazeta*, but on being promoted (?) to Chair of the State Committee on Films he was dropped to candidate membership. As first secretary of a rural raikom, U. F. Krishtalevich was on the Central Committee, but on becoming Deputy Minister of Social Security he was dropped from the roster. The President of the Grodno Oblispolkom, N. P. Molochko, lost his Central Committee membership on becoming Belorussian Minister of Trade. First Secretary of the Zavodskii Raikom in Minsk City, V. M. Semenov, lost his membership after becoming First Secretary of the Grodno Gorkom (a position qualifying as regularly, but not always, represented on the Central Committee). This list could be extended but the point is perhaps already clear. How can this indicator denote elite standing if a sizeable number of actors lose it as they advance upwardly in the hierarchy?

A second consideration brought to the fore by the method of stratification employed here touches on the matter of formal organizational hierarchies in the Soviet Union and calls into question the analytical utility of relying on the nominal rank of positions. Consider the case of the Organization-Party Work Department of the Central Committee of the KPB. Formally, the Department has in descending order of authority a Head (who is ranked in Stratum 2), a First Deputy Head (Stratum 4), two deputy heads, three heads of sectors, four inspectors and five instructors. Interestingly, the hierarchy which we have generated ranks the deputy department heads, sector heads and inspectors all in Stratum 5. Table 2.3 details the bases for these rankings by outlining the position transitions for each of these groups of jobs. Taken as a whole, these data show a tendency toward transition to other jobs in the apparatus of the KPB (17 of 22 transitions, six of which are intradepartmental). Secondly, four of the five transitions to other organizations involve jobs in the People's Control Committee of the BSSR, suggesting a close link between the Department and that organization. Most notable, however, is the similarity among each set of positions with respect to the subsequent career moves of their incumbents. We find, for instance, a deputy department head, a sector head and an instructor each making his next career move to the position of First Deputy Head of the Department. Likewise, individuals moved from jobs in each group of positions directly to one of the deputy chairs of the People's Control Committee of the BSSR (albeit an instructor's next career move was to the presumably more elevated position of First Deputy). If rank in a hierarchy has meaning in as much as it denotes a series of positions over which one's career develops, what are we to make of a case in which captains, majors and colonels, as it were, all share a more or less equal chance of being next promoted to general? And when such is the case, what might relations in such a hierarchy look like? Are formal subordinates and superiors likely to behave as such in practice? At the least, this exercise alerts us to what seems a significant gulf between nominal rank and rank as determined empirically by mobility, and suggests in this respect further cause for caution in applying the term 'bureaucracy' to the Soviet form of organization.

These considerations bear on a third question connected with elite stratification in the Soviet system, that of the 'importance' associated with certain jobs and the rank which might be assigned them on that basis. One way to regard 'importance' is to locate this quality in the job itself. The director of this organization or the first secretary of that obkom might be regarded as members of an elite because the organization or the obkom is itself 'important'. It should be clear, however, that this perspective has played a very small role in developing our Belorussian elite hierarchy. Consequently, some explanation might be in order as to why, say, the First Secretary of the Frunze Raikom in Minsk City or the Director of the Minsk Tractor Factory should be ranked in Stratum 3 with ministers of the BSSR. Are these positions that important? From the standpoint of the career mobility of the actors themselves they obviously were. These were the jobs that led directly to positions in the top strata, hence their high ranking in a hierarchy based on mobility. As we shall see in subsequent chapters, these jobs were apparently used by a clique within the KPB as stepping stones to advance the careers of clique members and, by the same token, the overall position of the clique within the system. Here we might note that these cases highlight the fact that the 'importance' of given positions may be radically altered when we approach it from the perspective of the relations among actors and their patterns of mobility rather than seeing it as some objective quality residing in the job.

The same is true in reverse for another position, Director of Gomsel'mash. A number of indicators would mark this job as an important one: the production of agricultural machinery figures prominently in the overall profile of Belorussian industry and, excepting the manufacture of tractors, Gomsel'mash is the Republic's leading producer of farm equipment;[16] Gomel', in which the plant is located, is the second largest city in the BSSR and Gomsel'mash is the largest firm in Gomel';[17] the Director of Gomsel'mash, as we have seen, is regularly a member of the Central Committee of the KPB, a status shared by only one other director of a firm, that of the Minsk Tractor Factory which ranks in Stratum 3 of the hierarchy. What justification, then, is there for ranking the Director of Gomsel'mash in the bottom stratum?

The answer to this question refers us back to the method of ranking and the purpose to which the hierarchy is to be put. Over the 21 year span of the data set, Gomsel'mash had only two directors, yielding one possible transition (the second director remains in the job) of which there is no record. This does not then imply that the position, lacking transitions, is unimportant; rather, it signifies that *this* position within the context of these data is of little consequence in as much as it is not connected to other positions or transitions among them, the investigation of which is the purpose for which this hierarchy has been designed. Hence, however 'important' this job may be in its own right, it plays no part in our study of mobility.

Summary and conclusions

The analysis of elite mobility presupposes some hierarchy of positions over which mobility takes place. Yet when we inquire into the issue of hierarchy we notice that it is always something that is imposed on the data by the analyst. The rankings in the hierarchy that we impose may be validated by certain characteristics of the system under investigation, but this does not alter the fact that we are imposing an analytic scheme in order to study mobility. And this 'in order to' seems the central point. The hierarchy, if it is to serve some purpose, should be designed with that purpose in mind.

Here we have generated a hierarchy of positions in the BSSR by reversing the hierarchy-mobility relationship, by taking mobility as the determinant of hierarchy in the first instance. In so doing, we have imposed some approximation of a *bureaucratic* hierarchy across the set of elite positions in Belorussia, a hierarchy developed out of transition probabilities to various strata in the model, one which in effect says that a job is to be ranked one rung below the stratum to which its incumbents move next. Beyond the utility intended for this hierarchy in subsequent chapters, what do the results of this exercise tell us about elite stratification in the Soviet system?

Judging from the Belorussian data presented here there is a considerable degree of similarity between hierarchy based on the formal rank of positions and hierarchy generated by transition probabilities to given strata. An examination of the rankings in Appendix A points up this congruence. At the same time, however, there seems to be enough departure from the formal ranking in the mobility-based hierarchy to raise some important questions regarding elite stratification generally and intraorganizational career ladders in particular, as our discussion of the Organization-Party Work Department of the Central Committee of the KPB would suggest. The implication would seem to be that a bureaucratic pattern of mobility is present to some extent, but the exceptions to such a pattern are sufficiently numerous and varied to cast doubt on the utility of the concept 'bureaucracy' as an accurate description of Soviet organization. At the least, the discrepancies between formal rank and the 'bureaucratic' hierarchy imposed on the data on the basis of the transition probabilities of positions indicate the influence of non-bureaucratic factors on mobility and, by inference, on the behaviour of actors and organizations in the system. We now turn to an investigation of such influences, beginning with the issue of centralization.

3 Centralization as a determinant of elite circulation

Centralization as a property of the system

The movement of actors across the array of political offices provides a particularly important index for power and policy in any political system. In the Soviet case, where effectively all social activity transpires through the medium of the party-state, the import of this proposition is especially pronounced. On the one hand, such activity is not so much regulated as it is (in principle) consciously planned, organized and directed by the central authorities whose formal lines of command run from Moscow to republic and provincial capitals whence they radiate outward to, ultimately, the basic units of political, economic and social organization. In the official parlance of the Soviet regime, there is a 'monolithic party' which directs a 'unified state structure' which in turn superintends a 'single economic mechanism.'

On the other hand, however, both our discussion of the Soviet form of organization and the discrepancies which we have observed between the mobility patterns evident in the BSSR and those which would be expected within a formal bureaucratic hierarchy would lead us to question the effectiveness of centralization, Soviet-style. As Lindblom has pointed out, the grand attempt at central direction which seems to be a defining feature of Soviet-type regimes is in fact fraught with a number of impediments embedded in the very structures that appear to privilege the role of the political centre.[1] We have summed up the consequence of these structural impediments as 'the tendency toward the personal appropriation of public office' and have noted in this respect the ability of those in subordinate positions to reinterpret, deflect or simply ignore the directives of superiors and to elude responsibility in doing so. Within this context, then, 'cadres policy' assumes crucial importance. Moscow can overcome to some extent the effect of personalized relations in formally subordinate organizations by manipulating the movement of personnel, by directly and indirectly offering the inducements of appointments and promotions in the apparatuses of the party-state in return for compliance with its directives. Centrally controlled appointments and promotions, then, constitute vertically structured incentives designed to offset the centrifugal pull of those horizontally structured incentive systems operating within the world of personalized administrative relations – personal enrichment via corruption, mutual security through collusion to deceive superiors, and so forth.

A great number of previous studies of Soviet elites have tended to frame their basic research questions, implicitly at least, around the idea of a centralized personnel system (see Figure 1.1). Their focus on the attributes of officeholders as indications of policy or systems change in the USSR appears to rest on assumptions regarding the categories of individuals who are favoured at one time or another by the appointments policy of the centre. If certain types of individuals are being recruited and promoted at certain points, the inference can easily be drawn that Moscow is consciously pursuing certain cadres policies in concert with its overall policy orientations. In as much as the *nomenklatura* system formally concentrates enormous appointment powers in Moscow (and, secondarily, in the capitals of the republics), the assumption that the right hand (cadres policy) knows what the left hand (substantive policy) is doing does not appear to be an unreasonable one to hold.

This assumption, however, has recently been called into question by a number of studies which indicate that the political centre uses its formal powers of appointment largely to ratify the results of the real process of selection taking place in the localities.[2] These studies represent a challenge to, and in certain respects an advance over, the conventional assumptions regarding central control over elite circulation in the USSR. The method which informs them, though, is continuous with the general orientation in the field which gives primacy to individuals rather than to the relations among them. As a result, the evidence that these studies adduce to support their overall conclusions regarding a declining importance of centralized direction in the Soviet personnel process is more suggestive than systematic. Take, for instance, the use of cross-regional transfers, an indicator commonly employed to measure the centre's influence on regional elite mobility. A diminishing frequency of such transfers and a concomitant tendency for officials to make their entire careers within a single republic or region are taken as indications of a weakening of the centre's influence over the movement of personnel and suggests that something of a *laissez faire* posture (summed up in Brezhnev's slogan of 'trust in local cadres') has been adopted with respect to the circulation of sub-national elites.

But, as plausible as this argument seems, it remains inconclusive because it seeks to address a systemic issue – the degree of centralization in the system – on the basis of individual-level data. As a consequence, it finds itself unable to engage a counter-argument constructed in terms of relations within the system, namely, that declining rates of cross-regional transfers may signal an increase in centralized control over personnel matters, in as much as the centre is now able to vet, groom and install local cadres on whom it can rely, thus obviating its need to shift personnel around among the various regions in order to secure compliance with its policy directives. Rather than a decline in centralization, a diminishing frequency in cross-regional transfers may indicate that centralization has been perfected to the point that the relatively clumsy method of moving subordinate officials around the map has become obsolete.

The point of this discussion is neither to suggest that indicators such as cross-regional transfers are useless nor that, in the present illustration, a decline in the rate at which actors are shifted among the regions of the USSR shows that central control over the movement of personnel has indeed been perfected. Rather, it merely points up the ambiguity that results when an analysis of a systemic factor such as centralization rests on the rather oblique individual-level data that are available at this time to scholars in the field. The vacancy model, which is designed to incorporate the relations among individuals, seems a sounder approach to answering questions of a systemic order. Here, we apply it to the question of whether centralization accounts for elite circulation in the BSSR.

Centralization and the circulation of vacancies in the system

An algebraic model

To the outline of the vacancy model developed in the first chapter, it is important at this point to add a word on its dynamics and to explicate its logic. As to the former, vacancy chains are a species of Markov chains, meaning that specifiable probabilities exist which govern the transitions in the system from one state to another. The 'states' in the system under consideration are the ten strata of jobs which comprise the hierarchical model generated in the previous chapter. The vacancy chain approach, then, postulates that the circulation process is a Markovian one wherein events in the system can be predicted solely on the basis of the distribution of vacancies among the strata in the system and the probabilities which effect their transitions among these strata.[3] Accordingly, the Markovian nature of the vacancy approach allows us to postulate a pure model of elite circulation in which central control plays no role, and then to compare empirical cases against this baseline. To the degree that the model fits the data, elite circulation across the array of positions in our stratified system of Belorussian offices can be regarded as Markovian. Vacancies can be taken as moving independently of one another in accordance with fixed transition probabilities which govern this movement. Effective, as opposed to nominal, central control over appointments would not add, if the model is successful, anything to an explanation of the circulation of elites within the system.

The vacancy approach relies upon the computation of probabilities in order to predict events in the system. We might, then, explicate the logic of this method by beginning with the simplest event under consideration, the movement of an individual vacancy.[4] Following conventional notation, we let q_{ik} represent the probability that in a given period of time a vacancy will move from some stratum (i) in our hierarchical model to a job in some stratum (k), and q_{i0} represent the probability that the vacancy will move outside the system. A square matrix, Q, can then be written in which the number of rows and columns corresponds to s, the number of strata in a hierarchical ranking of jobs, and q_{ik} can be found in the ith row and k^{th} column of Q. Similarly, let p be a column vector whose elements, q_{i0}, q_{k0} ... q_{s0}, are the termination probabilities of vacancies in the system (i.e., the probability for each vacancy appearing in any row of Q that its next move will be to the outside). Since by definition a vacancy must either move to another job in the system or to the outside, we can write: Q1 + p = 1, where 1 is a column vector with s components, each of which is unity.

Since vacancies trace chains of varying length as they move from one to another job in the system, let j represent the variable, chain length. Accordingly, let the mean lengths of chains initiated in each stratum be gathered in a column vector, λ. Finally, let P_j be a column vector, each of whose elements is the probability that, by the stratum in which a chain has originated, the chain will be of length j. The vector, P_j, is calculated according to the equation: $P_j = Q^{j-1}p$. As such, when the vector is multiplied by the variable, j, and summed, it is equal to λ, which in turn is equal to the inverse of p. This can be written:

$$\lambda = \Sigma jP_j = \frac{1}{p}.$$

In order to illustrate how P_j is calculated, consider a simple example in which all jobs have been grouped into a single stratum and the mean length of the vacancy chains involved is 2. The termination probability, p, would therefore be 0.5 (since $p = \frac{1}{2}$) and the Q matrix would have a single element which, according to the equation written above, $Q1 + p = 1$, would also be 0.5. Carrying out this computation, we would have:

j	Q^{j-1}	p	P_j	jP_j
1	1	0.5	0.5	0.5
2	0.5	0.5	0.25	0.5
3	0.25	0.5	0.125	0.375
4	0.125	0.5	0.0625	0.25
5	0.0625	0.5 =	0.03125	0.15625
6	0.03125	0.5	0.015625	0.09375
7	0.015625	0.5	0.0078125	0.0546875
8	0.0078125	0.5	0.00390625	0.03125
–	–	0.5	–	–

$$\Sigma P_j \approx 1.0 \qquad \Sigma jP_j \approx 2.0$$

It is evident in this example that the probabilities arranged in P_j represent a geometric series derived from the successive raising of Q to higher powers as the value of the variable j increases, and that the sum of the elements in P_j, were the calculation carried out infinitely, would equal unity. Similarly, we can see that were we to carry out the computation, $\lambda = \Sigma jP_j$, the mean length of 2 for vacancy chains in the illustration would equal the sum of all the elements of P_j multiplied by the variable j, and that the inverse of this sum would equal p.

Applying this method to our Belorussian data which are arrayed in a hierarchy that contains ten strata, we derive the 10 × 10 Q matrix of transition probabilities and the p vector of termination probabilities for all the vacancies recorded over the period, 1966–86. These are set out in Table 3.1. The matrix is read by taking any row entry as the stratum in which a given vacancy has arisen and matching it to any column as the probability that its next move will be to that stratum. For instance,

Table 3.1. *Q matrix of transition probabilities of vacancies among strata, 1966–86*

Stratum of origin	Stratum of destination										P
	1	2	3	4	5	6	7	8	9	10	
1	0.38	0.25	0.06	0.06	–	–	–	–	–	–	0.25
2	0.06	0.06	0.56	0.06	0.06	–	–	–	–	–	0.22
3	–	0.02	0.07	0.50	0.05	0.04	–	–	–	–	0.32
4	–	–	0.05	0.05	0.53	0.07	0.02	–	–	–	0.28
5	–	0.01	0.01	0.02	0.11	0.33	0.03	–	–	–	0.49
6	–	–	0.01	0.01	0.02	0.04	0.24	0.02	–	–	0.67
7	–	–	–	–	0.01	0.04	0.07	0.18	0.02	–	0.67
8	–	–	–	–	0.02	0.03	0.05	0.06	0.09	–	0.74
9	–	–	–	–	–	0.01	0.02	0.02	–	0.03	0.92
10	–	–	–	–	0.01	0.04	0.01	–	0.03	0.05	0.86

the first row reports that vacancies in the first stratum had a 0.38 probability of moving next to another job in Stratum 1, a 0.25 probability of moving next to Stratum 2 and an equal chance (0.06) of making their next moves to either Stratum 3 or Stratum 4. The p value in the right-hand column of Table 3.1 indicates a 0.25 probability that Stratum 1 vacancies will next move outside the system (i.e., the replacement who fills the vacancy will come from outside of the BSSR).

The primary test for a centralizing influence on the circulation of vacancies within the set of positions in the BSSR involves P_j, the column vector that predicts chain length by the stratum in which a given chain has originated. As in our simplified illustration, P_j expresses the probability that a certain percentage of chains originating in, say, Stratum 1 will be of length 1, a certain percentage will be of length 2, and so forth. If the observed distribution of vacancy chains originating in this stratum and others matches the predicted values in P_j, then the process is Markovian. In other words, the circulation of elites (taken as the circulation of vacancies) is not affected by a centralizing influence.[5]

Additional considerations

In addition to the main test for determining whether the system of positions in the BSSR exhibits the Markov property, three auxiliary measures of centralization are employed in this chapter. The first, and strongest, indicator of centralization involves a comparison of the career histories of those in the top three strata of the model (i.e., the strata in which effectively all jobs are subject to Moscow's *nomenklatura*) with the observed vacancy chains initiated by their exits from the system. If there are matches, that is, if we find the jobs in a certain actor's career history appearing again in the chain of vacancies set off by his departure from the system, then it is reasonable to infer that certain positions function as stepping stones to others, that the central authorities are grooming replacements for the top positions by installing certain individuals in stepping stone jobs and that the circulation of elites in the BSSR is determined from above.[6] To the degree that no significant overlaps of this type occur, however, the hypothesis that the central authorities are merely ratifying the results of a personnel process specific to the BSSR would be supported.

A second, and weaker, indicator of a centralizing effect on elite circulation in the BSSR involves the vetting of personnel in Moscow. Are vacancies in the Belorussian positions which numbered among the offices in the top three strata filled by replacements whose previous jobs were at the all-union level? A pattern of such would constitute evidence that candidates for high office in the BSSR regularly are placed in upper-level jobs after career detours that take them to Moscow where they are vetted by the central authorities.

The third, and weakest, indicator of centralization utilizes the p value (the probability that a vacancy will leave the system) for Strata 1 to 3. Increases or decreases in p over various periods in the time frame would suggest a concomitant tendency on the part of the central authorities to pack higher offices in the BSSR with individuals from outside (or those briefly holding jobs outside) of the Republic. As with the second indicator, above, this is a rather weak measure of centralization, 'weak' in as much as, unlike P_j which is based on the structure of elite circulation in the BSSR, it is confined to the particular movements of particular individuals. We might assume that Moscow, having vetted these individuals, has come to rely on them to carry out specific directives in the Republic. But this practice might be regarded as a rather poor substitute for effective personnel centralization in a systemic sense. Having been parachuted into high office in the BSSR, these same individuals must work with personnel already there in place. If the career mobility of the latter is shown to be beyond the effective reach of the centre either directly or indirectly, then these outsiders would be surrounded by 'natives' whom, even if they did not 'marry', they would likely find difficult to control.

The main test

The Q matrix presented in Table 3.1 reports the transition probabilities for individual vacancies to the ten strata in the model over the entire 20 year period encompassed by our study. As we would expect from the method used to stratify the sample of positions, the diagonal line in the matrix running through the intersection of row values and the column values found one step to the right of the corresponding row (2, 3; 3, 4; etc.) records in all but two cases the highest transition probabilities for vacancies in the system. So, for instance, vacancies which arrived in Stratum 2 had a probability of 0.56 of moving next to Stratum 3; those arriving in Stratum 3, a probability of 0.50 of moving next to Stratum 4, and so forth as one follows the diagonal toward the bottom-right quadrant of the matrix. The exceptions to this pattern occur at the top-left and bottom-right of Table 3.1. We notice in this respect that vacancies appearing in the first and last strata evince a higher probability to circulate within these same strata than they do to move to any other stratum in the model. In the case of Stratum 10, this simply reflects the fact that there are no lower strata from which to summon replacements. For Stratum 1, however, the relatively high probability (0.38) that a vacancy arriving there will make its next move to another job in the same stratum indicates a considerable degree of rotation of personnel among these top-level jobs and suggests that once an actor has filled one of these positions, his next career move will likely be to another top-level job.

Our main test for centralization is concerned with discrepancies between predicted and observed chain lengths by stratum of origin and involves the term, P_j, which predicts the distribution of chain lengths. Table 3.2 presents these data. In comparing the predicted distributions of chain lengths against their observed values, it is clear that the largest differences occur in the top three strata. Stratum 1 records two instances in which the differences between predicted and observed values reached or exceeded 10 percentage points, as does Stratum 3, while Stratum 2 involves one such case. Additionally, it will be noticed that modal values in the predicted and observed distributions agree in the case of Stratum 2 but diverge in the first and third strata.

Table 3.2. *Predicted (P) and observed (O) distributions of chain lengths by stratum of origin (in percentages)* N = 2774*

Chain lengths	Stratum 1			Stratum 2			Stratum 3		
	P	O	n	P	O	n	P	O	n
1	25.0	16.7	5	22.2	13.9	5	32.1	18.8	18
2	18.7	20.0	6	24.8	38.9	14	21.8	34.4	33
3	16.7	6.7	2	18.2	16.7	7	21.8	26.0	25
4	13.5	23.3	7	16.0	13.9	5	13.3	12.5	12
5	10.5	16.7	5	9.8	8.3	3	6.2	4.2	4
6	7.0	6.7	2	4.9	8.3	3	2.7	3.1	3
7	4.1	6.7	2	2.3	—	—	1.1	1.0	1
8	2.2	3.3	1	1.0	—	—	0.4	—	—
9	1.1	—	—	0.5	—	—	0.2	—	—

Chain lengths	Stratum 4			Stratum 5			Stratum 6		
	P	O	n	P	O	n	P	O	n
1	28.2	26.5	32	48.7	48.8	177	67.1	70.2	420
2	34.9	43.0	52	30.8	33.3	121	21.5	22.4	134
3	21.0	19.0	23	12.4	12.4	45	7.7	6.4	38
4	9.3	7.4	9	5.0	2.5	9	2.5	0.5	3
5	3.9	3.3	4	1.9	2.8	10	0.8	0.3	2
6	1.6	—	—	0.7	0.3	1	0.2	0.2	1
7	0.6	0.8	1	0.3	—	—	0.1		
8	0.2	—	—	0.1	—	—			

Chain lengths	Stratum 7			Stratum 8			Stratum 9		
	P	O	n	P	O	n	P	O	n
1	67.4	67.5	305	74.4	76.4	410	91.8	90.0	261
2	23.3	26.3	119	19.4	19.7	106	6.1	9.0	26
3	6.6	4.7	21	4.2	3.7	20	1.5	1.0	3
4	1.8	1.6	7	1.3	0.2	1	0.4	—	—
5	0.6	—	—	0.4	—	—	0.1	—	—
6	0.2	—	—	0.2	—	—			
7	0.1	—	—	0.1	—	—			

Chain lengths	Stratum 10		
	P	O	n
1	86.0	87.7	220
2	11.0	8.8	22
3	2.1	3.2	8
4	0.6	—	—
5	0.2	0.4	1
6	0.1	—	—

* 'N' refers to the number of vacancy chains.

Among the remaining strata, all differences between predicted and observed values are under the 10 percentage point mark. The largest difference in this group occurs in Stratum 4, a difference of 8.1 per cent. For these seven strata taken together, predicted and observed values are separated by a single percentage point or less in 29 of the 48 instances involved (60.4 per cent of the cases) and by 2 percentage points or less in 41 of the instances (85.4 per cent).

Although we are not attempting to generalize the findings in a sample to a larger population, there seems to be some utility in following White's suggestion[7] that the application of a significance test to data such as these would provide an indication of the meaning which we might attach to the differences recorded between predicted and observed values. A non-parametric statistic, the Kolmogorov Goodness of Fit Test, is appropriate to this purpose.[8] Setting the significance level at 0.5 (for we wish to test rigorously the predictive accuracy of the model and, hence, we want to make it difficult for ourselves to say that no significant differences obtain) we find that none of the differences between predicted and observed values is significant. This finding would support the predictive accuracy of the model and indicate that the circulation of elites in the BSSR resembles a Markovian process in which the centralized *nomenklatura* system in Moscow (or its counterpart in Minsk) has but a marginal influence.

Let us, however, examine this influence further. The data in Table 3.2 indicate that disruptions in our hypothesized Markov process for the flow of vacancies in the system are effectively confined to the top three strata. Since the jobs in question here overwhelmingly fall within the scope of Moscow's *nomenklatura*, this is to be expected on substantive grounds as well. However, a question remains

Table 3.3. *Predicted (P) and observed (O) distributions of chain lengths for the top three strata, with and without all-union jobs*

Chain Length	Strata 1–3 All-union jobs included		Strata 1–3 All-union jobs excluded	
	P	O	P	O
1	28.9	17.3	62.6	62.5
2	22.0	32.7	22.7	23.6
3	20.3	20.4	8.8	9.1
4	14.0	14.8	3.5	2.6
5	7.7	7.4	1.4	1.2
6	3.8	4.9	0.5	0.7
7	1.8	1.9	0.2	0.4
8	0.8	0.6	0.1	—
9	0.3	—		
10	0.2	—		

regarding the precise manner in which this centralizing influence functions. We can clarify matters by conceptually distinguishing between a direct form of centralization in which Moscow's cadres policies reach into the BSSR to alter the results of a personnel process which is endemic to the Republic, on the one hand, and an indirect form of central influence which derives from the interaction between the personnel system in the BSSR and that which exists at the all-union level, on the other. In so far as the latter is concerned, it may be the case that the influences which are disturbing a postulated Markovian flow of vacancies come about as a result of events taking place in Moscow rather than in Belorussia. Since a number of all-union positions appear among the jobs contained in the top two strata, we can determine whether the centralizing influence is directly or only indirectly at work by removing the all-union positions from the data set and repeating the analysis.

The results of this procedure are displayed in Table 3.3 which (owing to the small number of cases which remain in the data set for the top two strata once the all-union positions have been excluded) lumps together all jobs in the top three strata. These data show that an indirect form of centralization appears to be present in the system, but do not support the idea of a direct form of central control over elite circulation within the BSSR. The centralizing effect, which is evident in the marked disagreements between the columns of predicted and observed values on the left-hand side of Table 3.3 (differences larger than 10 percentage points show up in two cases) which include the all-union positions in the sample, disappears on the right-hand side where the all-union jobs have been excluded from the analysis and where the predicted and observed distributions of chain lengths come into very close agreement. To be sure, some of the closeness apparent in matching predicted and observed values on the right-hand side of Table 3.3 is a statistical consequence of performing the analysis after having excluded the all-union positions. Such skews the distribution in the direction of short chains, since we have artificially removed a number of the 'links' provided by vacancies in all-union positions which are evident in the greater proportion of long chains in the left-hand columns of Table 3.3. Nonetheless, the predicted values fit the observed results in the right-hand columns with such a high degree of accuracy (all differences are under one percentage point) that it seems safe to infer that to the degree that a centralizing effect on the circulation of vacancies in the model is apparent, it can be traced to the interaction of two separate personnel systems, one at the all-union level and another in the BSSR. Of course, in the real order of things, this division between personnel systems would appear somewhat artificial, but in drawing it we have been able to distinguish analytically between two varieties of centralization. One takes the direct form of a cadres policy that systematically manipulates the movement of actors among the offices in the BSSR; the other is indirect and consists of the implications which events taking place at one level of the system have for events at other levels. On the basis of the results from the main test, it appears that (a) a centralizing influence on elite circulation in the BSSR is of marginal import and (b) to the extent that the flow of vacancies in the Belorussian Republic is subject to such an influence, centralization is manifested indirectly as the interaction between personnel systems at the all-union and republic levels.

Auxiliary tests

The first, and strongest, potential indicator of centralization among the three auxiliary tests to be conducted is concerned with what matches might be found between the jobs contained in the career histories of those leaving the system by virtue of death, retirement, transfer to a position not included in the data set or simple removal from office, and the specific positions included in the vacancy chains initiated by their exits. We confine the application of this test to those actors whose departures from the system left a vacancy in some job

Table 3.4. *Job matches between career histories of officeholders and vacancy chains initiated by their exits, 1966–86 (Strata 1–3)*

	Chains initiated in Stratum 1	
	Chains initiated in Moscow	Chains initiated in BSSR
Total number of vacancies	13	66
Number of chains	7	17
Chain lengths	1,4	1–8
Number of matches	1	3

	Chains initiated in Stratum 2	
	Chains initiated in Moscow	Chains initiated in BSSR
Total number of vacancies	4	91
Number of chains	4	28
Chain lengths	1	1–6
Number of matches	0	3

	Chains initiated in Stratum 3	
	Chains initiated in Moscow	Chains initiated in BSSR
Total number of vacancies	—	159
Number of chains	—	54
Chain lengths	—	1–7
Number of matches	—	6

which is numbered among the top three strata. The focus on these strata follows both from their position atop the hierarchy and from the marginal impact of a centralizing influence on this sub-set of jobs which we observed in the results of the main test. Here, we are looking for another way in which centralization might manifest itself in the system. Job matches between the career histories of those leaving the system and the vacancy chains triggered by their exits would indicate the presence of a cohort of cadres, advancing through stepping stone jobs, who fill vacancies in the top jobs as they occur. Such would be demonstrable evidence of a centralizing influence on elite circulation, suggesting that Moscow has been effectively reaching into the personnel process in the BSSR and systematically staffing the top positions with replacements whom it had groomed and eventually installed in elite jobs.

Table 3.4 summarizes the results of this test for the top three strata. A total of 24 vacancy chains containing a total of 79 vacancies occurred in Stratum 1. Of these chains, as the upper-left portion of Table 3.4 shows, seven were initiated by a vacancy in an executive job in Moscow which had been held by an official whose former career had been in the BSSR. Five of these were of length 1 (indicating that these vacancies summoned no replacements from the BSSR), two were of length 4 and one of these contained a single match with the career history of the official whose exit initiated the chain.

A similar dearth of matches is observable in Stratum 1 for those chains begun by the exit of an officeholder in the BSSR (upper-right section of Table 3.4). In only three cases were there matches and each involved a single job in the replacement chain matching one of the positions in the career history of the exiting official (albeit, in one instance, the career history of the second person in the replacement chain evinced two matches with the other jobs in that chain). In as much as these 17 vacancy chains varied in length from 1 (the Head of the Belorussian KGB who in the two reported cases drew a replacement from outside the BSSR) to 8 and accounted for some 66 vacancies in all, the three matches recorded would not indicate that the centre has been grooming and installing replacements in Stratum 1 jobs in the BSSR.

The application of this same test to Stratum 2 yielded comparable results. No vacancies in Moscow summoned replacements from the BSSR (middle-left portion of Table 3.4). Of those 28 chains begun by a vacancy in a BSSR job (middle-right section) only three contained jobs which matched the career histories of those leaving the system (one in each case). Given that 91 vacancies were included in these 28 chains, three matches seems quite a negligible figure.

The data on the career histories of those leaving the system from jobs in Stratum 3 are incomplete. As a result, the analysis excludes 34 chains (with a total of 97 vacancies) begun by the exit of an official for whom no career history is available. The remaining 54 chains that were triggered by a vacancy first appearing in a job in this stratum were all initiated in the BSSR, owing to the fact that Stratum 3 includes no all-union positions. These 54 chains contain a total of 159 vacancies, of which only six (one in each case) match jobs in the career histories of those exiting officials on whom data are available. Again, the relative absence of matches indicates an absence of centralization measured in this way.

A sub-set of positions in Stratum 3, however, shows a slightly higher score on this indicator. That is, if we divide the jobs in Stratum 3 into one group which contains the executives of the state apparatus (ministers and deputy ministers, chairs and deputy chairs of state committees and so forth, as set out in Appendix A) and another group composed of all other positions in Stratum 3, we find that those leaving jobs in the state apparatus have career histories that match their respective vacancy chains more often than is true for the other group. In the case of the state executives, four matches were recorded against 49 vacancies contained in 21 chains (8.2 per cent), whereas the career histories of those exiting from the remaining positions in Stratum 3 evinced only two matches against 110 vacancies contained in 33 chains (1.8 per cent). While the percentage figures in either case are far too low to support the notion of centralization under this test, it is interesting to observe a muted 'bureaucratic' effect in the system, involving some (albeit, small) measure of predictability in the career paths to top jobs in the state apparatus. These results are consonant with those reported by other observers in the field, and apparently reflect the influence of the *nomenklatura* powers held by ministerial superiors at the all-union level.[9]

Even taking into account this (rather small) 'bureaucratic' effect which we have observed for certain jobs in Stratum 3, the overall results of this test indicate a decided absence of centralization in staffing the top three strata of positions in the BSSR through the use of a specifiable set of offices that function as stepping stones to jobs at the top of the hierarchy. The positions in these strata are clearly within the purview of the all-union *nomenklatura*, yet Moscow seems not to have used its formal authority to shape systematically the process of elite recruitment in the BSSR. One indication of what might be driving this process also emerges from these data, namely, the effect of region. In the present case, it takes the form of a disproportionate representation of organizations located in the capital city, Minsk, in the vacancy chains begun in the top three strata. Minsk is a city of republic, rather than oblast', subordination and consequently shares with the oblast' in which it is located a formally equivalent administrative status.[10] However, in terms of rank in the KPB, the party organization in Minsk City is apparently inferior to the Minsk Oblast' organization. The First Secretary of the Minsk Obkom has always been over the period of our study a full member of the Buro of the KPB while the First Secretary of Minsk Gorkom has never been included on the Buro as even a candidate member. Additionally, the First Secretary of the Obkom is the official head of the entire delegation from Minsk to congresses of the CPSU.[11] Therefore, we might expect that jobs in the city and oblast' organizations of Minsk would be more or less evenly represented in the vacancy chains initiated in the top three strata, with any edge going to Minsk Oblast'. We find, however, that the reverse is true. Among the vacancy chains begun in Stratum 1, jobs in Minsk City appeared 11 times while jobs in Minsk Oblast' turned up only twice; the comparable figures for chains begun in Stratum 2 are ten for Minsk City and four for Minsk Oblast'; and for Stratum 3, 15 for Minsk City and ten for Minsk Oblast'. Positions in Minsk City, then, are something of a fast track to high office in the Republic, a feature of this set of jobs that also accounts for the case, mentioned above, of two job matches between the career history of the second person in the replacement chain and the vacancy chain through which he was moving at the time (both job matches were Minsk City positions).

The prominence of Minsk City organizations as stepping stones to top elite positions in the BSSR may be better explained from the bottom-up rather than from the top-down. That is, an identifiable pool of positions with a relatively high frequency of transitions to higher office is not in itself evidence of an effective centralizing influence on elite circulation. It simply records the fact that a certain set of positions lines much of the avenue to higher office. As we see in the following chapter, a patronage group emerged in Minsk City organizations over the period encompassed by this study which, through ties with actors in Moscow, managed to distribute jobs in Minsk City to group members for whom these positions functioned as stepping stones to the highest offices in the Republic. In so far as a regionally based pattern of patronage is concerned, centralized control over elite circulation in the BSSR would be of the nominal variety. A centrally placed patron would be engaged in a particularistic exchange with clients in the BSSR; however, this could not be taken as evidence that Moscow has been pursuing a coordinated cadres policy in the Republic.

The results of the second auxiliary test indicate that Moscow makes very sparing use of a surrogate form of centralization, the vetting of candidates for higher office in the BSSR by means of sojourns in all-union offices which immediately precede their appointments to top positions in Belorussia. For Stratum 1 positions, such vetting seems to have occurred on four occasions. The position of First Secretary of the KPB was twice filled by Belorussian politicians who held jobs in Moscow prior to this appointment. The other two cases involve

Belorussians who held all-union jobs prior to being appointed secretaries of the KPB. Stratum 2 contains only two cases of vetting. In these the actors occupied Moscow positions before they were named Chair of Gosplan, BSSR, and Chair of the BSSR State Committee for Construction Affairs, respectively. For vacancies which appeared in Stratum 3 posts, the data record three instances in which replacements were drawn from Belorussian politicians who were occupying all-union offices at the time. In one case, the Ambassador to North Korea was recalled to fill the position of Belorussian Minister of Social Security, in another, the Head of the Main Administration for Repair and Technical Services of the USSR's State Committee for Agricultural Technology returned to Belorussia to become Head of the BSSR's State Committee for Agricultural Technology and, in a third, the Head of the Main Administration for Automotive Inspections of the USSR's Ministry of Internal Affairs came back to the BSSR to become its Minister of Internal Affairs. Taken together, the infrequency with which Belorussian politicians held all-union posts prior to taking up a position in the BSSR in any of the top three strata appears to indicate that, although vetting does occur, it does not seem to be a pronounced factor in shaping the circulation of elites in the Belorussian Republic.

The results of the final auxiliary test are displayed in Table 3.5. These data allow for a comparison between the probability (p statistic) and the relative frequency (observed rates) of vacancies passing out of the system over various periods of time. The figures in the two left-hand columns have been calculated from the full set of data while those in the right-hand columns have been derived from the same calculations but with all-union jobs excluded from the data set. This division permits us to make some further comparisons. The figures in the left-hand columns include data on those all-union positions that were at one time or another held by politicians from Belorussia who were replaced by individuals from outside the BSSR. The inclusion of such jobs tends to inflate somewhat the predicted and observed values in the table, adding to the turnover in specifically Belorussian positions a small fraction of the turnover in all-union jobs through which Belorussians had circulated. The figures in the right-hand columns are not affected by this consideration since they have been calculated solely on the basis of positions in the BSSR. As a consequence, however, vacancies in Belorussian jobs which have been filled by Belorussian politicians returning to the BSSR from posts at the all-union level are recorded as vacancies which have passed outside of

Table 3.5. *Probabilities and relative frequencies of vacancies passing out of the system in Strata 1–3 (combined), by time periods, with and without all-union jobs*

Time Period	All-union jobs included		All-union jobs excluded	
	Predicted	Observed	Predicted	Observed
1966–86	0.29	0.17	0.63	0.63
1966–76	0.29	0.20	0.58	0.52
1977–86	0.29	0.15	0.71	0.70
1966–71	0.24	0.21	0.48	0.57
1972–76	0.45	0.19	0.55	0.58
1977–81	0.25	0.18	0.68	0.70
1982–86	0.36	0.13	0.72	0.72

the system. This, as the figures indicate, raises predicted and observed values even more.

A comparison of the predicted and observed values in the left-hand columns of Table 3.5 shows that the probabilities for vacancies to pass to the outside consistently run ahead of the actual rates at which they do so. Although the figures in the fourth row of the table (1966–71) are close to agreement (0.24 versus 0.21), those in other rows, such as the fifth (1972–6), are clearly not (0.45 versus 0.19). The lack of overall agreement between predicted and observed values is apparently due to two things: the fact that the data used to calculate these values include all-union jobs and, relatedly, the method employed for calculating the predicted values. The former enables those vacancy chains begun in the BSSR to trace a path through jobs in Moscow, thus adding to their respective lengths. One result of this is apparent in the left-hand columns of Table 3.3 in which the predicted modal length of chains begun in the top three strata is a length of 1 (28.9 per cent) while the observed mode is a chain length of 2 (32.7 per cent). A similar difference between predicted and observed modes for chain lengths initiated in the top three strata obtains when the same analysis is performed on the data divided into discrete time periods.[12] The model's inability to predict modal lengths in the distribution of vacancy chains (Table 3.3) has already been traced to the inclusion of all-union jobs in the sample. This same factor seems to account for the differences apparent in the left-hand columns of Table 3.5. Recalling that the p statistic is the reciprocal of the mean chain length ($p = \frac{1}{\lambda}$) its tendency to 'overpredict' the rate at which vacancies in the top three strata make their next moves to outside the system is a consequence of the bunching of modal values for observed chain length distributions at lengths 2 and 3. Such distributions make for relatively low mean chain lengths and, hence, result in relatively high values for their reciprocal, p. Again, the presence of all-union jobs in the data set explains why the p values outrun the relative frequencies in Table 3.5. If, for instance, a job in any of the top three strata is filled by a Belorussian politician who leaves an all-union position, and this all-union job is, in turn, taken by an individual from some other locale in the USSR, the resulting chain attains a length of 2. Such a transaction does not then show up in the observed frequencies at which vacancies pass out of the system for the observed frequencies involve only chain lengths of 1, but it does tend to raise the probability estimate that they will do so because of the very small increment which a chain of length 2 adds to the score for mean chain length (the reciprocal of p). In the right-hand columns of Table 3.5, predicted and observed values come into close agreement precisely because all-union positions have been extracted from the data set, hence eliminating the pattern of chain length bunching around low values greater than one.

Focusing on the observed rates at which vacancies in Table 3.5 moved outside the system, we notice two patterns running in opposing directions over time. With all-union jobs included in the sample, rows 4–7 (i.e., those which cover the four periods of five years each) display a monotonic decrease in the relative frequency of movements to the outside; when the all-union jobs are excluded from the data, the relative frequency increases monotonically. The first pattern suggests a relative decline in the number of instances in which Moscow installed outsiders (i.e., officials from other parts of the USSR) in elite positions in the BSSR. Accordingly, the second pattern, which combines the installation of outsiders with the vetting of personnel in Moscow, indicates that over time Belorussian politicians who advanced to all-union posts were returning to top level jobs in the BSSR with increasing frequency. We take up this pattern in the chapter that follows. Here, having examined in the preceding test the matter of vetting and its relations to centralization, we turn our attention to the question of the direct packing of positions by Moscow.

Taken together, the individual cases represented in the data showed a limited proclivity on Moscow's part to exercise central control over elite circulation in the BSSR by packing positions in Belorussia with outsiders. For jobs in Stratum 1, such packing took place on three occasions, two of which involved outsiders who were installed as Chair of the Belorussian KGB, and in the third an outsider was parachuted into the position of Secretary of the KPB in charge of agriculture. No such parachuting occurred for any of the positions in Stratum 2. Among the 21 vacancies in Stratum 3 which were not recorded as having been filled by an individual who moved immediately from another job in the system, eight involved cases in which either no background information on the replacement was available or the jobs themselves were terminated by administrative reorganization. In the remaining 13 cases, eight recorded instances of vacancies filled by individuals who had career histories in the BSSR and who had either left the collection of positions assembled in the data set for brief periods (owing to health reasons, a return to full-time studies, or a posting described in the data sources as 'other work') or entered from a job in the BSSR that was not included in the data set. Hence, the data support only five possible instances of packing for Stratum 3 offices: Minister of the Belorussian Peat Industry, Minister of Rural Construction, Procurator of the BSSR, Chair of Gosteleradio and Deputy Chair of the Belorussian State Committee for Petroleum Products.

Two conclusions can be drawn from the third auxiliary test for centralization. First, the method of packing has been seldom used by Moscow as a means to manipulate elite circulation in the BSSR. Over the 20 year period spanned in this study, some 1,368 vacancies occurred in the Belorussian jobs numbered among those in the top three strata. The data record only nine instances in which these vacancies were filled by the transfer of an individual who had no previous career history in the BSSR. Even allowing for those few additional cases in which data are missing, the quantitative aspect of this method of centralized control over the personnel system bulks quite small.

Secondly, on the qualitative side, it is interesting to note something of a pattern in the positions that were packed. One sub-set of these, involving jobs in the area of political and legal control, includes the offices of Chair of the Belorussian KGB (twice packed) and Procurator of the BSSR (once packed). These cases appear to be particularly clear illustrations of cross-regional transfers that are designed to serve the purpose of enhancing Moscow's control over events in Belorussia through the insertion of outsiders into the leading positions in the law-enforcement apparatuses. By the same token, however, one may well wonder about the efficacy of this device, especially in as much as one of the individuals in question, V. A. Mogilnitskii (Procurator of the BSSR from 1973–83), was dismissed from office in the wake of a major scandal which also toppled a number of Belorussians in the Procuracy and Ministry of Internal Affairs (see Chapter 7). Perhaps in this instance the outsider sent in to control the natives ended up marrying one or more of them. At any event, these cases would indicate that Moscow has relied on packing certain sensitive positions in the BSSR in the interest of asserting central control, but the infrequency of same and the unreliability of the results would also caution against attaching much significance to this method.

Another sub-set of Belorussian jobs wherein some packing is evident involves the agricultural sector. Agriculture, including both the production of foodstuffs and the raising of crops for industrial use, has been an especially important component of Belorussia's economy.[13] It might be expected, then, that Moscow would take a particular interest in Belorussian agriculture and dispatch to the BSSR reliable cadres to superintend the agricultural sector. The data show three instances of such: V. S. Shevelukha served as Secretary of the KPB in charge of agriculture from 1974 to 1979, at which time he was transferred out of the BSSR and became Deputy Minister of Agriculture for the USSR; L. M. Chura was appointed Belorussian Minister of Rural Construction in 1980 but disappeared from the data sources after an administrative reorganization that terminated this office in 1985; I. Ya. Britov was named Minister of the Peat Industry, BSSR, in 1970 but drew an early pension in 1972 for reasons of health. Although this sub-set of jobs differs from that discussed above by virtue of the fact that these positions have more to do with implementing policy in order to make something happen, rather than to prevent something from occurring, which is the forte of law enforcement, the small size of the sub-set leads us to the same conclusion which we drew in reference to the first group.

Over the remaining policy sectors in the BSSR – light and heavy industry, education, health, cultural affairs and so on – only two instances of packing were recorded. G. N. Buravkin was named Chair of Gosteleradio, BSSR, in 1978 and continues in that post at present; V. S. Baranovskii became Deputy Chair of the Belorussian State Committee for Petroleum Products in 1980 and also holds that post currently. We draw from these rare instances in which outsiders were installed in jobs in the BSSR the inference that packing as a means by which Moscow might exercise control over Belorussian elites is distinguished by the infrequency of its use.

Summary and conclusions

The Soviet system concentrates enormous appointments powers in the hands of central authorities. The basic question addressed in this chapter, however, concerns the degree to which this control over appointments manifests itself in practice as a mechanism that structures the process of elite circulation. In order to treat the issue of centralization adequately, we have sought to view it as a characteristic of a system rather than as an aggregate of individual attributes. Accordingly, we constructed an analytic model of elite circulation, which derives from the method of vacancy chain analysis, and postulated that the circulation process is a Markovian one in which events in the system can be predicted solely on the basis of the distribution of vacancies among the 'states' in the system (our ten strata of hierarchically ranked jobs) and the probabilities that govern the transitions of vacancies to other states. By framing our model of elite circulation in these terms, we were able to test empirically for the presence of a centralizing influence on the flow of vacancies by means of comparisons drawn between the model's predictions and the observed results.

The findings produced by the main test that was performed on the data indicated that, while not statistically significant, some measure of centralization appeared to be present in the system and its influence was most pronounced among those offices ranked in the top three strata of positions (Table 3.2). In pursuing this line of inquiry, we learned that the influence of centralization was indirect. Rather than a mechanism that interfered with the movements of vacancies via direct and systematic manipulation of the personnel system in the BSSR, centralization emerged out of the interaction between vacancy flows at two levels of the Soviet system (Table 3.3). From this we drew two conclusions. First, effective (as opposed to nominal) centralization has no more than a marginal influence on the circulation of elites in the BSSR. Secondly, to the extent that such an influence is present, it appears to be a byproduct of the interaction between personnel systems at the all-union and republic levels.

The three auxiliary tests that were conducted in order to check further for traces of centralization in the circulation process tend to support the findings of the main test. The use of stepping stone jobs which function to groom replacements for higher office, the vetting of upwardly mobile actors by means of sojourns in all-union offices prior to entry into a top position in the BSSR, and the packing of elite jobs in

Belorussia with outsiders are all related to the matter of central control over the Republic's personnel process. Examples of each are evident in the data, but they are so few in number that they more resemble exceptions to the rule rather than explicit patterns of intervention on the part of the central authorities.

The narrative in this chapter has devoted the bulk of attention to these exceptions, isolating them as possible instances in which a centralizing influence has been manifest in the circulation process. Consequently, little emphasis has been placed on the larger pattern. Here, we might correct this imbalance somewhat by drawing attention to the overall predictive accuracy of the vacancy model. If some disturbances in the circulation process are apparent at the upper-end of the position hierarchy where two levels of the Soviet federal structure are joined, such disturbances have not been evident in the flows of vacancies at the middle and lower ranks (Strata 4–10). This, in turn, suggests an effective absence of a central personnel directorate within the BSSR that systematically shapes the process of elite circulation. As we see in the following chapter, a number of discrete personnel systems, organized around the foci of region and patronage, operate in the Belorussian Republic.

4 The regional structure of elite circulation

Regionalism connotes a *de facto* decentralization of authority in the Soviet system. It amounts to a form of slippage in the implementation of the centre's substantive policies, one which substitutes, as it were, the ongoing modifications of carpenters, bricklayers and so forth for the designs developed by the architect. In so far as cadres policy is concerned, regionalism functions as a countervailing influence on the centralized appointments mechanism through which the content of Moscow's *nomenklatura* is determined by personnel processes transpiring far from the capital. Behind the appearance of a central personnel office that directs the placement of cadres from the top-down, a number of studies have detected the presence of regionally based pockets of positions through which personnel circulate with little interference from the centre.[1] An upwardly mobile career for the great majority of Soviet politicians seems to hinge on, first, finding one's way into one of those networks which control local appointments and advancing on the basis of the patronage dispensed by holders of important regional posts. Secondly, it involves ascending the regional hierarchies to the point at which connections with potential patrons at higher levels might be cultivated.

The longevity and resilience of the regional factor in Soviet political life is in large measure a consequence of the manner in which that political life is structured. On the one hand, central actors seeking support against their rivals have actively nurtured regionalism through the beneficent extension of patronage to both cronies and potential allies alike.[2] On the other, attempts by the central authorities to exercise effective control over the affairs of this or that region have engendered defensive reactions on the part of local elites who collude in the interest of mutual security to elude the accounting to which they would otherwise be called.[3] Indeed, a number of observers have located the basis of regionalism's sustained presence in the Soviet system in the repeated cycle of attempts made by the political centre to enforce its dominion on regional elites who, in the face of this common threat, close ranks and cover their collective tracks by systematically deceiving the central authorities about the actual state of affairs in their respective bailiwicks, thus deepening further the problem of central control.[4] As our earlier discussion of weak structures and strong ties might suggest, the Soviet form of organization tends to favour a personalized style of interaction on which regionalism thrives and provides little by way of institutionalized means for reining in regionalism's centrifugal effects.

We have already encountered traces of regionalism in our analysis of elite circulation in the BSSR. In generating a hierarchy of positions in Chapter 2 we noticed that jobs in certain locales were empirically ranked in strata considerably higher than those to which their formal designations would appear to entitle them. Such positions seem to function as fast tracks to top elite office and their clustering in specific places suggests the influence of region in the patterns of mobility which we observed. Additionally, our findings in Chapter 3 regarding the effective absence of a centralizing influence on elite circulation *within* the BSSR would lead us to suspect that a number of personnel systems function in Belorussia at levels below that of the republic. In as much as a geographic base might be established for these, the practice of vetting upwardly mobile politicians by means of temporary postings in all-union jobs also takes on a new dimension. From the perspective of the centre, such vetting permits a determination of a given candidate's reliability; from that of the candidate, it provides an opportunity to cultivate patronage connections that can be used to advance not only his own career but those of other actors to whom he is tied by virtue of previous work in a given region.

The present chapter continues the methodological orientation that we have followed to this point. Our attention is focused on regionalism as a systemic factor in the process of elite circulation in the BSSR. Accordingly, we shall repeat the main test performed in Chapter 3, but modify its design by replacing the hierarchical strata with the regions of the Belorussian Republic.[5] In order to avoid confusion, we refer to the matrix of transition probabilities among the regions as R (instead of Q). Vacancy chains which begin at the all-union level are in some instances not germane to the issue of a regional structure of elite circulation in Belorussia and are therefore excluded from certain portions of the analysis. Chains which begin at the republic level, however, are relevant in all cases, and, hence, are consistently included. All other terms and calculations pertaining to the main test as set out in the previous chapters are retained here.

The logic employed in this examination of the effects of region on the circulation of Belorussian elites parallels that which was discussed in Chapter 3 regarding the effects of centralization. P_j, which here predicts the distribution of chain lengths by the regions in which chains originate, is again the key term. To the degree that the observed distribution of vacancy chain lengths matches the values predicted by P_j, the circulation of vacancies among the regions of the BSSR can be regarded as a Markovian process in which the flow of vacancies is explained by the present state of the system (the regional distribution of vacancies) and the probabilities that govern the movement of vacancies among the regions. Region, if the model's predictions prove accurate, would form the basis of elite circulation in Belorussia.

In addition to the main test for a regional basis of Markov chains in our model, we shall offer some comparisons between the regional and stratified models, and examine both the career origins of regional elites, and the representation of the regions among the top office-holders in the BSSR and USSR.

The main test

The first set of results of our analysis of elite circulation according to region are set out in Table 4.1. Here, the statistic, P_j, predicts the length distribution of vacancy chains for each of the regions, and for republic-level organizations, in which chains originated. The overall agreement between the predicted and observed distributions of chain lengths is quite high, and suggests considerable accuracy for the regional model. In fact, 38 of the 56 predicted/observed couplings (67.9 per cent) are separated by a single percentage point or less, 49 of the 56 (87.5 per cent), by 2 percentage points or less. Applying, again, the Kolmogorov Goodness of Fit Test to the results here, we find that none of the differences between predicted and observed values is significant at the 0.5 level. Hence, there seem to be particularly strong grounds for accepting the validity of the regional model.

Focusing on the individual regions for a moment, we notice that disagreement between predicted and observed values is greatest in Minsk City and Minsk Oblast'. Although the size of these differences is not large enough to be statistically significant, we note in passing the fact that the differences which appear have been somewhat exagger-

Table 4.1. *Predicted (P) and observed (O) distributions of chain lengths by place of origin (in percentages) N = 2739*

Chain lengths	BSSR			Minsk Oblast'		
	P	O	n	P	O	n
1	55.1	55.5	434	70.0	66.6	219
2	28.0	26.6	208	20.6	25.2	83
3	10.8	10.7	84	6.4	5.5	18
4	3.8	3.6	28	2.0	1.5	5
5	1.3	2.3	18	0.7	0.9	3
6	0.4	0.9	7	0.2	0.3	1
7	0.1	0.4	3	0.1	—	—

Chain lengths	Brest Oblast'			Vitebsk Oblast'		
	P	O	n	P	O	n
1	69.5	71.5	158	73.4	74.4	227
2	21.0	19.9	44	19.3	17.7	54
3	6.5	6.8	15	5.2	6.2	19
4	2.0	1.8	4	1.5	0.7	2
5	0.7	—	—	0.4	0.7	2
6	0.2	—	—	0.1	0.3	1
7	0	—	—	0	—	—

Chain lengths	Gomel' Oblast			Grodno Oblast'		
	P	O	n	P	O	n
1	71.4	70.8	225	74.9	78.5	179
2	20.1	23.9	76	18.5	15.8	36
3	5.9	4.7	15	4.8	4.8	11
4	1.8	0.3	1	1.3	—	—
5	0.5	—	—	0.4	0.9	2
6	0.2	—	—	0.1	—	—
7	0.1	0.3	1	0	—	—

Chain lengths	Mogilev Oblast'			Minsk City		
	P	O	n	P	O	n
1	70.3	68.8	201	72.4	76.2	198
2	20.7	24.3	71	19.2	19.6	51
3	6.2	5.1	15	5.7	4.2	11
4	1.9	1.4	4	1.8	—	—
5	0.6	0.3	1	0.6	—	—
6	0.2	—	—	0.2	—	—
7	0.1	—	—	0	—	—

ated by our method of coding in as much as we have in this case analytically separated what is geographically a single unit. Were we to subsume Minsk City within Minsk Oblast', predicted and observed values would come into closer agreement and the values recorded for Minsk Oblast' as a whole would more resemble those of the other oblasts. As we see below, however, there is considerable utility in maintaining the City and Oblast' as discrete units with respect to explaining the process of elite circulation in the BSSR over this period.

Minsk City stands out from the other units in the regional model on another count. The chains that originated there do not exceed a length of 3, while in the oblasts the longest chains reported vary from lengths of 4 to 7. Two factors account for this. First, the number of administrative levels is fewer in Minsk City as compared to the oblasts. Whereas each oblast' contains city, raion and enterprise level positions within it, the administrative hierarchy in Minsk City includes only raion and enterprise level organizations. Hence, when vacancies draw replacements from jobs at levels below them, vacancies occurring in Minsk City have one less level from which to draw. Secondly, and more importantly, vacancies arriving in Minsk City which traced chains through its organization of lengths greater than 3 were themselves initiated by vacancies at the republic or all-union levels. As a consequence, such chains are not reported in the results for Minsk City. This phenomenon not only explains the peculiar chain length distribution for the City but indicates a replacement pattern in which those occupying Minsk City jobs are drawn into republic and all-union positions with a particularly high frequency. We return in what follows to both of these anomalies and draw out some of their implications.

Table 4.2 introduces a second set of results associated with the main

Table 4.2. *R matrix of transition probabilities of vacancies among regions, 1966—86*

Place of origin	Place of destination								
	Minsk	Brest	Vitebsk	Gomel'	Grodno	Mogilev	Minsk City	BSSR	USSR	Outside
Minsk	0.22	0.01	—	0.01	—	—	0.03	0.03	—	0.70
Brest	0.01	0.28	—	—	—	—	—	0.01	—	0.69
Vitebsk	—	0.01	0.23	—	0.01	—	—	0.01	—	0.73
Gomel'	0.02	—	0.01	0.25	0.01	—	—	0.02	—	0.71
Grodno	—	—	—	—	0.22	—	0.01	0.01	—	0.75
Mogilev	0.01	—	—	—	—	0.26	—	0.02	—	0.70
Minsk City	0.01	—	—	—	0.01	—	0.22	0.04	—	0.72
BSSR	0.04	0.03	0.03	0.02	0.02	0.02	0.05	0.23	0.01	0.55
USSR	0.02	0.04	0.02	—	—	0.02	0.04	0.29	0.10	0.48

test. It involves the R matrix of transition probabilities among regions which figures into the calculation of the P_j statistic (here, $P_j = R^{j-1}p$). The table is composed of nine rows and nine columns, six of which designate jobs in the six oblasts of the BSSR, one represents jobs in the capital city, Minsk, while the remaining two refer to republic and all-union positions, respectively. The matrix is read by taking any row entry as the place in which a given vacancy has occurred and matching it to any column to find the probability that its next move will be to the place designated by that column. So, for instance, the first row reports that a vacancy that appeared in Minsk Oblast' had a 0.22 probability of moving next to another job within (or, what is the same thing, summoning a replacement from within) that same oblast, a 0.01 probability of moving next to Brest Oblast', and so forth. The values entered along the diagonal in the matrix represent, then, the probabilities that vacancies occurring in a given place will make their next moves to jobs within that same place. For the regions and capital city of the BSSR, these values on the diagonal again place in sharp relief the importance of region in the circulation of vacancies. Only in the case of Minsk and Gomel' oblasts did a vacancy have a greater than 0.01 chance of summoning a replacement from another region. In the case of Minsk Oblast' the replacements tended to come from Minsk City which is, of course, within the same region geographically speaking, while for Gomel' only in one instance did a vacancy have a greater than 0.01 chance of circulating to another region and this figure is still rather small (0.02). Below, we examine the case of Minsk Oblast' further, for it has much to do with the rise and decline of a particular faction in Belorussian politics during the period encompassed by our study.

As might be expected, incumbents in Minsk Oblast' and Minsk City jobs had a greater likelihood of moving next to jobs at the republic level than did their counterparts in the other regions of the USSR. Row 8, which reports these probabilities for the BSSR, indicates that a vacancy in a republic-level job had a slightly greater chance (0.05) of moving next to Minsk City than it did of moving to Minsk Oblast'. What may be rather unexpected, however, are the comparable figures in row 9. In this case, all-union vacancies summoned replacements from Minsk City and Brest Oblast' with equal probability (0.04) while the probability that vacancies in all-union jobs would be filled by an incumbent in a Minsk Oblast' position was no greater than that for Vitebsk and Mogilev oblasts (0.02). Recalling from our discussion in the previous chapter that the city of Minsk is the administrative equivalent of Minsk

Oblast' but is apparently outranked by the Oblast' as far as the party hierarchy is concerned, we would not expect that the formal standing of Minsk City in the BSSR is sufficient to explain the fact that officeholders there had, in comparison with their counterparts in Minsk Oblast', twice the likelihood of making their next career moves to positions at the all-union level. Minsk City does have the largest concentration of industry in the BSSR and the size of its party organization is larger than that of any of the oblasts taken separately (which would for Minsk Oblast', of course, require deducting the Minsk City membership from its total).[6] But, again, these differences do not seem large enough to account for the disparity in transition probabilities, especially in as much as the second largest oblast' by both industrial concentration and party membership, Gomel', evinced no transitions to all-union jobs while Mogilev, the smallest oblast in the BSSR, scored equally with the larger Minsk and Vitebsk oblasts as we have seen.

Industrial concentration and party membership do not, then, correlate with transition probability to all-union jobs. The high scores recorded by Minsk City (as we see in more detail, below) seem to be due to the factor of 'region', represented in this instance by the connections among officeholders in Minsk City and their relations with officials in Moscow.

Regarding the relatively high score recorded for Brest Oblast', we note that this seems to be the result of the small number of cases involved and the particular nature of the cases themselves. Of three transitions which summoned replacements from Brest, one involved the First Secretary of the Brest Obkom of the Komsomol entering the Academy of Social Sciences of the Central Committee of the CPSU as an *aspirant* (the only such case recorded in the data), and two concerned officeholders in Brest taking jobs in the Secretariat of the CPSU as instructors, a post that is well below the rank of offices in Moscow held by the great majority of BSSR politicians whose careers included jobs in the Soviet capital. As a consequence, the relatively high score for Brest Oblast' does not imply, as it does for Minsk City, a concommitantly high frequency of transitions to important posts in Moscow.

Are the transition probabilities in the R matrix stable over time? We might answer this question by dividing the 21 years spanned in our time frame into two discrete periods, 1966–76 and 1976–86, each containing ten possible changes of incumbent (1966/7, 1967/8, and so on) in each of the jobs, and then recalculating the R matrix for each of these two periods. In comparing the R matrix for the first period with that for the second, we notice that none of the differences in transition probabilities is greater than 0.02. We are led to the inference that the regional pattern of vacancy circulation appears to be quite stable over time across all jobs in the system.[7]

The data presented in Tables 4.1 and 4.2 suggest that elite circulation in the BSSR over this time period can be grasped as a process in which region seems to be the primary characteristic of the system. The high predictive accuracy of the model with respect to chain length distributions across the regions (Table 4.1), the high probability evinced by vacancies to circulate within the region in which they appear (diagonal in Table 4.2) and the relative stability of the regional pattern over time point up the salience of region as a characteristic of elite mobility in the BSSR. At this point, some comparisons might be made regarding the manner in which this process is construed in the regional and stratified models and the respective utilities associated with each.

The two models compared

The results of the main test performed on the regional model can be compared against those of the equivalent test conducted on the stratified model in the previous chapter. In general, the predictive accuracy of the regional model (Table 4.1) is clearly higher than that of the stratified model when all-union jobs are included in the data set (Table 3.2). The movement of vacancies in the system, therefore, seems in some respects to be better captured by an analytic framework constructed on the basis of lateral vacancy flows (movement within the same and among the other regions) than by the stratified model in which vacancies move in vertical paths across ranks in a hierarchy. On the other hand, the modification introduced in the stratified model (the exclusion of all-union jobs from the data set) yielded results (Table 3.3) that compare quite favourably with those of the regional model. On this basis, there appears to be no warrant for preferring one model over the other. Rather, we might view them as alternative explanations of the circulation process, each of which contributes something to the total picture.[8]

The similarity of chain length distribution in the regional model contrasts sharply with the differences in chain lengths recorded by the various strata in the hierarchical model (Table 3.2). As a rule, higher strata produce longer chains. That is, whenever a vacancy enters a job

in the upper strata and then circulates in the system by drawing successive replacements from jobs of lower rank, the result will be a relatively
long, hierarchically ordered chain. This effect is obviously present in a
model constructed on the basis of a stratified ranking of jobs (hence, the
particular pattern of chain length distributions reported in Table 3.2). It
also appears within the regional model. As noted above in our comparison of chain length distributions for chains begun in Minsk City as
opposed to those originating in the oblasts, the number of administrative levels in a region is related to the length of the chains which form
there. Consequently, we reach the conclusion that the movement of
vacancies within and among the regions is not independent of their
movement across jobs in a hierarchy. The stratified model contributes
to our comprehension of the regional pattern of vacancy circulation.

The converse of this proportion is also true. Region influences the
flow of vacancies within the stratified model. An inspection of those 13
chains reported in Table 3.2 which attained lengths of 6 or greater
points to the fact that in ten of them vacancies traced paths through
jobs situated in a single region, while in the remaining three vacancies
circulated among positions characterized by a particular functional
specialization (agriculture in two instances, Komsomol work in the
other) and, accordingly, cut across two or more of the regions of the
BSSR. In the same way that the distribution of chain lengths generated
by the regional model can be regarded in large measure as a function of
hierarchy, so the specific content of the longer chains which appeared
in the stratified model is primarily determined by the regional circulation of vacancies. Each model, as it were, complements the information provided by the other.

When the modification of removing all-union positions from the
data set is introduced into the stratified model, the results of the main
test for both the stratified and regional models are quite similar on two
counts. First, the termination probabilities in each are relatively high.
For the stratified model, the probability that a vacancy will make its
next move to outside the system is 0.63 (Table 3.3), while for the
regional model the probability varies from 0.55 to 0.75 (Table 4.2).
Secondly, the predicted and observed chain length distributions agree
closely with the observed results in each case (Tables 3.3 and 4.1).
Although this agreement is somewhat greater in the stratified model
when modified, we recall that it was brought about by the removal of
the all-union jobs from the sample. Since no such adjustments were
made in the regional model, it has the advantage of being a more
realistic representation of the data.

This final observation notwithstanding, our comparison of the two models underscores the interaction of hierarchical rank and region in the circulation process. Although rank and region on their face would obviously be considered as major factors determining the mobility patterns of Soviet elites, the utility of the vacancy chain approach employed here consists in its capacity to capture this interaction explicitly by preserving the relations among events which are themselves empirically linked. Particularly in those cases which involve relatively long chains, the vacancy models have enabled us to see how region contributes the bulk of the content to chains begun at the upper levels of the hierarchy, while hierarchy, in its turn, plays a key role in determining the sequence of moves made by a vacancy once it has arrived in a given region. In brief, these two models call attention to the relationship that obtains between region and rank as factors which structure mobility patterns within the system. When viewing the circulation process from the vantage provided by either model, we are at the same time observing the effects of the other. The interaction between rank and region is placed in yet sharper relief by the results of the auxiliary tests for the influence of regionalism on the circulation of elites in the BSSR.

Auxiliary tests

We direct our attention at this point to another facet of the interaction between the hierarchical and regional models of mobility by examining regionally based leadership systems in the BSSR and the manner in which these articulate with their counterparts at the republic and all-union levels. Accordingly, the auxiliary tests are designed to analyse the origins and destinations of those who at one time or another occupied the top positions in the regions.

The data presented in Table 4.3 concern the origins of the regional elites. Here, 'origin' is defined as the place in which one held a job prior to occupying a top position in a given region. Even allowing for the fact that a number of those appearing in the columns under 'BSSR' and 'USSR' in Table 4.3 were in effect returning to the regions in which their careers began, these data indicate that regionalism is much less a pronounced factor in accounting for movement into elite positions in the regions than it is with respect to the set of regional positions in general. For the seven regions considered together, 62.8 per cent of the top jobs were filled by someone whose immediately prior position was in the same region, yielding a ratio of recruitment from within the

Table 4.3. *Regional origins of Belorussian regional elites*, 1966–86*

	From inside region	Other BSSR region	From outside-region BSSR	USSR	Total
Brest Oblast'	26	8	7	3	44
Vitebsk Oblast'	24	11	8	4	47
Gomel' Oblast'	33	6	9	0	48
Grodno Oblast'	24	7	5	0	36
Mogilev Oblast'	33	5	7	0	45
Minsk Oblast'	31	29 (12)	8	0	68
Minsk City	43	4 (3)	6	0	53

* Elite positions include: oblast' party secretaries (for Minsk City, city party secretaries); the president and first deputy president of the oblispolkom (for Minsk City, the gorispolkom); and the first secretary of the largest gorkom in the region (since Minsk City is dealt with as the equivalent of a region, the Borisov gorkom is used for Minsk Oblast' and the largest raikom in Minsk City, Sovetskii Raikom, is used for the capital).

The numbers appearing in parentheses indicate the complement for Minsk Oblast' which came from positions in Minsk City and the complement for Minsk City which came from Minsk Oblast'.

respective regions to recruitment from without of 1.7:1. For the overall circulation of vacancies (Table 4.2) the comparable ratios vary from a low of 2.75:1 (Minsk Oblast') to a high of 14:1 (Brest Oblast').

Minsk and Vitebsk oblasts recorded the lowest scores (45.6 per cent and 51.1 per cent, respectively) on the internal recruitment of their top elites. The score for Minsk Oblast', however, approximates the mean score for all regions if we were to consider those arriving from Minsk City jobs as coming from within Minsk Oblast' (63.2). The other extreme case is clearly Minsk City with an internal recruitment rate to top positions of 81.1 per cent. If we apply to Minsk City the same qualification which we introduced for Minsk Oblast' and deduct those who moved from jobs in the latter to positions in the former, we note that in only one of 53 cases did a member of Minsk City's elite come from a job in another region. This exceptionally high rate of internal recruitment for elite positions in Minsk City suggests the existence of a closed personnel system in the capital. Particularly in the second decade of our study, we find that this closed Minsk City group has come to dominate the top offices in the Belorussian Republic.

Table 4.4 displays the data on regional access to elite jobs at the republic level. Here, 'elite' refers to those jobs whose incumbents were

Table 4.4. *Regions of origin of top elite in BSSR, 1966–86*

	1966–86	1966–75	1976–86
Minsk Oblast'	10 (8)	10 (8)	0
Brest Oblast'	2	1	1
Vitebsk Oblast'	7 (2)	3 (2)	4
Gomel' Oblast'	1*	1*	0
Grodno Oblast'	2 (1*)	1 (1*)	1
Mogilev Oblast'	1 (1)	0	1 (1)
Minsk City	7	0	7
Outside of BSSR	4	3	1

Note: Origin is defined as region in which last position was held before entering the top elite. Numbers in parentheses indicate number of identified Partisans; asterisks indicate established career outside of BSSR before entering BSSR elite; number with asterisk in parentheses indicate main career line in Minsk Oblast'.

regularly represented (i.e., elected to these positions after at least four of the five congresses of the KPB held within the time frame of this study) on the Buro of the KPB. The numbers enclosed by parentheses in the table record the frequency with which members of the Partisan faction in Belorussian politics, the dominant group by the mid sixties, left leading positions in the regions to occupy elite jobs at the republic level. The left-hand column of Table 4.4 points up the fact that Minsk Oblast' has been the regional stronghold of this group and that out of an overall total of 30 officials moving from regional positions to elite jobs in the BSSR, 11 of these could be identified as Partisans.[9]

Perhaps the most interesting contrast apparent in Table 4.4 concerns the shifting regional basis of recruitment to elite jobs in the Republic. The middle column which includes the first decade of the study indicates a decisive dominance of Minsk Oblast'. Of 16 politicians moving from regional jobs to elite positions in the BSSR, ten were from Minsk Oblast'. The second period (right-hand column of Table 4.4), however, witnesses the complete discontinuation of this line of recruitment and the emergence of Minsk City, which accounted for seven of the 14 recruits from the regions, as the dominant regional basis for entry into the BSSR elite. Were we to include in these figures those individuals who had begun their careers at the regional level, entered positions at the all-union or republic level, and then found their way into the set of elite jobs in the BSSR, this dominance on the part of Minsk City would stand out all the more.[10] When we compare the pattern of recruitment from the regions to the republic-level elite (Table 4.4) with that of recruitment into the regional elites, we notice that the faction emerging in Minsk City in the first decade of our study on the basis of high levels of internal recruitment was able during the second decade to replace the Partisans as the leading group in Belorussian politics. It seems reasonable to infer in this respect that what appeared under the category of vetting in our analysis of centralization also contained another element. Members of the Minsk City faction while posted in Moscow jobs were apparently able to utilize their offices and the access which they afforded to other influential actors at the centre in order to advance their own career interests and those of other members of the group.[11] It appears that by the mid seventies a certain axis had developed between the Minsk City group and its members and supporters in Moscow. Although a full treatment of this matter is reserved for the discussion of patronage in the chapters that follow, we note here that through sojourns in Moscow jobs three leading members of the Minsk City faction – N. N. Slyun'kov, A. A. Reut and V. A. Lepeshkin – enjoyed a close proximity to patrons at the centre and that this appears to have been a crucial factor in promoting the fortunes of the group in general.

In addition to the apparent all-union ties developed by leading members of this group, one of the striking things about the Minsk City faction is its industrial base. Contrary to the pattern that has prevailed for other groups of politicians in the BSSR who launched their careers in the Komsomol apparatus, the leading figures in the Minsk City group began their political activity in the industrial enterprises of the capital, particularly at the Minsk Tractor Factory.[12] (For a list of those who began their political careers in Minsk City industries, see Appendix B.) We notice in this respect a pattern familiar to students of elite recruitment in the USSR, namely, the tendency among rising leaders to bring with them to higher office those with whom they had previously worked.[13] In the Minsk City case, the dominant figure exercising such patronage seems to be N. N. Slyun'kov, who was First Secretary of the KPB from 1983 to January of 1987 at which time he became a secretary of the CPSU and, shortly afterwards, a full member of the Politburo. By the same token, however, it would be difficult to explain the ascent of the Minsk City faction in terms of the pattern commonly described in the literature whereby a single patron develops through his control over appointments a vertically structured network of clients who, in turn, may exercise patronage over their own sub-groups of followers. Slyun'kov and another leading member of the Minsk City group, A. A. Reut (currently First Deputy Chair of Gosplan, USSR), were both in Moscow from the mid 1970s to 1983, the former as a deputy chair of Gosplan, the latter as First Deputy Minister of the Radio Industry. Given the fact that this was the period during which the Minsk City faction began to replace the Partisans as the dominant group in the BSSR and that the offices then held by both Slyun'kov and Reut would not equip them with *nomenklatura* rights sufficient to ensure the promotions of their would-be clients from Minsk City, it seems logical to conclude that something other than the standard patron-client model was operative in this case. Likely, what we have here is a double-edged process which, from below, took the form of a cohort of individuals from industry entering, first, into prominent Minsk City jobs and, from above, the cultivation of lateral ties between Slyun'kov and Reut to other officials in Moscow with appropriate *nomenklatura* rights that facilitated this upward mobility for the Minsk City group. In sum, the process more resembles the actions of a team in which a certain division of political labour prevails; those in Moscow use lateral ties to other all-union officials in order to advance the fortunes of their colleagues back home, the latter, in turn, recruit new team members and build a bloc of supporters within the regional base.[14]

The other region for which distinctions are apparent in Tables 4.3 and 4.4 is Vitebsk, which recorded the lowest rate of internal recruitment to top regional posts (45.6 per cent) and, after Minsk Oblast' and Minsk City, the highest rate of recruitment to republic positions (23.3 per cent). The middle and right-hand columns of Table 4.4 indicate a presence and an absence, respectively, of Partisans among its upwardly mobile politicians. Although we have insufficient data to reach firm conclusions in this case, the available information would suggest that a regional clique there was instrumental in breaking the dominance of the Partisan faction both in Vitebsk Oblast' and in the BSSR as a whole. The most influential politician to have emerged from a position in the Vitebsk region is A. N. Aksenov. Work in the Belorussian Komsomol during the earlier postwar years (a stronghold of the Partisans at that time) has led one observer to infer that Aksenov had close connections with the Partisan faction.[15] Aksenov, however, was not himself a member of the Partisan resistance and he moved very early in his career to a job in Moscow (he worked as a Komsomol secretary there from 1957 to 1959). On returning to the BSSR he became a deputy chair of the Republic's KGB and then Minister of

Internal Affairs, appointments which suggest that he had been culti-
vating the patronage of important all-union officials during the period
of his Komsomol work in Moscow. Aksenov served as First Secretary
of the Vitebsk Obkom from 1966 to 1971, a period in which a certain
struggle seems to have gone on in Vitebsk between members of the
Partisan faction there entrenched and a group of younger politicians
whose careers were advancing under Aksenov's aegis.[16] L. S. Firisanov and V. I. Brovikov who became obkom secretaries in Vitebsk
during Aksenov's tenure as First Secretary there are cases in point;
each rose rapidly to higher office at the republic and (in Brovikov's
case) all-union levels in conjunction with subsequent promotions
enjoyed by their apparent benefactor, Aksenov.[17] Indeed, Brovikov's
career on leaving Vitebsk followed in the footsteps of Aksenov's. He
replaced Aksenov as Second Secretary of the KPB in 1978 when
Aksenov became Chair of the Council of Ministers of the BSSR; after
some two years as Deputy Head of the Organization-Party Work
Department of the CPSU, Brovikov returned to the BSSR in 1983 as
Chair of the Council of Ministers while Aksenov became Ambassador
to Poland, a position taken by Brovikov when Aksenov was named
Chair of Gosteleradio, USSR. It seems quite plausible that Aksenov
enjoyed important Moscow connections and that these were instrumental in his appointment to head the Vitebsk Obkom, the only
regional job in his career history. We might interpret this appointment
within the context of a larger struggle taking place in Moscow at the
time between certain Belorussian Partisans and rival groups in the
Kremlin leadership. Aksenov's move to Vitebsk enabled him to
schedule personnel appointments in that Oblast' in such a way as to
weaken the influence of the Partisans there. Moreover, his own
subsequent promotions to the positions of Second Secretary of the
KPB and Chair of the Council of Ministers of the BSSR can be read as
the installation of a political rival who would act as a check on the
republic-level leader of the Partisan faction, First Secretary of the KPB,
P. M. Masherov. Aksenov's influence would also account for the
relatively high rate of recruitment from Vitebsk to elite BSSR jobs in
the second decade of our study.

Summary and conclusion

The present chapter has aimed at drawing some distinctions
with respect to those factors that are contained in the rather broad
concept 'regionalism'. Accordingly, we have examined the influence

of region on the overall pattern of elite circulation, the manner in which it structures access to elite positions at both the regional and republic levels, and the way in which it articulates with the phenomenon of patronage whose presence in the system takes a regional form but whose deployment, since it often involves apparent connections to all-union political actors, may also work in the direction of inhibiting the influence of region. With these considerations in mind, we have approached the phenomenon of regionalism in two ways. First, we have placed it in macro-level perspective in order to determine to what extent regionalism can be regarded as a characteristic of the personnel system in the BSSR. Secondly, we have examined on a micro-level the specific origins and destinations of those who at one time or another occupied the top positions in the various regional hierarchies of Belorussia in order to locate links between regionalism and patronage.

As a macro-level phenomenon, we hypothesized that elite circulation in the BSSR could be viewed as a Markov process and explained by an analytic model constructed on the sole category of region. Testing the predictions of this model against the observed distributions of vacancy chain lengths (Table 4.1) served to confirm this hypothesis for the system as a whole. The circulation of vacancies within the system appears as a function of the regional configuration of vacancies that initiate chains and the transition probabilities contained in the R matrix (Table 4.2). From this we conclude that elite circulation in the BSSR tends to move according to its own rhythms, and that the structure evident in these rhythms is a regional one.

As we saw in the previous chapter, the formal control over elite circulation that is exercised by Moscow and Minsk does not necessarily translate into an effective method of centralization in personnel policy. Rather, such control takes place on a field where other systemic forces operate, forces that tend to limit, if not negate, the formal powers of *nomenklatura*. Regionalism is a broad name covering a number of these forces. With respect to cadres policy, regionalism represents both a centrifugal force in the system, and an integrating mechanism. It tends to pull the *loci* of personnel transactions outward toward a plurality of points by influencing the direction of initial recruitment and early career patterns in such a way as to provide constant opportunities for local elites to form bonds – in this regard, patronage arrangements – among themselves. The concept of regionalism, then, taps at the macro-level an important dimension of elite circulation, suggesting a process which from the perspective of the centre may well seem to be fragmented by region but, within a given region, one that appears rather ordered and, on the basis of our comparison of transition probabilities in two discrete time periods, one which seems quite stable and predictable.

The comparisons drawn between the stratified and regional models have enabled us to specify the connections that obtain between hierarchy and region as factors that structure the circulation process. Hierarchy accounts for much of the form in the process (e.g., the various distributions of vacancy chain length in Table 4.1) while region supplies much of the content (e.g., our finding that ten of the 13 long chains in the sample were regionally based). In this respect, each model might be regarded as the complement of, rather than as an alternative to, the other.

When we adjust our focus to the micro-level, however, the picture becomes a bit more complex. We begin to notice other factors, masked by the general concept of regionalism in macro-perspective, that modify our understanding of the role of region in the circulation process. In this respect, we remind ourselves that the concept 'region' is no more an exhaustive account of what drives the process of elite circulation than is the formal appointments mechanism of the *nomenklatura*. Each represents a factor in the equation, and each for the analyst constitutes more a point of departure than an ultimate destination. For studies of the circulation process are, in the end, studies of social action. Indirectly, at least, we are necessarily involved with the matter of what the actors themselves are doing, what they believe themselves to be doing, the ends that they intend to achieve or the things that they seek to prevent. What the macro-level concept of regionalism contributes to this enterprise is a framework that enables us to sort out the systemic effects that structure individual action. These effects are themselves but the combined results of the totality of actions in the system, but they appear to individuals or groups in that system as opportunities or constraints confronting them.

In comparing the general pattern of elite circulation with that of the recruitment of top elites in the various regions of the BSSR, we found that region was of considerable influence in structuring access to these elite positions (Table 4.3); hence, a certain comparability between the macro- and micro-level is apparent. However, we also noted that the influence of region on recruitment to these elite positions was considerably less than it was for the circulation process as a whole. It seems that for the great majority of cases, recruitment to elite positions at the regional level evinces both a convergence and a divergence between regionalism and the related phenomenon of patronage groups or factions. On the one hand, region is commonly regarded as a basis from which clientelistic relationships emerge. Leading political figures in the various regions of the USSR are equipped, as we know, with extensive *nomenklatura* rights over appointments to thousands of lower-level jobs in their territories. Not only are early political careers predicated upon such regionally controlled appointments, but, as we generally assume, the immediate proximity of the actors themselves in everyday working situations and a measure of shared responsibility before superiors at higher levels tend to induce that group identity and orientation which from the centre's perspective appears as 'localism' or *krugovaya poruka*.

On the other hand, however, patronage politics might be employed in order to dislodge some rival group from its regional base. The case of Vitebsk illustrates such an incidence in which region and faction appear to pull in opposite directions. Factional struggles in Moscow seem in this case to have reacted back on the region, disrupting extant patronage relations in Vitebsk and promoting the careers of a number of Vitebsk politicians whose connections and career patterns are more national than regional in their orientation.

Finally, our attention is drawn to the apparent beneficiary of the decline of the Partisan faction, the Minsk City group. Here again, the influence of region seems especially pronounced when we examine the origins of the elite in Minsk City. The data indicate that a tightly knit group formed there over the period of our study and emerged as the dominant faction in Belorussian politics during the latter part of this period (Table 4.4). This group is characterized by: (1) an exceptionally high level of regionally constrained access (Table 4.3); (2) numerous connections between its leading figures and officials at the all-union level; (3) a recruitment base in local industrial firms rather than in the Komsomol apparatus; and (4) the apparent absence of a single leader or patron. The first three of these characteristics seem to be variations on the regional theme in Soviet politics. However, they lend themselves to another interpretation when considered in the context of the fourth characteristic, the emergence of a patronage group lacking a single patron.

In comparative perspective, what we have observed with respect to the Minsk City group in Belorussian politics shows some striking similarities to changes in the structure of clientelism in Italy as reported by Luigi Graziano.[18] Traditionally, clientelistic relations in Italy have been forged on the basis of vertical links between individual patrons and their respective followings. With the advent of socio-economic modernization, clientelism persists but assumes another form, one in which horizontal linkages replace vertical ones and in which *groups* of individuals act in concert to advance group interests. In the Belorussian case, we seem to see a comparable phenomenon unfolding. The Partisan faction, dominant in the early years of our study, was initially organized around a single patron, K. T. Mazurov. The rise and decline of Mazurov's fortunes in the central leadership appear in retrospect as something of a barometer for those of the Partisan faction in Belorussia. This pattern is a familiar one to observers of patronage politics in the USSR. The Minsk City group, however, appears to be organized along lines analogous to Graziano's 'new clientelism' in which horizontal linkages supplant vertical ones. From this perspective, the other characteristics of the Minsk City group – highly restricted entry, multiple connections to all-union offices, an industrial base of recruitment – may well signal the advent of a 'new clientelism' on the Soviet scene, one congruent with the patterns of urban-industrial life in the same way as the traditional patron-client model is rooted in agrarian society.[19] In this respect, it is useful to recall the urban-industrial transformation of Belorussia referenced in the first chapter. Our initial evidence on the topic of patronage would lead to the inference that changes in patronage relations correspond to changes in the socioeconomic context in which these relations are embedded. The Minsk City group, from this point of view, emerged as the dominant faction in Belorussian politics in part because it succeeded in developing a form of organization functionally adapted to an industrial society.

5   The structure of patronage affiliations

Following the implications of the analysis conducted in the preceding chapter, we turn our attention here to tracing out the patronage ties that appear to bind the actors together into identifiable factions in mutual competition for political office within the BSSR. We take up, first, the matter of personnel flows within and among the several organizations – party, soviet, ministerial and so forth – that collectively comprise the formal framework of all offices in our sample. This exercise completes our study of those factors that make up the general anatomy of the personnel system in Belorussia – hierarchy, region and organization. The results of our investigations on this level enable us, in turn, to frame the more specific and concrete analysis of factional affiliation that follows. Secondly, a methodological orientation toward the question of identifying patron-client ties is developed, yielding two techniques for classifying members into patronage groups. These techniques are then applied to the data.

Mobility within and across organizations

The movement of personnel, when viewed in the light of its organizational dimension, is often regarded as at least a rough measure of elite integration in the USSR. This way of looking at things sees the tendency in the Soviet system that works in the direction of fragmenting the elite on the basis of numerous, organizationally based, interest groupings – what Jerry Hough has referred to as 'bureaucratic pluralism'[1] – as counteracted by the rotation of officials through a variety of organizations such that psychological attachments to any single one of them are unlikely to form, since extended interaction among the members of a given organization is regularly disrupted. It goes without saying, however, that the content of the concept 'integration' is determined by that of its opposite,

79

'disintegration'. If we view individual organizations as poles which attract interest groupings around themselves, fragmenting officialdom in the process into a number of elites with a potential for conflict,[2] then cross-organizational transfers would appear as a form of elite integration in such a system. From this perspective, fissures within the elite would result from a given organization's capacity to control its own personnel process, whether such control reflects advancement on grounds of merit[3] or on the basis of patronage[4] or both.[5]

Were we to alter our perspective on fragmentation, however, and replace the single organizational locus with a conception of patronage groups whose members span a number of organizations, our view of interorganizational transfers would change accordingly. From this vantage, the movement of personnel across organizations would reveal both integrating and disintegrating features. On the one hand, the rotation of group members through jobs in a number of organizations would promote interorganizational cooperation among those institutions wherein group members had been placed. Common activities involving individuals working in a variety of institutions would by the same token enhance the cohesion of the group itself. On the other hand, however, it is obvious that to the degree that this pattern obtains for specific patronage cliques, its implications for the system as a whole run in the opposite direction. A fractured personnel system organized around multiple patronage networks with an attendant rivalry among competing groups would be the expected consequences of such an arrangement.

Beginning with the idea that patronage groups distribute their members among a variety of organizations, a conception that follows from the data presented in the previous chapter and one that also accords with the consensus of specialists in the field,[6] we commence our search for the influence of patronage on the mobility patterns displayed by Belorussian elites with an examination of personnel interchange among the organizational hierarchies of the BSSR. In so doing, we are at the same time tapping the incidence of ties among actors in interorganizational networks at a general level.[7] Thereafter, the discussion moves to a consideration of the ties among particular actors whose relations one to another constitute interpersonal networks in the system.

The data presented in Table 5.1 concern the frequency with which various organizations in the BSSR have supplied recruits to other organizations and the frequency with which they have filled vacancies

Table 5.1. *Frequencies and relative frequencies of personnel supply among organizations, 1966–86**

	Party	Soviets	Ministries	State committees	Komsomol	Trade unions	Judicial organs	Cultural apparatus
Party	484 (0.58)	192 (0.23)	80 (0.10)	49 (0.06)	3 (0.004)	14 (0.02)	1 (0.001)	7 (0.01)
Soviets	136 (0.49)	81 (0.29)	42 (0.15)	16 (0.06)	—	1 (0.004)	—	—
Ministries	18 (0.11)	12 (0.08)	108 (0.69)	18 (0.11)	—	—	1 (0.006)	—
State committees	3 (0.07)	2 (0.05)	12 (0.27)	27 (0.61)	—	—	—	—
Komsomol	26 (0.46)	2 (0.04)	2 (0.04)	1 (0.02)	25 (0.45)	—	—	—
Trade unions	2 (0.33)	1 (0.17)	1 (0.17)	—	—	1 (0.17)	—	1 (0.17)
Judicial organs	1 (0.08)	1 (0.08)	3 (0.25)	1 (0.08)	—	—	6 (0.50)	—
Cultural apparatus	4 (0.40)	—	1 (0.10)	3 (0.30)	—	—	—	2 (0.20)

* Frequencies appear as numbers, relative frequencies appear in parentheses.

internally. The table is read by row. The first row indicates that some 484 actors left jobs in the party organs in order to fill vacancies that had opened in other party jobs and that this number accounted for some 58 per cent of all those who left a given party job and found some other position in the system. Continuing along the first row, we find that the party sent 192 individuals who had held a job in its ranks to replace officeholders who had left some position within the hierarchy of soviets, and that this figure represented 23 per cent of all those who left a party office to take up another position. Similarly, 80 individuals left party jobs for appointments in the ministerial apparatus (10 per cent of those exiting party jobs), and so forth.

The bottom three rows of Table 5.1 contain numbers which are unfortunately not large enough to support any meaningful conclusions regarding the rates at which the trade unions, the judicial organs (courts and procurators) and institutions in the cultural sphere (newspaper editors and heads of various Belorussian societies) supplied themselves or other organizations with recruits. The size of the numbers is itself a product of two factors: the relatively small proportions of these populations in the sample, and the fact that, especially in the case of trade unions, the jobs tend to involve terminal career moves (none of the presidents of the twelve trade unions represented in the sample, for instance, was known to leave office for another position). Focusing, then, on the top five rows, these data suggest four things. First, self-supply is the predominant tendency in recruitment. The diagonal in the table shows that the party, the ministries and the state committees 'send' the majority of those leaving an office in their respective organizational hierarchies to some other office in the same hierarchy.

Secondly, this pattern is particularly pronounced in the case of the ministries and the state committees. Indeed, when we consider the fact that these organizations are two wings of the same governmental hierarchy in the BSSR, the incidence of self-supply is even more striking. The inference that might be drawn here is that careers in these organizations tend more so than in others to be intraorganizational. This interpretation is congruent with the conclusions drawn by John Miller who examined personnel transfers across the USSR for senior officials.[8] Nonetheless, nearly one-fifth of those who left positions in Belorussia's ministerial apparatus found subsequent positions in either party or soviet organs, suggesting that the high rates of self-supply noted here would not preclude the existence of inter-organizational ties.

Thirdly, the rates of supply from party to soviet bodies (0.23) and from soviet to party bodies (0.49) are particularly high and indicate especially close connections between these two organizations.[9] The data here, in terms of the relative frequency of supply, differ from those recorded by Miller who found that 'transfers from party to state are more common than the reverse'.[10] For state sector organizations in the BSSR, we find that supply rates to and from party bodies are roughly equal in the case of ministries and state committees and, that for the soviets, the rate at which personnel are supplied to party bodies is more than double the rate of supply moving in the opposite direction.

Miller's related finding, that the party is a net supplier of personnel, is supported, however, when we examine the absolute frequencies in Table 5.1. Party organizations out-supplied all others combined by a ratio of 3:2 (830 incidencies of moves from a party job to some other job in the system out of a total of 1,391 moves). Two factors account for this. One, party jobs are more numerous in the sample than are those of any other single organization. Comparing the number of party positions with that of the next two organizations in terms of frequency of representation in the sample, we find that there are 839 party jobs, 598 soviet jobs, and 353 in the ministerial apparatus. Two, and more importantly in the present context, turnover is highest in party offices. Drawing the same comparisons between jobs in party organizations on the one hand, and those in the soviet and ministerial apparatuses, on the other, we find that 830 moves from some position in the system to some other position were initiated in party jobs. The corresponding figures for soviet and ministerial posts are 276 and 157, respectively. Hence, the party's role as a net supplier is in large part due to the fact that party jobs do not tend to hold their incumbents as long as do jobs in the other sectors. In addition to *nomenklatura* powers which would on the face of it make party bodies the prime candidates among Soviet organizations for generating patronage connections, we note at this point another characteristic of party offices, taken as a group, which increases their salience for the formation of interorganizational networks, namely, a relatively rapid movement of individuals into and out of positions in the party apparatus.

Finally, the data presented in Table 5.1 on personnel supplied by the Komsomol demonstrate that holding office in the Komsomol serves primarily as an apprenticeship for a party job. While this pattern is in no way surprising, it seems that in three instances the reverse was true. In as much as the Komsomol is the party's youth organization that prepares cadres for political careers, we would not expect those who have already embarked on such careers to leave full-time salaried positions in the party in order to assume posts in the Komsomol. Although the incidence of such is rare, the fact that it occurred on three occasions adds again something to our understanding of the relations that obtain between the party and other organizations, in this case, its junior league. Personnel flows from the party to the Komsomol would suggest the existence of a particular concern on the part of the party leaders responsible for these appointments regarding cadres work in the organs of the Komsomol. In so far as holding office in the Komsomol amounts to a preparatory phase in individual careers that opens onto subsequent jobs in the party organs (and our data would definitely support this interpretation), the dispatch of party officials to fill Komsomol offices provides the party organs with a more or less direct hand in supervising the apprenticeship of its future cadres. At the same time, however, we should not overlook the potential in this arrangement for the formation of patronage ties between, on the one hand, those who through prior work in the party organs have established connections to influential actors and, on the other, aspiring politicians in the ranks of the Komsomol. We examine this aspect of the matter below.

Do rates of supply within and across organizations vary over time? The evidence for the USSR in general seem quite mixed. Ronald J. Hill has observed that a number of Soviet authors claim that since the Stalin years mobility tends to occur within the individual organizational hierarchies of party and state. Yet, as Hill has noted, another group of Soviet authors maintains that cross-organizational transfer remains the pattern.[11] Surveying the recent period, Thane Gustafson and Dawn Mann point out that there may be more exceptions than there are rules in this area.[12] The Belorussian data, set out in Table 5.2, indicate very little change in the rates at which organizations supply personnel to fill vacancies elsewhere in the system. Aside from a higher relative frequency of personnel interchange between ministries and state committees in the second decade (and given both the organizations concerned and the small numbers involved we would do well not to attach any significance to this) the only change of any magnitude involves the soviets which supplied themselves a little less, and the party a little more, frequently in the second period. Overall, these data tend to demonstrate a considerable measure of stability in the rates of supply among organizations for these two periods of time. From the standpoint of interorganizational networks as reflected in

Table 5.2. *Frequencies and relative frequencies of personnel supply among five organizations for two time periods*

1966–76	Party	Soviets	Ministries	State committees	Komsomol
Party	268	112	45	22	2
	(0.58)	(0.24)	(0.10)	(0.05)	(0.004)
Soviets	75	53	27	9	—
	(0.46)	(0.32)	(0.16)	(0.05)	—
Ministries	6	7	52	7	—
	(0.08)	(0.10)	(0.72)	(0.10)	—
State committees	1	—	4	14	—
	(0.05)	—	(0.21)	(0.74)	—
Komsomol	15	2	1	1	15
	(0.44)	(0.06)	(0.03)	(0.03)	(0.44)

1977–86	Party	Soviets	Ministries	State committees	Komsomol
Party	216	80	35	27	1
	(0.58)	(0.22)	(0.09)	(0.07)	(0.003)
Soviets	61	28	15	7	—
	(0.55)	(0.25)	(0.14)	(0.06)	—
Ministries	12	5	56	11	—
	(0.14)	(0.06)	(0.66)	(0.13)	—
State committees	2	2	8	13	—
	(0.08)	(0.08)	(0.32)	(0.52)	—
Komsomol	11	—	1	—	10
	(0.50)	—	(0.05)	—	(0.45)

the transfer of personnel across organizational boundaries, we conclude on the basis of these data that such networks as a group have been maintaining themselves through more or less constant rates of personnel interchange. However, as we see below, this general pattern is not necessarily true of any of the networks taken separately. Individual expansions and contractions occur within the more or less uniform rates evinced by the system as a whole.

Table 5.3 orders the data in another manner. It concerns the reciprocal of personnel supply, viz., the rates at which individual organizations draw their replacements either internally or from some other organization in the system. The data in this case are read by column. The first column, for example, shows that replacements for

Table 5.3. *Rates at which replacements are drawn among organizations, 1966–86 (in percentages)*

	Party	Soviets	Ministries	State committees	Komsomol	Trade unions	Judicial organs	Cultural apparatus
Party	71.8	66.0	32.1	42.6	10.7	87.5	12.5	70.0
Soviets	20.2	27.8	16.9	13.9	—	6.3	—	—
Ministries	2.7	4.1	43.4	15.7	—	—	12.5	—
State committees	0.5	0.7	4.8	23.5	—	—	—	—
Komsomol	3.9	0.7	0.8	0.9	89.3	—	—	10.0
Trade unions	0.3	0.3	0.4	—	—	6.3	—	—
Judicial organs	0.2	0.3	1.2	0.9	—	—	75.0	—
Cultural apparatus	0.6	—	0.4	2.6	—	—	—	20.0

party jobs have come overwhelmingly from those already holding positions in the party organs (71.8 per cent) and that soviet officials have been the second leading source of replacements (20.2 per cent) for openings in the party apparatus.

The data in Table 5.3 contain two patterns. The diagonal in the table indicates that for the party, the ministries, the Komsomol, and the judicial organs, internal recruitment has been the norm. For the other organizations, replacements are most frequently drawn from the party organs. Taking this finding together with the proportion of recruits coming from party jobs into positions in those non-party bodies that rely primarily on internal recruitment, the data in Table 5.3 would reinforce our earlier observation regarding the role of the party as the net supplier of cadres in the BSSR. Additionally, as we have seen in the case of supply, the rates at which organizations have drawn their recruits internally and externally remain quite constant over the two decades of this study.[13]

This analysis of personnel movement within and among the organizational hierarchies of the Belorussian Republic supports some of Gerd Meyer's observations regarding 'core elites' in the Soviet system who occupy politically sensitive positions around which patronage groups are likely to form.[14] Specifically, the data presented here would indicate that party and soviet jobs would serve as the primary organizational *loci* for interorganizational networks. Indeed, from the point of view of organizations as discrete personnel systems, the exchange of cadres between party and soviet bodies would largely erase the organizational boundaries between them. The party, to be sure, bears heavy responsibilities for the conduct of soviet work, and no responsibility in this area surpasses that of cadres selection.[15] Despite ritualized criticism of party 'interference' in soviet affairs, however, the party's usurpation of the authority formally lodged with the soviets is not the result of some aberration in the subjective orientation of certain party members, as the criticism would imply, but the logical outcome of the structure of their relations. In simple and direct terms, it derives from the fact that 'up to the present time, clearly written limitations in party and state documents, distinguishing the functions of the party and soviet organs, do not exist.'[16] Unwarranted party interventions, which recently have been acknowledged by Soviet spokesmen to be the outgrowth of basic (dysfunctional) relations in the Soviet system,[17] appear as both the cause and consequence of the exchange of cadres noted here. We cannot expect that the party organs would refrain from intervening in the affairs of the soviets if, on the one hand, these organs bear responsibility *vis-à-vis* their superiors for the conduct of soviet work while, on the other hand, the rotation of personnel between these bodies is such that those who lead a given soviet at one point in time have previously been the direct subordinates of those party officials encharged with overseeing the work of that same soviet. The structure of this relationship consigns party/soviet distinctions to the field of fictive differentiation. In fact the soviet 'has become essentially a subordinate department of the party apparatus'.[18] Consequently, in using the variable 'organization' to detect patronage groupings in what follows, we allow for the fact that the soviets do not appear to represent autonomous or semi-autonomous personnel systems as do, say, the ministries and state committees.

The rates at which organizations supply one another with replacements and those at which organizations draw their recruits both internally and from other institutions further demonstrate the decisive position of the party within the system. The party is unique. It is the only institution that supplies, and is in turn supplied by, all other institutions. As such, the interorganizational circulation of elites in the BSSR can be understood as a process skewed in the direction of party dominance.

This dominance, however, is not absolute. Although rates of personnel exchange among other institutions are considerably lower than those displayed by the party, such rates are in many cases large enough to support the notion of elite integration across these institutions as well. Especially in light of what we learned in the preceding chapter with respect to the Minsk City group, many of whose members entered party and soviet jobs in the capital from positions in the industrial sector, this observation suggests the hypothesis that interorganizational transfers represent strategic links among institutional sectors that integrate the particular patronage groups whose members circulate through positions within them.

Detecting patronage groups

The conventional model of patronage is specified in terms of vertically ordered dyads that lock both patrons and clients into personalized relations governed by the norm of reciprocity and oriented toward the rendering of mutual assistance.[19] Larger networks are often constructed by aggregating these dyads together, both vertically and horizontally, such that a major patron who occupies the top position in such a network is connected to clients who in turn act as patrons *vis-à-vis* clients of their own who are found at lower levels in the patronage structure.[20]

This model of patronage aims to reduce to a common denominator great quantities of social phenomena occurring in numerous places, across different cultures and spanning centuries of time. In this consists an obvious and considerable advantage from the standpoint of conceptual scope. Nonetheless, it would be mistaken to reify a particular conceptualization of patron-client relations and regard it as some objective and eternal pattern that either invariably occurs or defines *a priori* a patronage relation in a given instance.[21] As we have seen in the previous chapter, patronage relations in the Soviet Union closely resemble the dyadic construct in some instances (e.g., the Partisan faction) but not in others (e.g., the Minsk City faction). In employing the concept of patronage, then, we would do well to leave open the matter of the precise form which patronage relations might take and seek closure via an empirical route.

While refraining from designating in advance a single form taken by patronage relations in our sample, we recognize at the onset that in directing our attention to such relations in the USSR we are travelling down a well-worn path.[22] Indeed, what T. H. Rigby has described as the 'second polity' – the informal world of personal relations that reshapes all manner of official decisions at the implementation stage, not least of which are those in the area of personnel[23] – has been openly identified in recent years by Soviet scholars themselves, who diagnose it as a leading cause of the various maladies that afflict the Soviet system.[24] Yet general agreement among specialists with respect to the presence and importance of patronage ties in the USSR has so far not led to an established method for detecting them.

If there are criticisms to be made here, the first might be directed to the question of specificity, or lack thereof, in setting out just what constitutes a patronage tie and what sorts of information are to be used to indicate the presence of such in a given case. It is, unfortunately, not at all uncommon to encounter statements in the field of Soviet elite studies on the order of 'actor X, who has ties to actor Y', or 'actor X promoted his client, Y', without learning in context anything about the methodological and empirical bases on which such statements rest. In any and all instances, the statements themselves may be valid. The point is that our knowledge of Soviet elites cannot advance in a cumulative and systematic way unless the criteria for specifying interpersonal ties are themselves specified and, hence, susceptible to a demonstration of their validity and reliability.

A second difficulty involves those cases in which the criteria for establishing patronage ties are specified but remain less than convincing indicators of clique affiliation. In this respect, indicators that are thought to measure clientelistic ties on the basis of the career histories of actors which show that two or more of them have worked in the same institution or in the same locale contain a large element of ambiguity that is not always acknowledged by those who employ them.[25] Work in, say, the same institution may mean that a tie has been established. It may also mean just the opposite. A rival group may have succeeded in 'planting' one of their members in an institution otherwise dominated by a particular patronage clique.[26] To be sure, a standard of absolute certitude in these matters would do nothing but paralyse research efforts. The closed world of Soviet politics divulges few of its inner secrets and the parties to patronage relations are not known for advertising their existence as such. In attempting an analysis of these relations we are, then, necessarily confronted with some degree of ambiguity in what we observe and consequently are forced to make interpretations which may not be as susceptible to verification as we would otherwise prefer. The point, again, is to reduce this ambiguity as much as possible in order to render our interpretations, if not valid, then at least sufficiently transparent to stand correction from further research.

The results of our analysis to this point enable us to identify in a preliminary way a small fraction of the total number of individuals in the data set as members of various factions or patronage groups in Belorussian politics. First, we have those who fought in the partisan movement during the Second World War and entered political life in the BSSR thereafter. From the available data sources, some 74 members of this faction, the Partisans, can be identified (see Appendix B). Secondly, as noted in the previous chapter, there appears to be a particular core to the regional grouping arrayed among jobs in Minsk City that is composed of individuals who initiated their political careers in the industrial organizations of Minsk. This core, the Minsk City Industrial Group (MCIG) has 51 known members (Appendix B). It is more than conceivable that others in the larger Minsk City grouping are also members of the MCIG, but the absence of data on their early careers prevents us from identifying more than 51 members of the MCIG proper. Finally, we are able at this point to identify explicitly only a small contingent of a third factional grouping in the BSSR which was discussed in the preceding chapter. This faction, which formed in Vitebsk Oblast', includes A. N. Aksenov, the apparent patron in the BSSR, and V. I. Brovikov and L. S. Firisanov, his clients. The following analysis will enable us to fill out the membership of this group and also to locate other patronage cliques which have operated in the BSSR over the period encompassed by this study.

Consistent with the methodological orientation that has guided the analysis to this point, we rely, here, on mobility as the principal means for indicating patronage affiliations. In so doing, we can appropriate some very useful ideas from two students of patronage relations in the Soviet Union. The first derives from Gyula Jozsa who has put forward the metaphor of a *seilschaft* – a roped party of mountain climbers – in order to suggest the manner in which patronage groups ascend the political heights of the Soviet hierarchy as a single unit.[27] The second has been developed by John P. Willerton, Jr, who has used, among other discriminating factors, upward mobility – in this case two or more promotions for a client within a region and/or institution headed by his would-be patron – to indicate patronage ties.[28] We begin our analysis of patronage by empirically interpreting the idea of *seilschaft*.

Replacement chains as seilschaften

A replacement chain, the cohort of actors who advance through the set of jobs contained in a given vacancy chain, represents a strict and empirically direct interpretation of a political *seilschaft*. The appearance of certain actors in the same replacement chain, however, need not in itself connote a patronage link among them. On the one hand, the composition of the replacement chain may be due in part or *in toto* to chance factors; say, the unexpected death of an officeholder which summoned a (perhaps temporary) replacement from among his immediate lieutenants which in turn created a vacancy which was filled by a new recruit as yet unconnected to some patronage clique. On the other hand, those in a given replacement chain may on occasion be the clients of different patrons. Their simultaneous movements through the chain might reflect the fact that the jobs within it belong to separate *nomenklatury* and may even have resulted from a negotiated arrangement among patrons whereby X's client received a promotion to one position as part of a bargain that brought about a similar promotion for Y's client to another. In order to minimize the ambiguity that obtains here, we stipulate that, unless we have reason to think otherwise, individuals occupying positions in replacement chains will be regarded as linked if and only if they have appeared together in the same chain on more than one occasion.

Applying this criterion to the data, we find that on 26 occasions two individuals appeared twice within the same replacement chain, and that on two other occasions two individuals were thrice members of the same chain. The relative frequency of such occurrences in the context of the total number of replacement chains in the sample is quite low (0.7 per cent for twice-appearing and 0.1 per cent for thrice-appearing pairs of actors) and would therefore suggest that these pairings are not likely to be the result of chance. Rather, we seem to have here a rather select group of cases in which the mobility of one of the actors in a given pair is predicated on the mobility of the other. From this relationship, we infer a tie between them.

The reoccurrence of certain individuals in the same replacement chains is in some cases already known to us. For instance, we noted in the previous chapter how the progression of V. I. Brovikov's career followed in the footsteps of A. N. Aksenov's. Our analysis here shows them to have been members of the same chain on three occasions and can be taken as further evidence of a patronage tie between them. The same holds for certain members of the MCIG, coupled in this analysis in the same chains on two occasions: N. T. Gulev and M. S. Senoko- sova, V. V. Gurin and V. N. Dragovets.

In three instances, pairs of actors were twice associated in replacement chains which occurred within individual ministries, indi- cating, perhaps, the presence of 'bureaucratic' patronage. In two of these cases, we seem to find a protégé whose career progressed in the wake of that of his formal superior – V. S. Voronov on the 'tails' of I. M. Mozolyako in the Belorussian Ministry of Industrial Construc- tion, A. G. Andreev on those of E. Yushkevich in the Administration of Belorussia Railroads. In the third case, the coupling of G. N. Zhabitskii and V. A. Piskarev was the only known incidence in this study of a 'negative' *seilschaft*. As we see in more detail, below (Chapter 7), Piskarev's fortune was made out of Zhabitskii's ruin, and each was associated with factions in the BSSR who vied for power during the political succession of the 1980s.

Two very useful pieces of information that this exercise has turned up are: (1) the coupling of actors not yet classified by factional affiliation with individuals previously identified as either Partisans or members of the MCIG; and (2) the presence of a given actor in more than one pairing. Each of these results allows us to expand our present

Table 5.4. *Clientele groupings established by association in replacement chains**

Clientele groupings

Minsk Oblast' Group (Patronage Affiliation, Partisans):
M. T. Radyuk (P) T. N. Strizhak (P)   A. N. Bychek   V. A. Mokhov
A. S. Bogdan   K. Z. Terekh   M. N. Khudaya   M. V. Mikhnevich

Minsk City Group (MCIG):
A. B. Zuev (MCIG)   V. D. Bysenko (MCIG)   V. N. Dragovets (MCIG)
V. M. Semenov   V. I. Mikhasev   B. A. Savchenko (MCIG)
I. M. Sidorovich   A. A. Sanchukovskii   A. K. Kurach
L. K. Sukhnat (MCIG)   N. T. Gulev (MCIG)   N. S. Nerad (MCIG)
G. S. Tarazevich   M. S. Senekosova   R. S. Pionova
(MCIG)   (MCIG)
V. A. Pechennikov   V. V. Gurin (MCIG)

Gomel' Oblast' Group (Partisans):
A. A. Malofeev   Yu. M. Khusainov   A. D. Gurban
A. S. Kamai   E. E. Savostenko   V. V. Shuvalov

Grodno Oblast' Group (Partisans):
G. F. Fomichev (P)   M. Z. Yadikin   O. E. Molyavko
S. T. Kabyak   E. I. Nagotko   V. V. Dekhtyarenko

Brest Oblast' Group (Brezhnev Clients):
A. P. Saenko   V. M. Khil'chuk
I. A. Stavrovskaya   V. A. Litvinchuk

Vitebsk Oblast' Group (Brezhnev Clients):
A. N. Aksenov   V. I. Brovikov

Mogilev Oblast' Group (Partisans):
N. N. Balashov   R. I. Kalugina
I. I. Kozlov   I. P. Lyudogovskii

* The groupings, here, have been determined on the basis of joint appearances in two or more replacement chains with a member of a known faction. The letters 'P' and 'MCIG' that appear in parentheses after the names of some individuals denote their membership in either the Partisan faction or the Minsk City Industrial Group, respectively.

factional rosters by including additional clients. The coupling of an as yet unclassified actor with an individual already identified as a member of a given faction is taken as evidence that the former is a client of the faction to which the latter belongs. Multiple pairings of a particular actor, the second pattern from which associations can be inferred, are treated as transitive (i.e., if X has twice or more appeared in the same chains with both Y and Z, we assume that Y and Z are both tied to X and tied to each other).

Taken together, these pieces of information can be used to designate a number of factionally affiliated actors (Table 5.4). The largest single bloc, containing 17 individuals, is grouped around offices in Minsk City. Given the relatively closed system of recruitment to these jobs, it is not at all unexpected to find the frequent appearance of these officials in the same chains, often paired with members of the MCIG. One other actor, A. A. Sanchukovskii, whose early career included jobs as an industrial executive and gorkom secretary in Mogilev, is linked to this group by virtue of his transfer to a Minsk City office (after an apparent sojourn in Moscow), a personnel move involving a seven-person replacement chain, three of whose links have been identified as members of the MCIG and a fourth appears as an MCIG client.

These data indicate that the Partisan faction had developed networks of clientele in four of the oblasts of the BSSR (Minsk, Gomel', Grodno, and Mogilev). As the dominant group in Belorussian politics for most of the period encompassed by this study, this too is not unexpected. Interestingly, the three regions that in this analysis do not appear as areas of Partisan strength (Minsk City, Vitebsk and Brest oblasts) comprise the regional bases for those factions in visible contention for the leadership of the BSSR during the succession that followed the death of P. M. Masherov in 1980. One actor identified here as a member of the Brest Oblast Group, I.A. Stavrovskaya, had begun her career in the Oblast' in the late 1950s when the Partisan faction was still dominant there. For this reason she is regarded in the analysis that follows as a Partisan client.

In Chapter 7 we deal with the shifting nature of factional oppositions and alliances in the BSSR during the Masherov and Brezhnev successions. Here, it remains to anticipate that discussion by appropriating from it some information relevant to the composition of the major factional groups that have formed in the Belorussian Republic. Hence, in addition to those Brezhnev clients holding republic level offices,[29] we note that two of the three regional bases that were not areas of Partisan strength were headed by Belorussian politicians with ties to the Brezhnev network – A. N. Aksenov in Vitebsk and E. E. Sokolov in Brest[30] – and that the MCIG, which operated in the third of the regional bases not controlled by the Partisan faction, had ties to the Andropov-Gorbachev group. With these classifications in place, and with the addition of those actors identified with various factions in Table 5.4, we are able to carry forward our analysis.

Patronage ties as repeated joint-mobility

The second method for detecting the factional affiliations of individuals in the sample also incorporates the ideas of mobility and recurrence. In this case, however, we aim to associate individuals who were not necessarily members of the same replacement chain and whose movements from one job to another did not necessarily take place within the same year. Rather, we are concerned with those cases in which a potential client made two or more career moves within an organization or region under the control of one of the patronage groups or sub-groups that we have detected. When such is the case, we draw the inference that a tie exists between the client and the patronage group in question.

The ambiguity that necessarily obtains when inferring such ties among actors is minimized by adopting again the rule of two or more moves. It is further minimized by specifying that the member of the patronage group, under whose wing the client's mobility took place, was himself mobile on both occasions. Consequently, we are assuming that, when an identified member of a patronage group found a new job, the influence of his faction was also used to promote certain other individuals who are to be regarded as clients of the group in question. Ambiguity is minimized again by adding the proviso that only those individuals are to be regarded as clients who (two or more times) moved in the same year as, or in the year following, the patron's move. Surely, patronage powers could be exercised at a greater remove than a one-year lag between the mobility of patrons and clients, and we are *a priori* screening out all cases in which such took place. In this respect, however, we are prepared to exchange a broader scope for more precision in the identification of clients. By reducing the time dimension to no more than one year after the move of the patron, we are able to identify what might be called 'hard' clients, i.e., those whose career fortunes are more or less directly linked to those of their patrons. Given the ambiguity that confronts such an exercise and our wish to reduce it as much as possible, adherence to these three rules – (1) movement by the client on more than one occasion within an organization or region controlled by a patronage group, (2) movement by the patron on each occasion, and (3) a time lag of no more than one year between the respective moves of patrons and clients – seems to be a price well worth paying.

The application of these three rules to our sample of Belorussian officeholders allows for the classification of some 398 individuals (12.7

Table 5.5. *Identification of clients by repeated joint-mobility for three patronage groups (N = 398)*

	Number Identified
Partisan clients	
Republic Level	87
Minsk Oblast'	27
Gomel' Oblast'	52
Grodno Oblast'	18
Mogilev Oblast'	40
Brezhnev clients	
Republic Level	50
Vitebsk Oblast'	58
Brest Oblast'	11
MCIG Clients	55

per cent of the total sample) as clients of one of the three main patronage groups (Table 5.5). Adding these cases to the group of actors whose patronage affiliations have already been identified brings our total count of members of the various networks to 557 (17.8 per cent of the total sample). Were we attempting simply to classify as many individuals as possible as members or clients of the various groupings, then the methods that we have adopted would serve that purpose rather poorly. Since the constraints built into the analysis perforce exclude from classification the great majority of the individuals in the data set, an attempt at a more comprehensive classification would require decision rules that are less rigorous and more inclusive. But in as much as our intention has been to reduce ambiguity in order to deploy some relatively solid results in subsequent stages of the analysis which treat various events in the system from the viewpoint of factional politics, the inclusiveness of the procedures used to determine factional affiliation presents no serious problem. To the contrary, the individuals identified by factional grouping on the basis of the methods adopted here are by definition the more mobile actors in the system and, by that measure, the ones who figure prominently in the events that we take up, below. Accordingly, the factional classification of *this* minority in the sample adequately suits the purpose of employing the variable 'faction' in the analyses that follow.

With respect to the data set out in Table 5.5, three observations might be made in anticipation of our use of 'faction' to account for certain events in the system. First, the number of Partisan clients identified is considerably larger than the corresponding number for either of the other two groups. Since the Partisans were the dominant faction in Belorussian politics throughout most of the period covered by this study, this is to be expected. With the death of their leader, P. M. Masherov, in 1980, however, we find that this faction rapidly disintegrated. Its members were retired from office and its appendages of clientele in the regions were often drawn into another network, that of the MCIG.

Secondly, the figures in the table show a rather larger number (119) of Brezhnev clients in the BSSR. This group represented the main challenge to the Partisan faction and many of its members had already secured important posts in the Belorussian party-state prior to Masherov's death. With Masherov out of the way, the Brezhnev forces rapidly replaced the Partisans in the Belorussian leadership, but their victory did not long survive Brezhnev himself.

Thirdly, the MCIG, owing both to its tight system of internal recruitment and to its connections to central figures in the Soviet leadership, appears to have been the most effective of the factional groups. In the next chapter, we observe the career advantages enjoyed by members and clients of the MCIG. In Chapter 7, we see how this relatively small but strategically placed faction was able to displace many of their leading rivals in the BSSR while simultaneously building a new ruling coalition from among a number of the members and clients of the other, defeated, groups.

6 Does faction make a difference?

In this chapter, we apply what we have learned so far about factions in the BSSR to three sets of events within the system. First, we inquire into the matter of the effect that factional affiliation has had on elite mobility patterns in the BSSR for those who entered political careers through the various channels that supply recruits. Secondly, we take up the particular case of women within the system. We are concerned in this respect to compare the range of political offices occupied by women in the BSSR against the profile of female political roles which has been established by a number of scholars for the USSR as a whole and to ask here, as well, if differences among Belorussian women with regard to career chances can be accounted for on the basis of factional affiliation. Finally, we examine the matter of negative sanctions – official criticism, reprimands and publicly announced dismissals from office – and ask again whether factional affiliation accounts for the patterns in the data.

The influence of faction on mobility patterns

One dimension of the influence of factional affiliation on our sample of Belorussian officeholders concerns mobility. Does membership in a particular patronage group enhance one's chances for promotion to higher office? We address this question by examining the career histories of 361 individuals who can be identified from the data sources as having begun their political activity as either, (1) party secretaries, trade union officials, or executives in industrial firms, (2) officers in the Belorussian Komsomol, or (3) skilled workers who rose to executive positions in various industrial enterprises but who did not previously occupy party or trade union offices within them. Partitioning this group of 361 officeholders according to their respective points of entry into the system makes it possible to compare the trajectories of careers launched from each of these points. Is it the case, for instance, that those who initially served as party secretaries in industrial firms climb higher than do their counterparts who worked in trade union organizations? More importantly for present purposes, however, this categorization by channel of entry allows us to control for the effect of the channels themselves and to determine, by comparing, say, trade union officials associated with one patronage group against others who entered via the same channel, whether factional affiliation makes a difference in the career histories of those coming into the system through these various portals. The number of officeholders of concern to us here is not large, and categorizing them by both faction and channel of entry would yield sub-groups too small in many cases to show any worthwhile results. In order, therefore, to distribute the sample in such a way as to fill all of the categories with a number of cases sufficiently large to draw comparisons regarding the influence of factional affiliation on the mobility patterns displayed by those entering through the various channels, we shall divide the 361 individuals in question into two sub-sets: members of the MCIG and all others.

Some 128 individuals can be identified as having begun their political careers in the BSSR in one of the industrial firms in the capital.[1] Of these, 68 (53.1 per cent) recorded no subsequent career moves to higher offices, 28 (21.9 per cent) advanced to positions in the party apparatus in their next career moves, seven (5.5 per cent) were appointed to an executive position in a soviet in their next career moves, and the remainder, 25 (19.5 per cent), made their next career moves to a job in the state apparatus (ministries and state committees). The comparable figures for the 233 non-MCIG members under consideration here are: 112 (48.1 per cent) recorded no subsequent career moves to higher offices, 75 (32.2 per cent) next took jobs in the party apparatus, 21 (9.0 per cent) found executive positions in soviets, and 25 (10.7 per cent) moved next to higher posts in the state apparatus. These figures indicate that members of the MCIG had a marginally smaller likelihood of upward mobility (46.9 per cent) than did their counterparts in other areas of the BSSR (51.9 per cent). They also indicate that members of the MCIG moved immediately into positions in the party and soviet apparatus with a lower frequency (21.9 per cent versus 32.2 per cent, and 5.5 per cent versus 9.0 per cent, respectively) and were more frequently promoted out of their entry-level jobs into positions in the state apparatus (19.5 per cent versus 10.7 per cent). Taken together, the relative frequencies reported here for the two groups would suggest that tracks to high-level political careers are slightly more competitive in Minsk City and that those from the capital who do manage to make their way upward on the job ladder tend more so than the others to take their next career steps on some rung within the hierarchies of the ministries or state committees.

The second of these distinctions between the two groups seems to be consonant with the profile of the MCIG which has been developed up to this point. As a group composed of individuals from the skilled sector of the working class in the capital, we would expect that members of the MCIG would provide a reservoir of talent from which appointments to managerial and administrative posts in the economy would be made. Such appointments were facilitated, no doubt, by those members of the MCIG who occupied administrative posts in Moscow where they were able to recommend for promotion others with whom they had previously worked or with whom they had prior association in Minsk by means of, say, common membership on a party committee or director's council. The first distinction noted above, however, would add another characteristic to the group, namely, a relatively high level of internal competition for advancement to higher office. The political structures in Minsk City constitute a somewhat more narrow funnel for passage from factory-level jobs to higher positions in party and governmental bodies. There are more KPB members in Minsk City, we recall, than in any of the oblasts of the BSSR and with some one-quarter of the BSSR's total industrial output, Minsk City represents the largest single source of potential recruits from factory-level positions to higher political office. Yet, within the capital, the number of jobs into which such recruits might move (e.g., raikom secretaries or raiispolkom chairmen) is comparatively much smaller than it is in the oblasts. Hence, in Minsk City there appears to be a larger number of potential candidates competing for jobs in a smaller pool of positions. This competitive aspect of the MCIG may, then, say something about the skills (technical, organizational and political) of those who managed to obtain subsequent promotions. It also, as the data in Table 6.1 suggest, indicates the influence that membership in the MCIG has on career advancement.

The data displayed in Table 6.1 were derived by taking the number of the stratum that corresponds to each of the respective positions in the data set (Appendix A) that were occupied at one time or another by one or more of our 361 individuals and calculating the mean scores for each group according to the five categories of entry-level positions.

Table 6.1. *Average ranks of first, second and highest positions held for two groups entering system through five channels* (N=361)

| | Entry jobs | | | | | | | | | |
| | P.P.O.s | | Trade unions | | Executives | | Workers | | Komsomol | |
	MCIG	Others	MCIG	Others	MCIG	Others	MCIG	Others	MCIG	Others
Job Rank										
First Job	7.7 (69)	8.6 (71)	7.3 (4)	10 (17)	7.4 (35)	7.7 (62)	5.6 (12)	6.7 (15)	6.6 (8)	6.4 (68)
Second Job	6.2 (18)	6.9 (29)	5.7 (3)	8.8 (4)	4.6 (13)	5.6 (21)	4.3 (9)	5.2 (12)	5.8 (5)	5.6 (49)
Highest Job	3.9 (9)	5.9 (12)	4.7 (3)	5 (1)	3.0 (3)	4.3 (12)	1.7 (7)	2.4 (10)	4.7 (3)	4.3 (29)

* Numbers in parentheses indicate respective number of cases from which average ranks of jobs were determined. Row totals for 'Second Job' are lower than the total number of second career moves mentioned on p. 99 for the MCIG and others by 12 and 6, respectively. These differences result from those cases in which known second career moves were not made to jobs in the set of ranked positions in Appendix A.

The first row in the table reports, then, that the average rank of the jobs first held by members of the MCIG when they entered into the positions contained in the data set was in some cases (secretaries in primary party organizations, chairmen of trade union councils, and skilled workers in industrial firms) considerably higher than the jobs first held by the others, recalling that the *higher strata* are designated by the *lower numbers*. For industrial executives and Komsomol officials, however, the rankings are by and large equivalent for the two groups.

The second row in the table reports on those who advanced from the entry-level positions to another position in the system. We note here an indication of the relative competitiveness of the personnel system in Minsk City with respect to party secretaries in industrial firms. Whereas 29 of the 71 actors (40.8 per cent) who entered the system as P.P.O. secretaries outside of Minsk City were able to advance to a higher position, only 18 of 69 (26.1 per cent) among the MCIG managed to do so. Those who entered the system as trade union officials in Minsk City, on the other hand, had a much higher incidence of promotion than did their counterparts elsewhere, but the numbers in this case are not large enough to support any firm conclusions. Otherwise, the two groups seem to compare rather evenly on the percentage of members who received promotions after having entered the system via one of the remaining three channels.

Excepting for the moment those who entered through the Komsomol channel, members of the MCIG who had advanced to another job in the system have been more successful than their counterparts in reaching highly ranked positions. For these individuals, a full rank separates members of the MCIG who entered as factory executives from their counterparts and, with respect to those entering the system as either secretaries of P.P.O.s or skilled workers, the better part of a full rank distinguishes MCIG members from the others. The largest difference recorded in this respect appears in the cases of those entering from factory-level trade union offices, a rank difference of 3.1, but here, again, the numbers involved are too small to sustain meaningful inference.

The data in the second row of the table indicate that the field of Komsomol work represents the only channel into elite positions in which MCIG members have been at a (slight) comparative disadvantage. Moreover, this disadvantage also appears in the third row, and suggests a number of things. First, recruitment to elite positions from among the ranks of Komsomol officers has been somewhat less pronounced in Minsk City than it has been in the oblasts of the BSSR.

Second, among non-members of the MCIG, the Komsomol apparatus has served as a faster track to top elite positions than have the
channels of party secretary and trade union officer in an industrial
enterprise, while industrial executives rank evenly with Komsomol
entrants with respect to highest rank attained, and skilled workers
come out considerably better (2.4 versus 4.3). With the exception of
this small group (ten individuals) it is possible to offer the generalization that Komsomol office has been the most advantageous site from
which to launch a political career outside of Minsk City. In addition to
the average rank of jobs attained, the numbers of non-MCIG members
that appear in the third row of the table indicate that a greater
percentage (42.6 per cent) of recruits from the Komsomol reach top
elite jobs than is true of those entering through the other channels.

This generalization is reversed when we apply it to members of the
MCIG. In this respect, either channels other than Komsomol office
have led to higher ranking jobs or, as is the case with trade unions, the
respective rates of attrition have been greater for those entering the
elite through the channel of Komsomol work. Consequently, one part
of the answer to the question of what difference does faction make
regarding one's chances for upward mobility can be supplied with
reference to entry via the Komsomol. For MCIG members, Komsomol
work has been the least important path to the top, for non-members of
the MCIG, excepting again the small number of those in the sample
classified as 'skilled workers', it has been the most important one.

The data in the third row of the table also indicate that MCIG
members were able to reach higher ranking offices than were their
counterparts in all cases except Komsomol entrants. Attrition rates
here vary. For instance, comparatively fewer MCIG executives
received promotions after having reached 'second job' status (row 2),
and comparatively fewer non-members of the MCIG who entered
through the channels of party secretary or trade union chairman in an
industrial enterprise received promotions after having reached the
'second job' plateau. Combining entrants from all channels, however,
we find that the percentage of members who were promoted after
having reached 'second job' status is effectively equivalent for the two
groups – 52.1 per cent for members of the MCIG, 55.7 per cent for
non-members, and, with Komsomol entrants excluded, the comparable figures become 51.2 per cent and 53.0 per cent, respectively. Given
this overall equivalence in rates of attrition between the two groups,
we can add a second part of the answer to our question regarding the
difference made by faction. Members of the MCIG who advanced

beyond the 'second job' plateau and who had entered elite positions through any of the channels except Komsomol work were able as a group to attain higher ranking positions than was true for non-members of the MCIG. Moreover, this difference between the groups is especially pronounced in the case of those who entered the elite from positions as either party secretaries (3.9 versus 5.9) or executives (3.0 versus 4.3) in industrial enterprises. In sum, the influence of factional affiliation on the careers of MCIG members appears to be strong, especially for those who entered the Belorussian elite after having served their political apprenticeships in the factories of Minsk.

Women in the system

Western studies of women who occupy positions in the politico-administrative hierarchies of the USSR underscore the fact that there is a place for women in the Soviet system. This place, moreover, can be relatively well defined. On the one hand, among the highest offices of the Soviet party-state, women are conspicuous by their absence.[2] As one observer has put it: 'In substantive rather than ceremonial roles, in the key hierarchies of political and coercive power, and at the apex of the system as a whole, politics remains a male affair.'[3] On the other hand, women who occupy political roles in the USSR tend to cluster around those positions that carry on support-ive and/or nurturing activities of one sort or another. In both respects, Belorussian women appear to be a relatively undifferentiated sub-set of Soviet women. The type and importance of the offices that they have held seem to fit closely the larger Soviet pattern.

The numerical representation of women in the ranks of the KPB has increased moderately over the period covered by this study, as has their representation on local party committees.[4] In this regard, the proportion of KPB members who are female is relatively equal, give or take a percentage point, to the same proportions in the other republics of the USSR, excepting Estonia, Latvia and Lithuania where women participate at somewhat higher rates.[5] During the first ten years covered by this study, the proportion of women among secretaries of primary party organizations of the KPB nearly doubled and reached the 30 per cent mark by 1976,[6] a figure comparable to the overall average for the USSR.[7]

Like their counterparts in the other republics, women in the BSSR are commonly associated with a relatively narrow range of supporting political roles, foremost among which is that concerned with political socialization.[8] In our sample, it has been possible to identify 230 actors as females[9] and to identify further 125 of these as working in one or more jobs within a particular functional specialization. Among the 125 for whom such specifications could be made, 57 (45.6 per cent) have occupied positions in the general area of political socialization – party secretaries in charge of propaganda, cultural officers in soviets and so on. The second leading occupational specialty present in these data locates women within a select group of managerial positions concentrated in the light and food industries, health, social security and trade. Some 36 women (28.8 per cent) in our sub-sample could be so classified and this figure again seems to be representative of the USSR as a whole.[10] Only five women are identified as having held posts in the area of heavy industry and three in the agricultural sector, while the internal 'housekeeping' specialization – such as secretary of a soviet – accounts for the remaining 24 (19.2 per cent).[11]

These comparisons suggest that Belorussian women in political roles very much resemble the profile of women in the Soviet polity wherein under-representation, distance from *loci* of power and concentration within a select group of activities are the relevant characteristics. It may also be true that the same factors that have produced this profile of politically active women in the USSR operate with more or less equal effect in the BSSR.[12] Having established a rough comparability between the USSR and the BSSR on this score, however, our concern here is to examine the influence of faction on this particular sub-set of Belorussian officeholders. Consequently, we are content simply to draw the inference that there seems to be nothing unique to the BSSR as far as the role of women in politics is concerned.

One of the occupational characteristics of women in the sample, their concentration in lower-level positions, limits the utility of the methods developed in the previous chapter for identifying factional affiliation. Since a majority of women in our sample (139 of 230) have held only a single job in the system, the method of inferring a patronage relation on the basis of two or more career moves could not be applied in most cases. In order, then, to generate a sample of factionally affiliated females large enough to discern differences among groups, another approach has been added to the methods employed thus far. This approach designates factional affiliation by appointment to a position within a set of offices thought to be controlled by one of the factional groups already identified. The accuracy of this less rigorous technique has been improved to some degree by assigning all borderline cases to the category labelled 'unknown'. Through a combination of the methods previously developed and the somewhat less rigorous technique introduced here, it has been possible to classify 174 of the 230 women as clients of one patronage group or another.

The data set out in Table 6.2 point up a relationship between the factional affiliations of women in the sample and their access to elite positions in the BSSR (defined here as those jobs included in the top four strata of positions in Appendix A). The left-hand column of the table lists the various factional groupings together with the number of women who could be associated with each; the column in the centre provides the number of women from each of these respective groups who have gained access to one of the elite jobs; and those on the right-hand side list the names of the women in question and the highest offices that they have reached. Perhaps the first thing that might be said about these data is that they suggest something about the place of women in the system, namely, that their place is not at or near the top of the hierarchy. Whether we view these results from the perspective of the proportion of women in the sample who reached these elite jobs (ten of 230) or from the even more revealing standpoint that the 212 jobs in these four strata over 21 years yield a total of 4,452 possible year-long tenures in this set of elite positions of which only some 60 involved females, it would follow that women's access to elite jobs in the BSSR is very highly constrained.

Secondly, for those women who have managed to reach elite positions, the influence of factional affiliation is apparent in these results. Only 14.3 per cent of the women in the sample can be identified as either members or clients of the MCIG, yet this group accounts for half of the women who have held elite jobs. Owing to the small number of cases, however, we cannot establish a clear difference among the groups in a statistical sense. Moreover, the highest ranking position held by a woman, Deputy Chair of the Belorussian Council of Ministers (Stratum 2), has been occupied on two occasions (N. L. Snezhkova, 1968–85, and N. N. Mazai, 1985–) by the clients of other patronage cliques. Even with these two qualifications in mind, however, these findings would support the inference that factional affiliation is associated with the career chances of women in the system. Taking women as a group, the data indicate that each had a one-in-thirty-three chance of reaching an elite job. For members and clients of the Partisan faction, the comparable figure would be one-in-twenty-three, for clients of the Brezhnev group, one-in-forty-one, and for members and clients of the MCIG, a little better than one-in-seven.

Table 6.2. *Factional affiliation of women and access to elite positions** (N=230)

Factional groupings	Number reaching elite	Name	Highest office
Partisans and Clients:			
Republic level (n=12)	2	V. A. Klochkova	First Dep. Chair, Belkoopsoyuz, 1977–82.
		I. A. Stavrovskaya	Minister of Food Ind., 1980–.
Mogilev Oblast' (n=19)	1	N. L. Snezhkova	Dep. Chair, Council of Ministers, 1968–85.
Gomel' Oblast' (n=23)	–		
Grodno Oblast' (n=23)	–		
Minsk Oblast' (n=23)	–		
MCIG and Clients (n=33)	5	T. T. Dmitrieva	Dep. Minister, Higher and Middle Spec. Ed., 1968–78.
		M. S. Kononova	Minister of Light Ind., 1972–75.
		M. S. Senokosova	Director, Minsk Worsted Factory, 1976–78
		N. S. Nerad	Chair, BSSR Soc. for Friendship and Cultural Ties, 1982–.
		L. K. Sukhnat	Minister of Education, 1985–.
Brezhnev Clients:			
Brest Oblast' (n=12)	1	N. N. Mazai	Dep. Chair, Council of Ministers, 1985–.
Vitebsk Oblast' (n=29)	–		
Unknown Affiliation (n=56)	1	M. T. Dekhta	First Dep. Minister of Communic., 1976–82.

* 'Elite positions' is here defined as those jobs in Strata 1–4 of the hierarchy which is set out in Appendix A.

The use of negative sanctions

Patronage affiliation, as we have seen thus far, can exercise a discernible influence on one's chances for gaining access to higher office in the BSSR. Does it also play a role in determining the relative frequencies at which punishments ('negative sanctions') are visited on officeholders? In this section we examine three types of negative sanctions not uncommonly faced by officials in the USSR: reprimands, authoritative criticism and publicly announced dismissals. In so doing, we are interested to determine whether and to what extent patronage affiliation serves to protect members of a given clique and, conversely, to what degree and under what conditions it might increase their vulnerability to the use of negative sanctions.

Studies of crime and punishment in Soviet officialdom have called attention to the pronounced personalistic element embedded in the formal rules and procedures purporting to govern the conduct of officeholders.[13] For those operating within a milieu in which legal codes and administrative regulations are often contradictory, in which the demands of political superiors for performance are often a matter of greater urgency than is following the officially prescribed procedures, and in which personal contacts and the trading of favours may well have more to do with getting things accomplished than does the method of 'going by the book', following the formally established rules becomes at best an uncertain guarantee against the threat of punishment and, at worst, an indication (under the charge of 'formalism') that punishment may be warranted in a given case. Indeed, one student of Soviet affairs has gone so far as to refer to the process of rule-enforcement as simply another phase in a cycle of extra-legal, if not corrupt, administrative behaviour, arguing that negative sanctions are in context less a means of impersonally discouraging illegal behaviour than they are a weapon in the hands of one clique or another to be used against the more vulnerable members of rival groups.[14]

Reprimands

We begin our analysis of the use of negative sanctions on officeholders in the BSSR with 99 recorded cases of official reprimands issued by the People's Control Commission (Narkontrol'), the KPB and governmental authorities in the BSSR against individuals in the data set over the 21 year period encompassed by this study. To be sure, the total number of reprimands generated by these organs in this period runs into the thousands, but the great bulk of them have been directed at lower-level officials – chairmen of collective farms, rank-and-file party members, and so forth – who do not appear in the data set. Consequently, the small fraction of the total number of reprimands that is of concern to us refers to those rather special cases in which an individual, who occupied an office of sufficient status to be included in the data set, has received this negative sanction.

The data presented in Table 6.3 are arranged according to the source of the reprimands, their relative severity (whether of the ordinary or strict variety), the alleged reasons as to why they were issued (whether for poor work or corruption) and what effect, if any, they seem to have had on the careers of those who received them. The figures listed in the bottom row of the table, which show the net effects of reprimands, suggest that this form of negative sanction is a rather mild one. Among the 99 officials who have been reprimanded, only 17 are known to have been sacked within the following year, 62 retained their posts for at least the following two years, 12 received subsequent promotions, while the outcome in 20 of the cases was indeterminate.[15] Among those cases in which terminations are known to have occurred after reprimands had been issued, we find that only one individual has been removed from office after a reprimand for corrupt activities and that this case involves an 'ordinary' reprimand from Narkontrol'. In the two instances involving strict reprimands from Narkontrol' for corruption, the subsequent careers of the officials in question are unknown, perhaps indicating that terminations occurred. For the two cases of corruption in which the KPB had issued strict reprimands, however, one individual is known to have been retained in office while the results in the other case are indeterminate. Overall, the data suggest that the use of this negative sanction on Belorussian officials has not followed the pattern one might expect to find were the system governed by impersonal bureaucratic norms. Even if we were to assume that all of the cases which fall under the category of 'unknown results' in fact resulted in terminations, then it appears that one's odds of surviving a strict as opposed to a regular reprimand from Narkontrol' were not much different (7-in-12 versus 8-in-11), one's odds of surviving KPB reprimands were actually greater for the strict (2-in-3) than for the regular variety (9-in-22), and that reprimands issued by governmental authorities have been followed as often by promotion as they have been by termination.

Does factional affiliation shed any light on these outcomes?

Table 6.3. *Official reprimands and their effects on careers*

	Number	Infraction		Result			
		Poor work	Corruption	Termination	Retention	LP*	Unknown
Source and type of reprimand							
Narkontrol'							
Ordinary	44	34	10	4	32	5	8
Strict	12	10	2	1	7	2	4
Party Organs							
Ordinary	22	22	–	7	9	1	6
Strict	15	13	2	3	10	2	2
Government							
Ordinary	6	5	1	2	4	2	–
Strict	–	–	–	–	–	–	–
Totals	99	84	15	17	62	12	20

* 'LP' refers to those cases in which an official, having retained his job after receiving a reprimand, was *later promoted* to a higher office.

Regarding the members of the three groups listed in Appendix B, only two received reprimands and each managed to retain his job thereafter.[16] Some 37 additional members of this collection of reprimanded officials can be identified as clients of one or another of three patronage groups. In as much as the particular time at which a reprimand was issued has a bearing on the factional politics at play (see the following chapter), it is useful, here, to divide our time-frame into two periods, 1966–76 and 1977–86. During the first period in which a jockeying for position was evident between the Partisans and Brezhnev clients, we find that eight of the latter received reprimands and all eight retained their jobs, while 14 of the former were reprimanded and three terminations ensued. Two clients of the MCIG were issued reprimands during this period; one retained his job and, in the other case, the result is unknown.

In the second period, four Brezhnev clients were issued reprimands. One, who was reprimanded in February of 1980 on the eve of the (brief) accession of this group to the dominant position in the BSSR's leadership, managed to retain his office. Two were reprimanded in March of 1982 when the Brezhnev succession was getting underway in Moscow and (as we see below) at a time in which anti-Brezhnev forces were mustering themselves in the BSSR. The outcomes of these two cases are unknown. The final case occurred at the end of 1983 after the Brezhnev faction had been displaced as the dominant group in the Belorussian leadership by the MCIG. This reprimand resulted in termination. Clients of the Partisan faction received reprimands on nine occasions during this second period. None is known to have resulted in a termination while in five of the cases the officials in question retained their offices. Finally, three reprimands were issued to members of the MCIG during this period yielding no known terminations and two retentions.

Although the number of cases in which clients of the various patronage groups were issued reprimands is not large enough to support firm conclusions regarding the influence of factional affiliation on the use of this negative sanction, the results of the analysis seem to be suggestive on two counts. First, the institution of reprimands in the BSSR does not appear to conform to a bureaucratic pattern in which reprimands have marked, negative effects on the careers of officials who receive them. Leaving aside the matter of what personalistic or factional motives might have prompted the various authorities to issue reprimands in the first place, the data indicate little difference in the outcomes of cases in which strict, as opposed to ordinary, reprimands were employed, and further show that officials had at least a roughly 2-in-3 chance of surviving a reprimand and a 1-in-8 chance of being promoted thereafter. Secondly, the use and consequences of this negative sanction appear to be consistent with phases of factional rivalry. During the first period, the Partisan faction, as the dominant group in Belorussian politics, was under challenge from the Brezhnev forces. The only cases in which termination followed a reprimand involved Partisan clients. In the second period, when the pendulum had swung the other way, clients of each of these groups were issued reprimands but the only known termination involved a Brezhnev client who lost his job shortly after his group had lost its dominant position in the leadership.

Authoritative criticism

What happens to those officials who either have been singled out for blame by an authoritative spokesman at a party gathering or who have been named in critical articles published in the press? The incidence of such events is relatively rare. Among the 3,127 individuals in our sample, only 20 are known to have been the targets of these forms of authoritative criticism. Again, these rather special cases may indicate something of particular importance with respect to the use of negative sanctions and their relation to factional politics in the BSSR. If it is not an everyday event for members of officialdom to be held up to authoritative criticism, then we would do well to pay close attention to those rare occasions on which they have been.

In late 1969, *Pravda* published an especially critical article on poor agricultural performance in Gomel' Oblast', replete with calls for sacking certain members of the regional elite.[17] Four of the five officials who were singled out for blame lost their jobs in a matter of days.[18] In as much as each of the five held but a single job within the time-frame of this study, our methods for determining factional affiliation do not apply here. Nonetheless, there are two reasons to infer a motivation based on factional considerations in these incidences of authoritative criticism. First, *Pravda* was the medium for articulating the negative sanction and its editor at the time was M. V. Zimyanin, a leading member of the Partisan faction. Secondly, all four of the vacancies that resulted from the terminations were filled by individuals who have been identified as clients of the Partisans.

On four occasions, leading members of the MCIG and prominent clients of the Brezhnev group subjected various officials in the BSSR to authoritative criticism. Taking, first, the Brezhnev clients, we find A. N. Aksenov as Second Secretary of the KPB singling out for blame four raikom secretaries whom he alleged to be poorly discharging their responsibilities in the agricultural sector.[19] Two of the individuals in question were clients of the Partisan faction and one of them was removed from office shortly thereafter. The factional affiliation of the other two is unknown, but in so far as one of them was terminated shortly after Aksenov's charges, and this individual had only recently been decorated with the Order of Lenin for outstanding work in the agricultural sector, factional politics may have played a role in motivating these criticisms as well. The final case in which an official was criticized by a leading client of the Brezhnev faction involved T. Ya. Kiselev, as First Secretary of the KPB, charging another raikom secretary with poor performance in agricultural work.[20] The individual in question, who lost his job shortly thereafter, has been identified as a client of the Brezhnev machine. If factional identification was accurate in this instance, then we would assume that Kiselev sought the removal of this official for reasons other than those associated with factional rivalry *per se*.

The factional affiliations of those criticized by A. A. Reut[21] and G. G. Bartoshevich,[22] leading members of the MCIG, are not known, as is the case with three other officials who were criticized by party authorities for unsatisfactory performance in office. The four remaining officials who were subjected to this negative sanction have all been identified as clients of the Partisans. The criticisms were levelled during a period (1969–74) in which the Partisan faction was dominant in Belorussian politics but under challenge from clients of the Brezhnev group, and the outcomes of these criticisms are predictably mixed. Two Partisan clients retained their jobs, another was soon promoted and the fourth was sacked.

Publicly announced dismissals

In some 30 instances, the Belorussian press reported the outright termination of individuals whose names appear in our data set for reasons ranging from poor leadership to corruption. Thirteen of these dismissed officials have been identified as clients of either the Partisan or Brezhnev factions. The timing of the dismissals of these 13 actors coincided with the phases of factional rivalry discussed in the following chapter. Ten of the dismissed officials have been identified as clients of the Brezhnev group. Terminations in all ten cases occurred after 1983, that is, after the MCIG had replaced the Brezhnev clients as the dominant group in Belorussian politics. The other three cases involved the dismissal of officials identified with the Partisan faction and these took place at various times: one occurred in 1976 during a period of rivalry between the Partisan and Brezhnev groups; another took place in 1981 when Brezhnev clients had succeeded in ousting the Partisans from control of the Belorussian leadership; and the final instance was announced in 1986 by which time the MCIG had assumed the dominant position in the BSSR.

Whereas the dismissal of ten Brezhnev clients after the fall of the Brezhnev faction seems a straightforward case of redividing the spoils of office, the termination of the three Partisan clients is more difficult to account for in terms of factional rivalries. Under the assumption that these three terminations had been motivated by factional considerations, the first two might be explained as blows struck by the Brezhnev machine against their Partisan rivals. The third case, however, occurred during a period in which the MCIG was in collaboration with the remnants of the Partisan group (see Chapter 7) and was busy, as we just noted, sacking clients of the vanquished Brezhnev clique. N. N. Slyun'kov, then First Secretary of the KPB who announced this and three other dismissals in his speech to the Thirtieth Congress of the KPB, listed 'corrupt and deceitful leadership' as the reason for the terminations.[23] The most plausible explanation might be, then, that while prepared to reach accommodation with clients of their defeated rivals – and such seems to be true for clients of the Brezhnev group as well as for those affiliated with the Partisans – the MCIG was also prepared to be selective in doing so.

Conclusion

The evidence presented in this chapter tends to support the idea that faction makes a difference for the career prospects of those individuals associated with one or another patronage group. In those instances in which the available information is relatively plentiful, i.e., for those who entered the system through one of the five channels discussed and for those whom we identify as females, the effect of faction stands out rather distinctly. In either case, actors affiliated with the MCIG have regularly displayed a greater potential for promotion than have their counterparts. These findings can be regarded as evidence of a personalistic basis for elite circulation in the BSSR. Rather than considerations of merit or talent which we would associate with promotion mechanisms operating under bureaucratic conditions, we note in all cases, excepting those involving individuals who had begun their political careers as Komsomol officials, that affiliation with a particular patronage group coincides with the career chances of the actors.

The available information related to the use of negative sanctions is somewhat more sketchy, and whatever conclusions are to be drawn from it should, therefore, be rendered in more provisional terms. Nonetheless, we have observed with respect to the issuing and results of reprimands little of the pattern one might expect under a bureaucratic mode of organization. The consequences of a reprimand, if not the motives for issuing it, seem to be determined by forces other than those associated with a modern bureaucracy. Specifically, the timing and results of reprimands appear to be related to phases of factional conflict in the system. If officials are in fact reprimanded on the basis of poor performance or corruption, it would seem that phases in the rivalry among factional groups account for much of the variance over time regarding who is reprimanded and with what result. The use of the other two negative sanctions that we have discussed also appears to have a factional element in it, but the infrequency of the cases in which authoritative criticism or publicly announced dismissals have occurred cautions against drawing firm conclusions. However, taking the employment of all three types of negative sanctions together, we can say that the pattern that prevails – in one instance strongly, in another, weakly – points consistently to factional affiliation as an influence on events within the system.

7   Political succession

The political succession that transpired in Belorussia during the first half of the 1980s was a multi-phased process that developed in tandem with the Brezhnev succession. In the BSSR, leadership change was in some respects determined by the events that unfolded in Moscow while in others it anticipated them. Here, our intention is, first, to provide a narrative overview of this period of extraordinary flux in the personnel system by recounting the various factional alignments that formed, disintegrated and reformed over the course of the succession. Thereafter, our attention turns to the personnel changes that took place in the upper strata of the Belorussian hierarchy. We are concerned in this respect both to chronicle the rise and fall of contending groups according to their respective numerical representations within the Republic's elite at one stage or another in the process, and to look beneath the surface of these ratios in order to locate their basis in (shifting) factional coalitions. Lastly, we consider the outcome of the succession and offer some observations on apparent structural changes in the personnel system of the BSSR that seem to correlate with the direction of such changes in the USSR as a whole.

Succession in the BSSR in the context of Kremlin politics

For their participation in the coalition that deposed N. S. Khrushchev in 1964, Belorussia's Partisan faction profited handsomely. K. T. Mazurov, First Secretary of the KPB since 1956 and leader of the Partisans, was within months promoted to the post of First Deputy Chair of the Council of Ministers of the USSR and elevated to full membership on the Politburo. Probably as part of the same bargain, he was able to bring to Moscow two of his close associates from the partisan movement who had also established political careers in the BSSR after the War: M. V. Zimyanin who was named Editor of *Pravda* in 1965 and became a Secretary of the CPSU in 1976, and V. F. Shauro who took up the post of Head of the CPSU's Department of Culture. Zimyanin and Shauro remained in these positions until 1987 and 1986, respectively. Mazurov's lieutenant, P. M. Masherov, succeeded him as First Secretary of the KPB while other members of the Partisan group dotted the offices of the Belorussian party-state (see Appendix B).

Mazurov had frequently clashed with Khrushchev on a number of issues, foremost among which were agricultural policy and the proportion of investments allocated to his native republic.[1] Substantive issues in this field brought Mazurov into a close working relationship with the new General Secretary, L. I. Brezhnev, whose agricultural programme was consonant with that of Mazurov.[2] Hence, substantive policy benefits accrued to the BSSR as well as career advancement for members of Mazurov's faction in return for their role in the grand manoeuvre that ousted Khrushchev.[3]

Mazurov's alliance with Brezhnev, however, was a tactical one based on the common objectives of the moment. Indeed, the political gains which it brought about were sufficient to establish a national presence for the Partisans which they sought to exploit and enhance through coalition politics in Moscow. In the same way that Mazurov's group soon found itself at odds with the Brezhnev faction,[4] the latter seem to have cultivated ties with certain Belorussian politicians in order to infiltrate the Partisan base in the BSSR. T. Ya. Kiselev, Chair of the Council of Ministers of the BSSR since 1959, figured prominently in this relationship. As an apparent ally of Brezhnev,[5] he had been serving in the number two position in the Republic for nearly 20 years. He now moved to Moscow to become Deputy Chair of the USSR's Council of Ministers immediately after Mazurov lost his job as First Deputy Chair and his seat on the Politburo in 1978. A. N. Aksenov, another of the Brezhnev clients in the BSSR, moved from his post as Second Secretary of the KPB to fill the opening created by Kiselev's departure, and Aksenov's client, V. I. Brovikov, took over the job of Second Secretary of the KPB.

Mazurov's fall left the leader of the Partisan faction in the BSSR, First Secretary of the KPB P. M. Masherov, without a reliable patron in Moscow. Zimyanin, to be sure, remained a secretary of the CPSU, but with the decapitation of the Partisan's leadership, he seemed to have shifted his allegiances to Yu. V. Andropov,[6] KGB chief and contender in the Brezhnev succession already underway owing to Brezhnev's advanced age and failing health. Moreover, Masherov was further isolated at home. Not only did his rivals, Aksenov and Brovikov, now occupy the number two and three positions within the power structure in the BSSR, but two of the other four positions on the KPB's Secretariat had been filled by clients of the Brezhnev machine (L. S. Firisanov and N. I. Dementei) and only one was at this time held by an identified client of Masherov's Partisan faction (Yu. B. Kolokolov). Then, in October of 1980, Masherov died in an automobile collision under rather mysterious circumstances. This was the first recorded instance in Soviet history in which a member of the Politburo (who have always travelled under heavy guard, down the middle of highways cleared of traffic) was ever involved in an automobile wreck, much less a fatality in one. Moreover, the automobile collision that claimed Masherov's life was the first in a series of similar accidents (with or without inverted commas) that struck a number of high-ranking Soviet officials.[7] To this highly suggestive circumstantial evidence might be added the import of personnel changes occurring immediately before and after Masherov's death.

In August of 1980, the retirement of Ya. P. Nikulkin, Chair of the Belorussian KGB, presented Yu. V. Andropov with the opportunity to install one of his men, V. G. Baluev, in a strategic position at a particularly important juncture in succession politics at both the national and republic levels. If the accident was in fact a murder prepared by the KGB, then Andropov's hand and Andropov's man, Baluev, were surely behind it. But regardless of whether Masherov's death was accidental, both Andropov and Brezhnev gained with Masherov out of the picture. Kiselev, a Brezhnev client, returned from Moscow to replace Masherov as First Secretary of the KPB. Aksenov, who had previously worked in the Belorussian KGB and therefore may have had organizational ties to Andropov, was also apparently connected to the Brezhnev group via ties to G. N. Zhabitskii who had become the BSSR's Minister of Internal Affairs some two years prior to Masherov's death. At any event, Aksenov apparently shared with both the Brezhnev and Andropov factions an interest in removing the Partisan faction from power.

The succession struggle occurring in the BSSR seemed to be, then, something of a microcosm of the struggle taking place simultaneously in Moscow. Its early stages in either case evinced an apparent cooperation between the Brezhnev and Andropov factions in Moscow, and their supporters in the BSSR, to remove their common opponent, the Belorussian Partisans. Subsequent stages of the process, however, became more complex. Once the Partisans had been effectively eliminated, cooperation between the other factions at each level gave way to a contest between them. This contest reached a turning point in Moscow, of course, with the death of Brezhnev in November of 1982. In the BSSR, the decisive moment came two months later with the death of Kiselev.

The interval between the deaths of Masherov and Kiselev witnessed a lull in the succession in the BSSR and involved no extraordinary personnel changes. A sense of ebb and flow in factional politics during this period can be gained from a comparison of yearly rates of turnover in republic-level jobs numbered among the top four strata in Appendix A (excluding positions that we have regarded as sinecures) and the leading offices in each of the regions (the five obkom secretaries – or, for Minsk City, the four gorkom secretaries – and the chair and first deputy chair of the regional soviet executive committees). In 1980, the year of Masherov's death, 13 of these top 108 republic-level positions changed hands (12 per cent) and turnover occurred in seven of the 48 regional jobs under consideration (14.6 per cent). In 1981, seven republic-level jobs changed hands (6 per cent) as did four regional positions (8.3 per cent). The comparable turnover figures for 1982 are similarly low, six jobs were shuffled at the republic level (5.6 per cent) and five at the regional level (10.4 per cent). Outside of the two cases in 1980 that we have already noted, the death of Masherov and the retirement of Nikulkin, the only personnel changes during these three years that seemed to be in any way out of the ordinary were the demotion of N. V. Gordikov from Secretary of the Grodno Obkom to the post of Director of the Oblast' bee-keeping industry in 1980 and the transfer of B. A. Gvozdev, Chair of Gosplan, BSSR, and a Partisan client, to 'other work' in 1981.

With the death of Kiselev in January of 1983, however, changes came in a rush. Among the 108 republic-level jobs, 29 changed hands (26.9 per cent). In the regions, turnover occurred in 21 of the 48 positions (43.8 per cent). Moreover, the content of the changes indicated that the Aksenov group, which had ties to both the Andropov and Brezhnev factions, fared rather poorly. Aksenov was himself transferred out of the post of Chair of the BSSR's Council of Ministers and made Ambassador to Poland. He was replaced by his lieutenant, V. I. Brovikov, but his other client on the Secretariat of the KPB, L. S. Firisanov, was demoted to Deputy Chair of the Republic's Council of Ministers and was removed from the Buro of the KPB. The clear winner at this stage of the struggle was the MCIG, whose leading figure, N. N. Slyun'kov, was brought back to the BSSR from his position as a Deputy Chair of Gosplan, USSR, to fill the office of First Secretary of the KPB.

The appointment of Slyun'kov was the first major act by newly elected General Secretary Andropov in the area of personnel. The rapidity with which Slyun'kov was installed (one day after the death of Kiselev) and the fact that Slyun'kov had been working in Moscow for the previous eight years, signalled an abrupt end to the Brezhnevian 'trust in local cadres' and portended deeper personnel changes in the BSSR.[8] Slyun'kov returned to Belorussia wielding a sizeable broom, sweeping out his rivals and advancing members and clients of the MCIG to the vacancies thereby created. With Brovikov's move to Chair of the Council of Ministers, the vacancy in the post of Second Secretary of the KPB was filled by G. G. Bartoshevich, a leading member of the MCIG who had been serving as First Secretary of the Minsk Gorkom. Other members of the MCIG who advanced in the Belorussian hierarchy at this time included V. A. Lepeshkin, who returned from Moscow to fill the position on the Secretariat of the KPB left vacant by Firisanov's demotion, V. I. Kritskii, who was promoted to Deputy Chair of the Council of Ministers BSSR, and M. V. Kovalev, who moved up the ladder from Deputy Chair to First Deputy Chair of the Belorussian Council of Ministers to fill the vacancy created by the death of V. F. Mitskevich, a Partisan client. Another MCIG member, A. I. Bulgak, was shuttled to Moscow where he became a sector head in the apparatus of the Central Committee.

As for the broom, it was brought out into full view in December of 1983. Under the official explanation of sloppy work on a murder investigation involving a criminal gang operating in the Belorussian countryside,[9] heads rolled in the law enforcement apparatus of the BSSR. Dismissed from their posts were: G. N. Zhabitskii, Minister of Internal Affairs along with three of his deputy ministers (P. S. Zhuk, I. O. Timoshenko, and V. F. Maidanyuk), V. A. Mogilnitskii, Procurator of the BSSR and his First Deputy, P. V. Dudkovskii. This sweep of the law enforcement organs was, of course, part and parcel of the anti-corruption campaign that Andropov had got underway shortly after he replaced Brezhnev.[10] Within the world of factional politics in Belorussia, however, it represented the demise of a key group of politicians who had been closely associated with Aksenov and Kiselev, and a decisive victory for the MCIG. First, the purge was likely prepared by V. A. Lepeshkin while he was Deputy Head of the CPSU's Department of Administrative Organs, the department that supervises law enforcement agencies, prior to his return to the BSSR in late April of 1983. Secondly, the timing of the move against this group, following as it did Firisanov's removal from the Buro of the KPB and Aksenov's transfer to Poland, suggested that these individuals in the law enforcement organs were hit as soon as they had become sufficiently vulnerable. Finally, members of the Minsk City group advanced into the vacancies created by the purge. V. A. Piskarev, former Head of the Department of Internal Affairs in Minsk City, was alone among deputy ministers of Internal Affairs in surviving the shakeup. He had been posted to Moscow just before the purge took place and returned to the BSSR shortly thereafter to become the new Belorussian Minister of Internal Affairs. B. I. Matushevich, Deputy Chair of Minsk Gorispolkom, was promoted to fill one of the deputy minister positions in the Ministry and L. Dedkov, Procurator of Minsk City, became the new First Deputy Procurator of the BSSR. Excepting V. S. Egorov, a Partisan client who was promoted to the position of First Deputy Minister of Internal Affairs, the others who filled the offices left vacant by the purge have no clear factional ties and regional affiliations which are either mixed or absent in their career histories.

The Egorov promotion is symptomatic of another turn in the succession, namely, the recruitment of certain members and clients of the old Partisan faction into a new governing coalition headed by the MCIG. Given the relative sparsity of MCIG members and clients across the range of offices in the BSSR – a fact which reflects the narrow regional base of the group – it would seem clear that the dominant faction was in need of coalition partners and that these were to be found among those whose former patrons were now either removed from office in the BSSR or demoted. Equally, we should not overlook the fact that at this juncture the succession in Moscow was yet a long way from having run its course and that those pulling the personnel strings in the Soviet capital were certainly engaged in their own negotiations regarding appointments in Belorussia. Since clients of the Brezhnev machine represented at this juncture rivals to both the MCIG and their supporters in Moscow, those politicians who had been associated with the anti-Brezhnev forces, the Partisans, became rather natural allies in many cases. Accordingly, B. I. Petrov, a member of the Partisan faction, was brought out of retirement in 1983 to replace A. I. Bulgak, who had moved to a sector head position in the CPSU apparatus, as First Deputy Minister of Local Industry.

In the provinces we find more evidence of a MCIG–Partisan partnership at this time. A. M. Fomich, Second Secretary of the Minsk Obkom and a Partisan client, became Chair of the Belorussian State

Committee for Labour, a position opened up by the retirement of a member of the Partisan faction, F. D. Romma. A client of the MCIG, M. A. Knyazuk, took over as Second Secretary in the Minsk Obkom, while his job as Obkom secretary there was filled by K. I. Turovich, a Partisan client. S. M. Shabashov, another Partisan, retired as First Secretary of the Vitebsk Obkom and his job was taken by S. T. Kabyak, a Partisan client, who was transferred in from Grodno Oblast where he had been Chair of the Oblispolkom. This transfer suggested an easing out of the Aksenov faction from Vitebsk in as much as they were unable to fill this key post with one of their own clients. A similar change involved V. V. Prishchepchik, also a Partisan, who retired as First Secretary of the Mogilev Obkom and was replaced by yet another Partisan client, V. S. Leonov, who had been First Deputy Chair of the Oblispolkom in Mogilev.

After the dramatic changes in the composition of the Belorussian elite that took place in 1983 and following Andropov's death and his replacement by the last political gasp of the Brezhnev machine, K. U. Chernenko, in early 1984, a brief period of tranquillity ensued in the personnel system of the BSSR. Turnover rates receded considerably. Among the 108 top jobs at the republic level, only 13 changed hands in 1984 (12 per cent). In the regions only four personnel changes (8.3 per cent) occurred in that year. Although proceeding at a slower pace, turnover in 1984 continued to reflect advances for the MCIG and former clients of the Partisans. Among the 13 individuals who filled republic level vacancies in that year, nine have been identified by factional affiliation – four of whom were former Partisan clients, three were members of the MCIG and the remaining two were associated with the Brezhnev group. In the provinces, V. S. Rusak, a Brezhnev client, was retired as a secretary of the Vitebsk Obkom and his job went to a former Partisan client, T. I. Misuno. Additionally, M. A. Knyazuk of the Minsk City group was rotated from his job as Second Secretary of the Minsk Obkom to a position in Moscow while his job on the Obkom was filled by V. F. Kebich of the MCIG who had been heading up the KPB's Heavy Industry Department, a post which went to A. I. Trutnev, yet another client of the Minsk City faction who was returning from a position in the Soviet capital.

The throttle of personnel change was again opened in Belorussia when M. S. Gorbachev was named General Secretary of the CPSU in March of 1985. Slyun'kov, who has definite ties to Gorbachev dating back to his work in Gosplan in the agricultural machine-building sector which was supervised by Gorbachev while he was a Secretary of the CPSU in charge of agricultural affairs (1978–82),[11] clearly benefited from the outcome of the succession in Moscow, and his group in Belorussia reaped the rewards of office. Gorbachev's first year in power witnessed the largest turnover in the Soviet elite since the 1930s,[12] and although the comparable figures in the BSSR, where succession had already been underway for some five years, would not bear out this generalization fully, turnover in 1985 was nonetheless substantial. Among the 108 top posts at the republic-level 22 changed hands (20.4 per cent), while in the regions turnover was even higher, involving some 20 of the 48 offices in question (41.7 per cent). In this respect, Belorussia seems to be an exception to the larger pattern that prevailed in the USSR in which relatively few personnel changes occurred in the regions during Gorbachev's initial year in office.[13] Perhaps the question of timing, if we were to draw parallels between the successions occurring at the national and republic levels, is the reason for these differences. If we regard the Brezhnev succession as a continuous process which was interrupted by the death of Andropov and the period of relative respite that ensued for Brezhnev clients during the Chernenko interregnum, we arrive at the view that the Brezhnev succession did not get underway fully until the advent of Gorbachev. Consequently, during his first year as General Secretary, Gorbachev's personnel changes focused primarily on the upper layers of the Soviet hierarchy. In contrast, succession in the BSSR began with Masherov's death in 1980. By the time that Andropov became General Secretary, a Belorussian faction was already prepared to take power in the BSSR. Hence, as Gorbachev supporters, the Minsk City group was already sweeping away opponents in Belorussia some two years before Gorbachev himself emerged as the victor in the Kremlin. Once this had occurred, a second phase of personnel changes commenced in the BSSR, one which concentrated on regional offices at a time at which Gorbachev was occupied with removing opponents from national positions. In this respect, and in others discussed below, the Minsk City group represents something of a forerunner to the Gorbachev leadership.

Personnel changes in republic-level offices in the BSSR during 1985 continued the trends established earlier in the succession. Two members of the Partisan faction left office in that year: I. E. Polyakov, who retired from his post as President of the Prezidium of the Supreme Soviet of the BSSR, and F. A. Tsekhanovich, who was removed from his job as Minister of Grain Products. The former was replaced by G. S. Tarazevich, a member of the MCIG who had been serving as First Secretary of the Minsk Gorkom, the latter by N. S. Yakushev, a former Partisan client, who was transferred in from his position as Minister of the Vegetable Economy. Four members of the MCIG were promoted to high-level jobs in the state apparatus. V. F. Kebich moved from his post as Second Secretary of the Minsk Obkom to fill the vacancy created in the Chair of Gosplan, BSSR, when A. A. Reut, another member of the MCIG, left for Moscow to become a Deputy Chair of Gosplan, USSR. T. M. Bezruchko became a Deputy President of the Prezidium of the Supreme Soviet, BSSR, when G. Z. Lopanik, another member of the MCIG left that post. N. N. Kostikov took over as Belorussian Minister of Local Industry from L. V. Rusakov, a client of the Brezhnev faction who left for Moscow to become the BSSR's Representative to the USSR Council of Ministers, and L. K. Sukhnat replaced M. G. Minkevich as Minister of Education, a post which he had occupied for some 17 years. A fifth member of the MCIG, N. T. Gulev, became Head of the KPB's Department of Light Industry and Consumer Goods, replacing V. K. Lesun, a former Partisan client, who was named Chair of the Belorussian Chamber of Commerce, while a sixth, V. V. Gurin, took over as First Secretary of the Belorussian Komsomol.[14]

With respect to the exceptionally high rate of job turnover (41.7 per cent) recorded in the 48 leading regional posts in 1985, a number of the personnel changes indicate that factional realignment was continuing to alter the composition of the provincial elites. In Vitebsk, V. I. Kagalenok, whose career history contains regional ties to the Aksenov group, was demoted from Chair of the Vitebsk Agro-Industrial Council to Head of the Fuel Department of the Oblispolkom. A. A. Malofeev was transferred to the office of First Secretary of the Minsk Obkom from Gomel' where he had built his entire 23 year career history, serving in a variety of party positions and in one soviet post. The job left by Malofeev, that of First Secretary of the Gomel' Obkom, was in turn taken by A. S. Kamai, who had been Chair of the Gomel' Oblispolkom since 1982, but whose previous career history of 19 years involved postings in Mogilev Oblast' exclusively. In Mogilev Oblast' itself, a third inter-regional transfer took place when A. A. Yanovich, who had worked for some 13 years in a number of positions in Grodno Oblast', left his job as Head of the Agricultural Department of the KPB (to which he had been appointed in 1982) to become Chair of the Mogilev Oblispolkom. Malofeev, Kamai and Yanovich have all been closely identified with the Partisan faction. Their promotions and transfers across regions suggest that these politicians had succeeded in shifting their affiliations from the now defunct Partisan faction to those who had emerged from the succession process as the dominant group in the Republic. Equally, they show that the MCIG was expanding its governing coalition by adding to its network former clients of those patrons who had been displaced during the succession.

The inter-regional transfers that occurred in 1985 seem to antedate the policy announced at the Twenty-Seventh Congress of the CPSU in 1986 which involved a return to the pre-Brezhnev practice of rotating cadres across regional lines.[15] Thane Gustafson and Dawn Mann, who concern themselves only with the office of obkom first secretary and who appear to rely on a given official's last prior position, rather than on a more extensive career history, to indicate his/her regional affiliation, have concluded on the basis of their data that there had been by mid 1987 little evidence that the new policy regarding cross-regional transfers had been implemented to a significant extent in either the RSFSR or the non-Russian republics.[16] Our data tell a similar but, in part, slightly different story. During the period of the succession under consideration here (1980–June, 1986), cross-regional transfers in our sample of 48 elite positions occurred in each year. One took place in each of the first three years, in both 1983 and 1984 three were recorded (albeit in each of these years one of the transfers was not inter-regional in a geographic sense as it involved a move from a Minsk City organization to one in Minsk Oblast'), while three took place in 1985 and one occurred during the first half of 1986 when V. V. Grigor'ev, a Brezhnev client, with a career background in Brest Oblast' returned from work in the CPSU apparatus to become First Secretary of the Vitebsk Obkom. This move was the first in a series that seems to indicate that one segment of the old Brezhnev network in the BSSR, namely those with career histories in Brest Oblast', were drawn into the new governing coalition. Interestingly, Grigor'ev's transfer was to Vitebsk – the other regional base of the Brezhnev machine. Brezhnev clients among the regional elite there had not fared well during the succession, having recorded no promotions, one demotion and two removals from office. With the possible exception of the transfers in 1985 which seem to anticipate the new policy announced for the USSR in the year that followed, however, the overall rates of inter-regional rotation among leading cadres in the BSSR during the period of the succession do not seem to be markedly higher than the rates for same which were registered over the full period of this study (Table 4.3).

The significance of the transfers which occurred during the succession, then, appears under a double aspect. On the one hand, they can be taken as evidence that the dominant faction ensconced at the political centre of the BSSR was utilizing such transfers to disrupt the patronage bases of their rivals in the regions. On the other hand, we note that in so doing, they were simultaneously extending their own roster of clients by promoting officials previously associated with other patronage networks.

To conclude our discussion of personnel change during the succession, we note that, in the first half of 1986, 13 of the top 108 republic-level jobs changed hands (12 per cent) while changes occurred in four of the 48 regional positions (8.3 per cent). These figures, since they refer to only a six-month period, indicate a continuation of the relatively high rates of turnover associated with the succession. At the republic level, three personnel changes merit consideration. Aksenov had been recalled from Poland in December 1985 to become Chair of Gosteleradio, USSR, a position from which he would supervise much of the new approach in Soviet mass media inaugurated by the Gorbachev leadership.[17] His client, V. I. Brovikov, replaced him as Ambassador to Poland and Brovikov's previous post of Chair of the Council of Ministers of the BSSR was taken by M. V. Kovalev, a member of the MCIG. Secondly, D. V. Tyabut', a member of the Partisan faction retired from the post of Chair of the Auditing Commission of the KPB. His place was taken by I. F. Yakushev, thus creating a vacancy in the strategic position of Head of the KPB's Department of Organization-Party Work which was filled by V. I. Boris, a former Brezhnev client from the Brest Obkom. This was the second major promotion enjoyed by this now apparently favoured group from Brest previously associated with the old Brezhnev machine. Finally V. I. Liventsev of the Partisan faction retired from his position as Head of the KPB's Business Department and was replaced by V. L. Pavlyukevich, a member of the MCIG.

Succession in the perspective of factional contests

We might sum up the matter of winners and losers in the succession struggle that occurred in Belorussia by arranging our data on personnel changes in this period according to the factional affiliations of the participants, and charting out thereby the numerical rise and fall of the various contending groups. Table 7.1 can be read as something of a scorecard for the various factions *vis-à-vis* the top offices in the Republic. Each of the columns in the table lists the

Table 7.1. *Number of identified members of patronage groups in top elite positions* (Selected years)*

	1979	1982	1983	1986
Partisans	5	4	4	1
Partisan Clients	6	5	4	4
Brezhnev Clients	5	6	4	4
MCIG	1	2	6	8

* Top elite positions refer to those offices in the BSSR included in strata 1 and 2 of Appendix A

numbers of factionally identified actors found in elite positions at four key junctures in the succession. The first column shows that in the year prior to Masherov's death, the Partisans and their clients held nearly two-thirds of these jobs. By 1982, the high-water mark of the Brezhnev forces in the BSSR, both the Partisans and their clients had lost one job, while Brezhnev clients and the MCIG had each gained one. The actual positions held by Brezhnev clients at this time, however, are more indicative of the dominant position of the group than is their mere numerical plurality. Brezhnev clients in 1982 held four of the six positions on the Secretariat of the KPB (of the remaining two secretaries, only one can be identified by factional affiliation, and he was a Partisan client), and the posts of Chair and Deputy Chair of the Belorussian Council of Ministers. By the following year, however, Brezhnev clients had been removed or demoted from half of these jobs while the MCIG's representation among the elite positions had increased three-fold. Finally, the right-hand column of the table shows the MCIG and their new-found clients in complete control of the top jobs in the Republic. By 1986 only one Partisan remained in these positions (N. N. Polozov, head of the trade unions). Former clients of the Partisan group, by now apparently attached to another set of patrons, the MCIG, held four of these jobs, as did clients of the defeated Brezhnev machine. However, only one of the Brezhnev clients, who as a group dominated the leadership in 1982, had managed to retain his post (KPB Secretary N. I. Dementei). The other three former Brezhnev clients found in elite positions in 1986 were L. S. Firisanov, who had been demoted from KPB Secretary to Deputy Chair of the Council of Ministers, and two new arrivals from Brest, V. I. Boris who took over the KPB's Organization-Party Work Depart-

Table 7.2. *Number of identified members of patronage groups among heads of departments of the secretariat of the KPB* (Selected years)*

	1979	1982	1983	1986
Partisans	2	2	2	–
Partisan Clients	6	7	7	4
Brezhnev Clients	–	1	1	1
MCIG	2	3	3	4
MCIG Clients	–	–	–	3

The Secretariat of the KPB contained nineteen departments in this period. The data in the table refer to that sub-set of department heads who could be identified by factional affiliation. Since the Head of the Organization-Party Work Department appeared in Table 7.1, this table includes the First Deputy Head of that Department whose factional affiliation, at any event, is not known.

ment and N. N. Mazai who was appointed Deputy Chair of the Council of Ministers. Again, the numerical plurality enjoyed by the MCIG in 1986 is less indicative of the group's dominance than is the set of positions that its members held. By the end of the succession, three of the five secretaries of the KPB who can be identified by faction were members of the MCIG (including the first and second secretaries), as was the Chair and the two first deputy chairs of the Council of Ministers, the President of the Prezidium of the Supreme Soviet and the Chair of Gosplan.

Tables 7.2 and 7.3 concern the respective numerical representations of the various factional groupings for middle-level positions in the Belorussian party-state (i.e., those jobs that are listed among the third and fourth strata in Appendix A). Like the previous table, each displays snapshots at four important junctures in the succession which show the relative numerical strength of each faction in these offices. Table 7.2 involves the apparatus of the KPB and indicates, again, the substantial gains made by the MCIG and its clients over this period. Also of note in this regard is the fact that these gains were made at the expense of the Partisans and their clients who together had dominated these organs since 1966, and that the Brezhnev group had small success in installing clients in this set of positions.

Table 7.3 provides the comparable statistics for the state apparatus. Here the pattern evident in the four snapshots shows a more or less continuous decline in Partisan representation together with a con-

Table 7.3. *Number of identified members of patronage groups in upper levels of the state apparatus* (Selected years)*

	1979	1982	1983	1986
Partisans	6	3	3	1
Partisan Clients	15	16	21	17
Brezhnev Clients	13	17	10	7.
MCIG	4	7	7	10
MCIG Clients	1	2	3	4

* Positions include all those in strata 3 and 4 of Appendix A which are republic-level, non-KPB jobs. In addition to ministers, (first) deputy ministers, and chairs of state committees, the table includes other positions, such as Chief Justice of the Supreme Court, Procurator and First Deputy Procurator.

comitant increase in the numerical representation of the MCIG and its clients. Those associated with the Partisan and Brezhnev groups fluctuate in their numerical representation with the latter, having reached their peak in 1982, declining precipitously thereafter due to early retirements and dismissals from office. Another aspect of the data assembled in this table bears mention, namely, the high rate of turnover experienced by those who held jobs in the state apparatus. Of the 73 positions under consideration, 54 of them experienced at least one personnel change during the succession. Were we to examine only that fraction of these positions that includes the top jobs in the ministries of the BSSR, however, this turnover rate is considerably reduced. Accordingly, 17 of the 45 top positions (37.8 per cent) did not change hands at all in these years. It would seem, then, that a large minority of incumbents at the top of the ministries were unaffected by the succession as was a similarly large minority (42.1 per cent) of heads of departments in the KPB's Secretariat.

The data in Table 7.4 complete our series of snapshots of factional representation, focusing in this instance on elite jobs in the regions of the BSSR. An initial examination of these figures would suggest that continuity in factional representation was the salient characteristic of regional elites during this period, with the possible exception of Minsk City where MCIG members moved, in the main, to republic-level positions while the vacancies thereby created were filled by clients of the same group. A closer inspection of these data, however, reveals a somewhat different story. If we were to compare regions by the

Table 7.4. *Number of identified members of patronage groups in elite jobs**
in the regions (Selected years)

	1979	1982	1983	1986
Minsk Oblast':				
Partisan Clients	6	6	6	7
MCIG Clients	1	1	1	–
Brest Oblast':				
Partisan Clients	4	1	1	–
Brezhnev Clients	2	5	5	6
Vitebsk Oblast':				
Partisans	1	1	–	–
Partisan Clients	–	–	2	1
Brezhnev Clients	6	6	5	5
Gomel' Oblast':				
Partisans	1	1	–	–
Partisan Clients	6	6	7	6
Grodno Oblast':				
Partisan Clients	4	5	6	6
MCIG	1	1	1	1
Mogilev Oblast':				
Partisans	1	1	–	–
Partisan Clients	4	5	6	6
Minsk City:				
MCIG	3	3	2	1
MCIG Clients	2	2	3	4

* 'Elite jobs' refer to secretaries of the regional party committees (5 in each
oblast; 4 in Minsk City), and the president and first deputy president of the
regional soviet.

number of job changes that occurred in these positions, we would
locate Minsk Oblast' at the high end of the scale with 11 and Vitebsk
Oblast' at the low end with six. If we were then to ask in each case how
many actors were involved in the job changes that took place in these
two oblasts, we notice that they numbered 16 in Minsk and 13 in
Vitebsk. Consequently, we observe that in Minsk Oblast' the turnover
in positions involved a rotation of actors among offices while in
Vitebsk Oblast', the regional base of the Brezhnev grouping that fared
poorly during the succession, the turnover that occurred was of a
different order entirely. Although only six job changes took place
there, not a single member in the regional elite who left office was
known to have been assigned to another position in the data set. Their

replacements included two former Partisan clients transferred in from Grodno, a former Brezhnev client brought in from Brest where affiliations as we have seen, appeared to have shifted to the MCIG, and an individual whose factional affiliation is not known. Two other former Brezhnev clients in the Vitebsk region were elevated to elite positions in this period, but in the overall context of the personnel changes occurring there, not to mention in the BSSR as a whole, their factional affiliations, too, had apparently shifted toward the MCIG.

Implications of the succession for elite circulation

The outcome of a political succession in any of the republics of the USSR is, of course, closely linked to the politics prevailing in Moscow at the time. In the case of Belorussia, this relationship is perhaps especially pronounced in as much as succession struggles at the republic and national levels were going on more or less simultaneously. Moreover, it is possible to observe in this instance not only relationships between national and republic actors but some rather intriguing analogues between the process of leadership change that transpired at these two levels.

First, we might mention the aspect of leadership style. In the same way that the most prominent member of the MCIG, Slyun'kov, does not have a career history that typifies the classical single patron (such as Mazurov with respect to the Partisans), so Gorbachev has assembled a political team at the national level in which traditional patron-client relations are scarcely evident.[18] This leadership style seems to favour an emphasis on ability and commitment to programmatic goals[19] rather than fealty toward a patron which has been established over the course of longstanding personal relations.[20] In this respect, the association which we observed for Belorussia in Chapter 4, between, on the one hand, the emergence of the MCIG and its novel form of organization as a 'political team' whose members came from the ranks of skilled workers in the industrial enterprises of Minsk and, on the other, the transformation of Belorussia in the same period into a predominantly urban-industrial society, represents something of a precursor to the organizational pattern that has been displayed by the Gorbachev leadership whose avowed goal is to tackle the problems of an industrial society that have been rendered all the more acute by long years of neglect.

Secondly, as we noted in the foregoing, the Belorussian succession commenced in earnest some time before the Brezhnev succession gathered full force in Moscow. Consequently, the pattern in the BSSR appears in retrospect as a preview of some of the events that unfolded at the political centre. The overhaul of the personnel system in Belorussia during 1983 antedated by two years the measures introduced by Gorbachev at the all-union level, just as the increase in inter-regional transfers in the BSSR anticipated the announcement of such a policy at the Twenty-Seventh Congress of the CPSU in 1986.

Of course, these events in the BSSR did not take place without the involvement of the authorities in Moscow. At the same time, however, we should avoid viewing such involvement as a one-sided imposition of some ready-made cadres policy coming from the Kremlin. As we learned from the analyses conducted in earlier chapters, central direction of the personnel process in the BSSR cannot be accurately regarded as the mere reflex of Moscow's *nomenklatura*. In so far as Belorussian offices fall within the domain of the central appointments mechanism, we would do well to remember that the pool of candidates from which selections might be made is determined primarily by the influences of region and faction on the personnel system of the Republic. It goes without saying that Moscow installed Slyun'kov as First Secretary of the KPB. The significance of this event, however, was prepared years in advance when the MCIG began to organize itself as a political force in the BSSR. The installation of Slyun'kov, viewed from this perspective, signalled far more than placing an Andropov/Gorbachev supporter at the top of the Belorussian leadership. Rather, it involved the passing of political power in the BSSR to a new political team which was, as it were, already in the wings awaiting its chance.

Finally, a particularly sharp contrast is apparent between the Partisan faction and the MCIG with respect to geography. The Partisans were able to assemble a political machine at the republic-level that enabled them to emerge as the dominant group in the BSSR by the late 1950s. Thereafter, they extended their influence to the national level when Mazurov, Zimyanin and Shauro took up high-level posts in Moscow. Throughout the period of their hegemony in Belorussia, members of the Partisan faction were distributed among all of the oblasts of the BSSR (see Appendix B). In short, the Partisans were a republic-based faction with representation in Moscow.

The MCIG, on the other hand, is geographically structured on a Minsk–Moscow axis. The only evidence of its presence in the oblast organizations of the BSSR involves the brief tenures of M. A. Knyazuk (1983–4) and V. F. Kebich (1984–5) as Second Secretary of the Minsk

Obkom and that of V. M. Semenov as Secretary of the Grodno Obkom (1974–). Rather than factional dominance at the republic level which resulted in a factional presence in Moscow (the Partisan pattern), members of the MCIG were able to take over the leading posts in the BSSR only after, and apparently because, a presence for the group had already been established in the Soviet capital. The MCIG does not, then, constitute the sort of national political grouping represented by the Partisans. Neither are its members distributed throughout the regional structure of offices in the Republic, nor has the MCIG developed a political identity oriented to the concept of nation as the Partisans managed to do.[21]

The novel characteristics of the MCIG shed some light on two significant personnel changes at the all-union and republic levels that took place after the mid 1986 terminus of this study. The first involves the appointment of K. Z. Terekh to the post of Minister of Trade, USSR. The second refers to the replacement of Slyun'kov, who was named Secretary of the CPSU in January, 1987, by E. E. Sokolov, a former Brezhnev client, who had been First Secretary of the Brest Obkom since 1977. The career histories of neither Terekh nor Sokolov show any direct affiliation with either Slyun'kov or the MCIG. Prior to becoming First Deputy Chair of Belkoopsoyuz in 1970, Terekh's career had been entirely within the trade sector organizations of Minsk Oblast'. He was named Chair of Belkoopsoyuz in 1977 and Deputy Chair of the Council of Ministers of the BSSR in January of 1984. Since this last promotion came while Slyun'kov was First Secretary of the KPB and occurred during the period in which extensive personnel changes were being made under his leadership in republic-level posts, it seems reasonable to infer that Terekh was an addition to Slyun'kov's political team undertaken on the basis of his abilities as a political administrator and in conjunction with his programmatic orientation. Assumedly, it was these same qualities and Slyun'kov's endorsement that brought him to the attention of Gorbachev who began his renovation of the Soviet ministries in the following year.

The appointment of Sokolov as First Secretary of the KPB is even more difficult to account for in terms of conventional patronage politics and the jockeying for position displayed by contending factions. In conventional terms, one would expect that Slyun'kov would have been succeeded by a member of the MCIG, especially in as much as six of its members were already on the Buro of the KPB. Instead, the promotion went to Sokolov who at the time was not even a candidate member of the Buro. A number of factors, however, would make the appointment of Sokolov less of a surprise than it might at first seem.

First, attention can be called to the fact that Brest had experienced over the years of Sokolov's tenure as Obkom First Secretary the best record of agricultural performance among the oblasts of the BSSR,[22] and that a number of its farms now boast the highest grain yields in the Soviet Union.[23] Sokolov, whose entire career had been in the agricultural sector prior to assuming his position on the Brest Obkom in 1977, can surely take credit for these results, which have been rumoured to have made a very favourable impression on Gorbachev during his visit to Belorussia in July of 1985.

Secondly, in his report to the Thirtieth Congress of the KPB in January of 1986, Slyun'kov had many words of praise for Sokolov's work in Brest while the only other obkom secretaries whom he mentioned by name, L. G. Kletskov of Grodno and V. S. Leonov of Mogilev, came in for some sharp criticism.[24] Slyun'kov's report, when considered in the context of the promotions awarded in 1985 and 1986 to former Brezhnev clients from Brest, can be read as an announcement of a new coalition in the BSSR which included the Brest group as important partners.

Finally, one of the promotions in question stands out as particularly significant. By appointing V. I. Boris, a former client of the Brezhnev group in Brest, to lead the Organization-Party Work Department of the KPB and by naming him a full member of the Buro of the party's Central Committee, those in control of the top of the Belorussian *nomenklatura* were cementing this new coalition with the award of these important posts to someone previously associated with a rival clique. Taken together, the accolades for Sokolov and the promotion of Boris suggest that Slyun'kov's replacement may have been decided long before he left for Moscow in 1987. Although the Minsk–Moscow connection might have accounted for the MCIG's victory in the succession, the victory itself has placed squarely before the victors the larger task of governing the BSSR, a task that seems all the more challenging in light of the urgency of the problems and the scope of the reforms required to solve them which have been outlined by the Gorbachev leadership. Whether in Minsk or in Moscow, we seem to be witnessing a new chapter in the political history of the Soviet Union, one in which the rather comfortable relations of patronage and the escape from responsibility that they afford are giving way to a greater emphasis on talent and performance as operative criteria in cadres policy. For the MCIG, this emphasis has been coupled to the requirement of expanding the narrow regional base of the MCIG by bringing other political actors[25] into a ruling coalition that is capable of governing effectively.

8 Conclusions, implications and the question of levels

Elite circulation in the Soviet system is, as we have seen, a complex process. A number of studies that have sought to disentangle the many factors involved, to single out some collection of causes and to relate these to specific effects by way of a comprehensive set of propositions which explain the process have not met with great success. There is no reason to suppose that the analysis conducted here, although its methodological orientation sets it apart from other works in the field, is an exception in this respect. It may be that the indeterminacy of the results found in a great many studies of Soviet elites that have searched for correlations between a set of independent variables (the attributes of officials, the economic performance of the units that they superintend, and so forth) and the dependent variable of elite mobility is traceable to the question of levels of analysis. Individual-level data, for instance, may show some correlation with systems-level phenomena such as policy or systems change, as the model depicted in Figure 1.1 would have it. Yet the interpretation of such, not to mention the weakness of the correlations commonly reported in the literature, generally leaves much to be desired from the standpoint of conceptual adequacy. It is not at all clear, for example, that the Soviet Union is becoming more or less 'modern' or 'developed' because its political elite is becoming older or younger, more or less educated, or practiced in one or many occupational categories. Nor is it clear, were we to point the same finger at ourselves, that elite circulation in the BSSR is structured more by, say, regionalism than by the centralizing institution of the *nomenklatura*, although our findings, *on one level*, could certainly be read that way.

With this thought in mind, we might use the idea of levels of analysis to explicate the conclusions of the present study and to draw out what implications it may hold. First, on the highest level of abstraction, we find that the influences on the circulation process that

136

we have examined – centralization, regionalism and patronage – would be reduced to hypostatizations were we to regard them as individual causes that register discrete effects on the circulation of elites. Rather, we have seen how these factors are themselves inter-connected. In some contexts, they appear to operate in tandem, as when a regional pattern of elite circulation is maintained via the use of patronage in drawing in new recruits. In others, they appear to pull in opposite directions as, for instance, in those instances in which centrally controlled appointments serve to disrupt some cozy relation-ship established among members of a regionally based clique. In still others, we find that one may appear in the guise of the other, as when, say, the central appointments mechanism is employed by one patron-age group in such a way as to alter the flow of personnel in a region dominated by a rival group. We remind ourselves in this regard that in singling out these factors for analysis, we are doing no more than naming aspects of a process. Removing any one aspect from its object, asking what it alone effects, and so forth does violence to the totality in which it is embedded.

Secondly, and moving downward on the ladder of abstraction, we note that each of the factors that appear to structure the circulation of elites is conditioned by the other factors. The influence of each, that is, presupposes the presence of the others. We observed, for instance, in the third and fourth chapters how the circulation of vacancies in the system is structured by the simultaneous effects of both centralization and regionalism. On the one hand, long chains tend to begin at the centre but commonly trace paths through a single region. On the other, the mobility patterns of regional elites, as the history of the MCIG demonstrates, is accounted for in large part by their access to authorities in Moscow. In this respect we can draw a distinction between those aspects of the circulation process, centralization and regionalism, that function on the macro-level, conditioning the move-ment of actors in the system as a whole, and patronage as a phenom-enon closer to the micro-level that involves the relations established among individual actors themselves. From this perspective, the macro-level factors appear as the context within which the micro-level process transpires; patronage powers are deployed through the medium of the *nomenklatura* and function primarily on a regional basis. In drawing this distinction, however, we remind ourselves that its validity would be confined to the particular level of abstraction on which it has been advanced. For were we to shift levels, we can readily see how patronage might be regarded as the context within which, for instance, central appointments are determined or regional patterns of circulation are maintained.

Thirdly, our analysis of the political succession in Belorussia has brought to light yet other ways in which the aspects of the circulation process are intertwined. We have observed how patronage and regionalism, for example, have positively reinforced one another in the case of the MCIG and for certain of the regional groups previously affiliated with rival factions, and, at the same time, how the reverse has been true in the Vitebsk region where a number of former Brezhnev clients did not manage to survive the succession. Equally, we noted how the Minsk–Moscow axis appeared from one vantage as an arrangement in which the MCIG functioned as an extension of the centre and, from another, as one in which a regional group exploited its ties to central patrons in order to oust its rivals at the republic and sub-republic levels. In the face of this, it becomes clear that we cannot attribute a particular influence to any of the factors in question without at the same time specifying its contextual relations with the other factors.

Fourthly, the individual-level data reported in Chapter 6 on those entering the system through different channels of recruitment, on women, and on the incidence and effect of negative sanctions have highlighted the importance of a supra-individual phenomenon, faction, in accounting for certain events within the system. On this level of abstraction, we have examined the career histories of individual actors but have viewed these in relational terms, namely, in reference to their respective factional affiliations. Here we have drawn the conclusion that mobility has been more an attribute of collectivities than of individuals *qua* individuals. This is perhaps an obvious point, but in as much as the obvious is often overlooked, in the same way in which the crafty might conceal things by hiding them in plain view, it bears repeating and merits some discussion.

A purely meritocratic approach to mobility would hold that it is individuals who advance in job hierarchies, and that they do so on the basis of their performance as measured against some impersonal set of standards. An approach to this same phenomenon that is oriented to a narrowly construed concept of patronage inverts the picture and sees cronyism as the overriding factor. The perspective adopted here, however, reserves comment on individuals. Given our discussion of the Soviet form of organization, we find it difficult if not impossible to determine whether impersonal standards of performance exist in a meaningful sense. Factory A, for instance, may well have overfulfilled its plan, but we have no way of telling whether this achievement was brought about by efficient industrial management and effective labour organization or whether it resulted from personal connections that enabled the firm to secure low production targets, in the first place, and privileged access to scarce resources, in the second. Equally, because the career mobility of a given actor may be closely linked to that of a patron, we need not infer any deficiency on the client's part *vis-à-vis* the issue of merit. In fact, we might suppose that incompetent clients who mishandle responsibilities represent real liabilities for their patrons, and live ammunition for their rivals. The question of meritocracy versus patronage seems insoluble when formulated in terms of individuals alone. When viewed within a relational framework, however, one in which individual actors appear as members of patronage groups and in which the groups themselves are regarded as the operant units, we can see how meritocracy and patronage do not necessarily appear as antipodes. Actors, we might suppose, have an interest in securing career advancement through patronage, just as patronage groups have an interest in recruiting talented and capable members.

Merit, however, cannot be specified outside of context. Consequently, it is those who perform well according to criteria relevant to the Soviet form of organization who display merit and, as we have maintained, such criteria often place personalized relations at a premium. Taking the matter from the standpoint of individuals in the system, this proposition can be translated simply as: factional affiliations afford varying degrees of access to positions. Whether factional affiliation in a given case owes more to talent than to fealty is a question that cannot be decided in the absence of information on that case. Were we to move up the ladder of abstraction and refer this same proposition to supra-individual entities, however, another reading would result. Faction in this sense represents more than a collection of individuals. It connotes above all their relations one to another and the relations among factions themselves as structured by the form of organization in which they operate. Our argument has been that the Soviet form of organization tends to personalize the ostensibly 'bureaucratic' relations among individuals such that in cases in which considerations of merit conflict with those of patronage, the advantage would go to patronage. Those who have followed the Soviet press since the onset of *perestroika* would find ample support for this proposition in the innumerable articles and speeches that refer to talented cadres who perform well but are too often passed over when vacancies have appeared in jobs with greater responsibility. Moreover, the thrust of this oft-repeated comment is congruent with the argument advanced here; it holds that considerations of merit have been given short shrift because of the form of organization itself. *Ergo*, the expressed need for *perestroika* in general and, in particular, the necessity of changing the mechanism of cadres selection from a *nomenklatura* manipulated by cliques in the *apparat* to one in which a genuine electoral process fills vacancies in responsible posts. Presumably, the new mechanism would tilt the balance in favour of merit.

What implications might this study hold for the issue of elites in the Soviet political process? In addressing this question we are, of course, not prepared to go beyond the confines of our data and the conclusions that we have reached about them. At the same time, however, the notion of implication suggests that we take up something of an imaginative posture toward these things, walking, as it were, the borders of our study and hazarding a few remarks on what from this perspective seems to lie beyond. Under this flexible restriction, we might, then, name three.

First, the results of our analysis of centralization in Chapter 3, as well as our discussion of the succession in Chapter 7, would indicate that Soviet federalism is no mere fiction. Although federalism in the USSR may be deficient by Western standards in a number of important respects, from the vantage of the process of elite circulation it emerges as an identifiable characteristic of the system. A centralizing influence on the circulation of vacancies, as we have seen, results more from the interaction of personnel systems at the national and republic levels than from the systematic shaping of mobility patterns in the BSSR by the central authorities in Moscow. The federal pattern is also apparent in the succession. Central patrons may have installed their clients in the Belorussian leadership, but the clients themselves, of course, have not appeared out of thin air. They have histories. They have risen through the ranks of office in the BSSR and they have done so in consort with others with whom they have established relations over a considerable period of time. To say that Andropov installed Slyun'kov is in fact shorthand for saying that the central authorities participated in a thoroughgoing leadership change in the BSSR that brought the MCIG, its clients and its allies to power.

Secondly, these thoughts touch on another issue; namely, the concept of the circulation of elites itself. In this study we have preferred to treat it in a direct, empirical sense, rendered as vacancies that circulate in chains. Nonetheless, this way of studying the circulation process has yielded results that appear to have some definite implications for the issue that occupied the classical theorists, viz., the transfer of power from one social group to another as new elites replace older ones in the circulation process. In the Belorussian case, we have observed a variation on this theme in which the development of a largely agricultural society into a modern industrial one has been accompanied not only by the emergence of a new elite drawn from the skilled sector of the working class in Minsk but also by the transformation of relations within the elite itself in congruence with the pattern of life associated with an industrial order. In short, clientelistic relations of a vertical type, focused on a single patron, seem to have been succeeded by those of another order wherein horizontal relations among members of a group count for more and, correspondingly, personal loyalties to a single patron count for less. We might expect that 'merit' under this new arrangement has more to do with task accomplishment than has been true heretofore.

Finally, the question of political change in the USSR. The surface life of the Soviet system is characterized today by a degree of frankness in political discourse and a measure of innovation in reform initiatives that could scarcely have been imagined only a few years ago. These changes have surprised and, at times, baffled us. Unless we are to lapse into a mode of thought that apprehends the current changes in the Soviet system as yet another replay of 'revolution from above', as one involving no more than a leadership standing somehow over society, issuing proclamations and exhortations for change – a way of thinking that doubtless accounts for much of our present perplexity – then we would do well to inquire into the social bases and political antecedants of *perestroika*. As a working assumption, we might entertain the idea that the changes that burst so rapidly to the surface of Soviet political life express something that had been developing and even maturing for some time. Our analysis seems to have caught a glimpse of one such factor, namely, the transformation of patronage relations in the direction of 'new clientelism'. Ironically, patronage relations, so much to the fore in this study, appear to be altered in form and diminished in influence as their social context has been restructured by the exigencies of modern industrialism, just as Gorbachev, whose own career in many ways typifies the new clientelism, is now articulating a project of social restructuring, the fruition of which spells the eclipse of clientele by a new category, citizens.

APPENDIX A (N = 2,034)

Stratification of positions in the Belorussian Republic 1966–86

(Positions marked with asterisk were initially inserted into Stratum 1 and Stratum 2; numbers appearing after position title indicate the number of such positions found in the stratum; the Russian word, *predsedatel'*, has been translated as 'president' for those, usually elected, offices with some general political or social significance, while it has been rendered as 'chair' in those instances in which it refers to an office, filled by appointment, that is more administrative in its formal orientation)

Stratum 1 (n = 25)

Secretaries of KPB* (6)
First Secretary, Minsk Obkom*
President of the Prezidium of Supreme Soviet, BSSR*
Chair of the Council of Ministers, BSSR*
First Deputy Chair of the Council of Ministers, BSSR*
Chair of State Committee of People's Control, BSSR*
Chair of KGB, BSSR*
President of Trade Union Council, BSSR*
Deputy Head, Organization-Party Work Department, CPSU*
Deputy Chair, Council of Ministers, USSR*
First Deputy Minister of Agriculture, USSR*
Deputy Minister of Agriculture, USSR*
Ambassador to Poland*
Deputy Minister of Light Industry and Consumer Goods, USSR*
Minister of Machinery for Animal Husbandry and Fodder Production*
Deputy Chair, Gosplan USSR*
Chair, Goskom for Television and Radio, USSR*
Chair, Goskomsel'khoztekhnika, USSR*
Chair, Central Union of Consumer Cooperative Societies, USSR*
Deputy Chair, Gossnab, USSR*

Stratum 2 (n = 27)

Head, Organization-Party Work Department, KPB*
Head, Propaganda Department, KPB

142

Obkom first secretaries (5)
First Secretary, Minsk Gorkom
First Deputy President of Prezidium of Supreme Soviet, BSSR*
Deputy Chairs, Council of Ministers, BSSR (6)
Chair of Gosplan, BSSR*
Minister of Industrial Construction, BSSR
Chair, Gosstroi, BSSR
Sector Head, Organization-Party Work Department, CPSU*
Sector Head, Propaganda Department, CPSU*
Sector Head, Construction Department, CPSU*
Sector Head, Light Industry and Consumer Goods Department, CPSU*
Ambassador to North Korea*
Ambassador to Pakistan*
Head, Heavy Trucks Division, Ministry of Auto Industry, USSR*
Head, Main Admin. for Auto Inspections, Ministry of Internal Affairs, USSR*
Head, Admin. for Repair and Tech. Services, Goskomsel'khoztekhnika, USSR*

Stratum 3 (n = 67)

Department Heads, Secretariat of KPB (6)
Chairs of Party Commission and Auditing Commission, KPB (2)
First Secretary, Mogilev Obkom
Second Secretary, Minsk Obkom
First Secretary, Frunze Raikom, Minsk City
Presidents of oblast' soviets (7)
Ministers of BSSR (30)
Head, Admin. for Development of Poles' region
First Deputy Minister of Industrial Construction
Director, BelAvtoMAZ
Director, Khimvolokno (Mogilev)
Director, Minsk Tractor Factory
First Deputy Chair, Gosplan (1 of 2)
Chair, Goskom for Prices
Chair, Goskom for Phys. Culture and Sport
Chair and First Deputy Chair, Goskomsel'khoztekhnika (2)
Chair, Goskino
Chair, Goskom for Television and Radio
Chair, Goskom for Industrial and Mining Safety
Deputy Head, Main Administration for Supply of Petroleum Products
Chair, Union of Cooperative Societies
President, Supreme Court
Procurator
President, Society for Friendship and Cultural Ties with Foreign Nations

Stratum 4 (n = 93)

Assistants to First Secretary of KPB (2)
Director, Institute of Party History
Rector, Higher Party School
First Deputy Head, Organization-Party Work Department, KPB
First Deputy Head, Administrative Organs Department, KPB
Department Heads, Secretariat of KPB (10)
Deputy Heads, Agriculture Department, KPB (2)
Deputy Department Head, Industry and Transportation Department, KPB
Deputy Head, Machine Building Department, KPB
Instructors, Chemical Industry Department, KPB (2)
Secretaries, Minsk Obkom (3)
Second secretaries of obkoms (Brest, Vitebsk, Gomel', Grodno)
First Secretary, Orsha Gorkom
Secretaries, Gomel Obkom (3)
Second Secretary, Minsk Gorkom
First Secretary, Borisov Raikom (Minsk)
First Secretary, Lida Raikom (Grodno)
Secretaries, Minsk Gorkom (2)
Secretary of P.P.O., Bobruisk Lumber Factory
First deputy presidents, oblispolkoms (Minsk, Brest, Vitebsk, Gomel',
    Mogilev)
Deputy Presidents, Vitebsk Oblispolkom (3)
First Deputy President, Minsk Gorispolkom
President, Mogilev Gorispolkom
Head, Forestry Department, Brest Oblispolkom
Deputy chairs, Gosagroprom (4)
First deputy ministers (11)
Deputy ministers (12)
First Deputy Chair, Gosplan (1 of 2)
Deputy chairs of state committees (6)
Chair, Goskom for Publications
Permanent Representative to Council of Ministers, USSR
Head of Belorussian Railways
First Secretary of Komsomol
Procurator, Vitebsk Oblast'
Editors of *Kommunist Belorussii*, *Sel'skaya gazeta*, *Sovetskaya Belorussiya*
Instructor, Party Control Commission, CPSU*

Stratum 5 (n = 253)

First deputy heads of departments, KPB (11)
Deputy heads of departments, KPB (7)
Deputy Chair, Party Commission, KPB
Sector heads, Organization-Party Work Department, KPB (3)
Inspectors, Organization-Party Work Department, KPB (4)

Instructors, Propaganda Department, KPB (3)
Instructor, Admin. Organs Department, Minsk Obkom
Second Secretary, Mogilev Obkom
Secretaries of obkoms (12)
First secretaries of gorkoms (10)
Secretaries of gorkoms (2)
First secretaries of raikoms (18)
Second secretaries of raikoms (2)
Department heads, Minsk Obkom (5)
Department heads, Gomel Obkom (2)
Secretaries of industrial P.P.O.s (5)
Secretary of Prezidium, Supreme Soviet
Deputy presidents, Minsk Oblispolkom (3)
Deputy presidents, Minsk Gorispolkom (5)
Department heads, oblispolkoms (5)
First Deputy President, Grodno Oblispolkom
President, Vitebsk Gorispolkom
Head, Department of Capital Construction, Minsk Gorispolkom
Presidents of raiispolkoms (3)
Assistant to Chair of Council of Ministers
First deputy ministers (16)
Deputy ministers (58)
Directors of enterprises (4)
Chairs of state committees (10)
Deputy chairs of state committees (31)
Heads of main administrations (8)
Head, Department of Admin. of Affairs, Council of Ministers
Second Secretary, Komsomol
Secretaries, Trade Union Council (4)
Deputy Director, Minsk Tractor Factory
Deputy procurators (3)
Procurator, Brest Oblast'
Deputy Procurator, Grodno Oblast'
President, Academy of Sciences
Editor, *Zvyazda*
Editor, *Minsk Pravda*
Editor, *Grodno Pravda*
Student, Higher Party School, CPSU

Stratum 6 (n = 454)

Deputy heads of departments, KPB (4)
Sector heads in departments, KPB (16)
Inspector, Agriculture Department, KPB
Instructors in departments, KPB (4)
Deputy Head, Organization-Party Work Department, Minsk Obkom
Head, lecturers group, Propaganda Department, Minsk Obkom

First secretaries, gorkoms (14)
Secretaries, gorkoms (18)
Heads of departments, obkoms (25)
First secretaries of raikoms (31)
Secretaries of raikoms (16)
Secretaries of industrial P.P.O.s (3)
Heads of departments of Supreme Soviet (4)
Deputy presidents of oblispolkoms (12)
Department heads, oblispolkoms (14)
Deputy head, Minsk Oblast' Consumer Cooperative
Presidents of gorispolkoms (24)
Deputy presidents, Mogilev Gorispolkom (2)
Presidents of raiispolkoms (19)
Deputy presidents of raiispolkoms (2)
Deputy ministers (3)
Heads of departments in ministries (135)
Directors of enterprises (6)
Chair, Belbyttekhnika
Deputy chairs of state committees (5)
Deputy heads of main administrations (7)
Chief Arbiter
Heads of departments of state committees (14)
Heads of departments of Council of Ministers (18)
Deputy Head, Administration of Affairs, Council of Ministers
Secretaries of Komsomol (5)
First Secretary, Brest Komsomol Obkom
Heads of trade unions (19)
Presidents of oblast' trade union councils (6)
Deputy chief justices, Supreme Court (3)
Chief Justice, Vitebsk Oblast' Court
Procurators of oblasts (5)
Rectors of higher educational institutions (5)
Head of department, Komsomol, USSR

Stratum 7 (n = 336)

Deputy Head, Construction and City Economy Department, KPB
Sector Head, Construction and City Economy Department, KPB
Instructors of departments, KPB (23)
Heads of departments of obkoms (36)
Deputy heads of departments of obkoms (3)
Instructors of departments of obkoms (4)
First secretaries of gorkoms (3)
Secretaries of gorkoms (29)
Heads of departments of gorkoms (2)
First secretaries of raikoms (74)
Secretaries of raikoms (23)

Heads of departments of raikoms (3)
Secretaries of industrial P.P.O.s (8)
Deputy chairs, Supreme Soviet (2)
Secretaries of oblispolkoms (7)
Heads of departments of oblispolkoms (17)
Deputy heads of departments of oblispolkoms (2)
Presidents of gorispolkoms (4)
Deputy presidents of gorispolkoms (28)
Secretaries of gorispolkoms (2)
Presidents of raiispolkoms (21)
Deputy presidents of raiispolkoms (4)
Heads of departments of raiispolkoms (7)
Deputy Minister of Foreign Affairs
Directors of enterprises (5)
Heads of departments of state committees (5)
Chairs of oblispolkom units of state committees (9)
Heads of departments of Komsomol (2)
First secretaries of obkoms of Komsomol (2)
President, Brest Oblast' Trade Union for Agricultural Workers
Editor, *Bloknot agitatora*
Editor, Brest Oblast' newspaper, *Zarya*

Stratum 8 (n = 361)

Head, Department of Light and Food Industry, Brest Obkom
Deputy Head of Propaganda Department, Mogilev Obkom
Instructors of departments of obkoms (2)
First Secretary, Pinsk gorkom
Secretaries of gorkoms (2)
Heads of departments of gorkoms (24)
First secretaries of raikoms (14)
Secretaries of raikoms (84)
Heads of departments of raikoms (5)
Heads of departments of oblispolkoms (113)
Deputy heads of departments of oblispolkoms (2)
President of Bobruisk gorispolkom
Deputy presidents of gorispolkoms (5)
Secretaries of gorispolkoms (6)
Head, Department of Internal Affairs, Grodno Gorispolkom
Presidents of raiispolkoms (86)
Deputy presidents of raiispolkoms (4)
Heads of departments of raiispolkoms (2)
Director, Belvtorchermet
First Secretary, Grodno Komsomol Obkom
Chief justices, oblast' courts (4)
Editor, *Gomel' Pravda*

Stratum 9 (n = 243)

Deputy heads of departments of obkoms (2)
Sector head, Agriculture Department, Mogilev Obkom
First Secretary, Kobrin Gorkom
Secretaries of gorkoms (3)
Heads of departments of gorkoms (2)
First Secretary, Rogachev Raikom (Gomel' Oblast')
Secretaries of raikoms (116)
Heads of departments of raikoms (8)
Heads of departments of oblispolkoms (2)
Deputy heads of departments of oblispolkoms (6)
Secretary of Gomel' Gorispolkom
Heads of departments of gorispolkoms (8)
Presidents of raiispolkoms (6)
Deputy presidents of raiispolkoms (79)
Secretaries of raiispolkoms (2)
Heads of departments of raiispolkoms (3)
Director, Belarusskali
Deputy President, Minsk Oblast' Trade Union Council

Stratum 10 (n = 175)

Instructors of departments of obkoms (2)
Secretaries of raikoms (4)
Heads of departments of raikoms (22)
Secretaries of industrial P.P.O.s (32)
Deputy heads of departments, Supreme Soviet (2)
Deputy presidents of raiispolkoms (3)
Secretaries of raiispolkoms (37)
Heads of departments of raiispolkoms (9)
Directors of enterprises (48)
Deputy directors of enterprises (2)
Deputy heads of departments of Supreme Soviet (2)
Heads of trade union committees in enterprises (12)

APPENDIX B

A roster of factional groups in the Belorussian Republic 1966–86

The Partisan Faction

Members	Highest Offices Attained, BSSR and USSR
Avkhimovich, N. E.	Minister of Social Security, BSSR, 1961–73.
Astapenko, P. E.	Head, Department of Foreign Tourism, Council of Ministers, BSSR, 1965–70.
Astashenok, A. S.	Sector Head, Organization-Party Work Department, KPB, ?–1973.
Barminskii, V.	President, Sennenskii Raiispolkom, Vitebsk Oblast', ?–1968.
Bartashevich, E. F.	Deputy President, Bobruisk Gorispolkom, Mogilev Oblast', ?–1971.
Belogub, I. A.	Chair, People's Control Commission, Gomel' Oblast', 1965–79.
Bobrovskii, A. I.	Head, Organization-Instruction Department, Brest Oblispolkom, 1976–83.
Bondar', A. G.	Chief Justice, Supreme Court, BSSR, 1967–84.
Borisevich, N. A.	President, Academy of Sciences, BSSR, 1969–.
Bykovskii, V. I.	Secretary, Central Council of Belorussian Trade Unions, 1975–83.
Volozhin, P. F.	Deputy Minister of Agriculture, BSSR, ?–1967.
Volostnykh, E. F.	Deputy Minister of the Food Industry, BSSR, 1965–73.
Goncharov, P. N.	President, Dzerzhinskii Raiispolkom, Minsk Oblast', 1967–73.
Gorbachev, M. K.	Secretary, Primary Party Organization, Belorussian State University, 1970–3.
Gorelik, L. Ya.	Head, Main Administration for Material and Technical Supply, BSSR, 1965–77.
Demin, I. M.	General Director, BelavtoMAZ, 1975–81.
Denisevich, A. Yu.	Inspector, Central Committee, KPB, 1966–70.
Zimyanin, M. V.	Editor of *Pravda*, 1965–76; Secretary of CPSU, 1976–87.
Ivanov, F. M.	Deputy Chair, Gosplan, BSSR, 1967–79.
Kalilets, I. M.	Chair, Brest Oblast' Trade Union Council, 1969–?

Kachan, Ya. I.	Editor, *Kommunist Belorussii*, ?–1972.
Klimov, I. F.	Deputy President, Supreme Soviet, BSSR, 1968–74, 1980–1.
Klochkova, V. A.	First Deputy President, Belkoopsoyuz, 1977–82.
Kozhar, I. P.	Chair, Auditing Commission, KPB, 1963–7.
Kozlov, V. I.	President, Supreme Soviet, BSSR, 1948–67.
Kosyr', V. G.	Chair, KGB, Gomel' Oblast', ?–1971.
Kononovich, I. S.	Secretary, Central Council of Belorussian Trade Unions, 1963–75.
Krishtalevich, U. F.	Deputy Minister of Social Security, BSSR, 1975–?
Liventsev, V. I.	Head, Business Department, KPB, 1978–86.
Lobanok, V. E.	Deputy President, Supreme Soviet, BSSR, 1974–84.
Luzgin, V. I.	Minister of Social Security, BSSR, 1974–83.
Lyzhin, N. M.	Head, Trade Dept., Brest Oblispolkom, 1973–9.
Mazurov, K. T.	First Secretary, KPB, 1956–65; First Deputy Chair, Council of Ministers, USSR, Member of Politburo, 1965–78.
Makarov, I. N.	Chair, Auditing Commission, KPB, 1971–6.
Masherov, P. M.	First Secretary, KPB, 1965–80; Candidate Member, Politburo, 1965–80.
Mashkov, G. N.	Head, Business Department, KPB, 1968–78.
Minkovich, M. A.	Minister of Culture, BSSR, 1964–71.
Mitskevich, V. I.	First Secretary, Novogrudskii Raikom, Grodno Oblast', 1962–73.
Morozov, A. I.	Deputy Minister of Lumber and Wood Working Industry, BSSR, 1964–70.
Onipko, M. P.	Chair, Trade Union Council, Gomel Oblast', ?–1979.
Petrov, B. I.	First Deputy Minister of Local Industry, 1983–.
Pilotovich, S. A.	Deputy Chair, Council of Ministers, BSSR, 1978–83.
Pobol', A. K.	Chair, People's Control Commission, Grodno Oblast', 1963–71.
Poznyak, V. N.	Head, Department of Foreign Tourism, Council of Ministers, BSSR, 1970–85.
Pokrovskii, N. P.	Head, First Department, Council of Ministers, BSSR, 1960–71.
Polozov, N. N.	Chair, Central Council of Belorussian Trade Unions, 1970–.
Polyakov, I. E.	President, Supreme Soviet, BSSR, 1977–85.
Pritytskii, S. O.	President, Prezidium of Supreme Soviet, BSSR, 1968–71.
Prishchepchik, V. V.	First Secretary, Mogilev Obkom, 1974–83.
Pron'ko, S. A.	First Deputy President, Grodno Oblispolkom, 1976–81.
Radyuk, M. T.	Chair, Goskom BSSR for Mining Safety, 1969–75.

Romma, F. D.	Chair, Goskom BSSR for Labour, 1967–83.
Rubakhov, I. K.	Chair, Belorussian Association for Inter-Kolkhoz Construction, 1969–75.
Rudak, A. D.	Deputy Chair, KGB, BSSR, ?–1971.
Ryabinin, L. F.	President, Krichevskii Raiispolkom, Mogilev Oblast', 1967–71.
Savitskii, A. P.	Head, Sector on Artistic Literature, Department of Culture, KPB, 1969–77.
Sakevich, A. D.	Head, General Department, Minsk Obkom, 1971–?
Sambukh, F. I.	Business Manager, Council of Ministers, BSSR, 1969–80.
Sen'kin, N. V.	Head, Department of Local Industry, Brest Oblispolkom, ?–1974.
Snezhkov, V. L.	First Secretary, Rechitsa Gorkom, 1965–8.
Stepantsov, I. F.	Head, Agricultural Department, Mogilev Oblispolkom, 1965–8.
Strizhak, T. N.	President, Belkoopsoyuz, 1970–7.
Surganov, F. A.	President, Prezidium of Supreme Soviet, BSSR, 1971–6; Second Secretary, KPB, 1965–71.
Sysoeva, O. A.	Deputy Minister, Food Industry, BSSR, ?–1972.
Tyabut', D. V.	President Minsk Oblispolkom, 1965–76; Chair, Auditing Commission, KPB, 1976–86.
Fomichev, G. F.	President, Grodno Oblispolkom, 1972–8.
Tsekhanovich, F. A.	Minister of Grain Procurement, BSSR, 1983–5.
Shabashov, S. M.	First Secretary, Vitebsk Obkom, 1971–83.
Shauro, V. F.	Secretary, KPB, 1960–5; Head, Culture Department, CPSU, 1965–86.
Shirokikh, F. T.	Head, Department of Internal Affairs, Vitebsk Oblispolkom, 1965–9.
Shkundich, V. M.	Deputy Minister of Internal Affairs, BSSR, 1967–75; Chair, Central Council of Sports Societies, BSSR, 1975–?
Shubitidze, I. G.	Head, Department of Food Industry, Vitebsk Obkom, ?–1967.
Yudin, V. V.	Head, Cadres Administration, Ministry of Industrial Construction, BSSR, 1960–71.
Yakovlevich, P. G.	First Secretary, Polotsk Gorkom, Vitebsk Oblast', 1965–72.
Yarmol'chik, N. Z.	First Secretary, Uzdenskii Raikom, 1966–71.

The Minsk City Industrial Group*

Members	*Highest Offices Attained, BSSR and USSR*
Afanasenko, V. N. (W)	Deputy Minister of Auto Transport, BSSR, 1966–71.

Bartashevich, L. P. (W)	Head, Main Administration for Gasification, BSSR, 1970–3.
Bartoshevich, G. G. (S)	Second Secretary, KPB, 1983–.
Barkhanov, V. N. (S)	First Secretary, Lenin Raikom, Minsk City, 1979–83.
Bezruchko, T. M. (E)	Deputy President, Supreme Soviet, BSSR, 1985–.
Bil'dyukevich, V. L. (E)	Minister of Industrial Construction Materials, BSSR, 1979–.
Bulgak, A. I. (W)	First Deputy Minister of Local Industry, BSSR, 1977–83;
	Sector Head, Light Industry and Consumer Goods Department, CPSU, 1983–5.
Bysenko, V. D. (S)	Head, Department of Machine-Building, KPB, 1983–.
Vakhtin, A. N. (S)	First Secretary, Sovetskii Raikom, Minsk City, 1977–84.
Galko, V. G. (S)	Second Secretary, Minsk Gorkom, 1985–.
Glamazdin, A. N. (E)	Deputy Minister, Industrial Construction, BSSR, 1982–.
Gotal'skii, V. N. (T)	President, Union of Auto Workers, BSSR, 1972–.
Grib, A. L. (S)	Minister of Consumer Services, BSSR, 1977–.
Gulev, N. T. (S)	Head, Light Industry and Consumer Goods Department, KPB, 1985–.
Gurin, V. V. (K)	First Secretary, Komsomol, BSSR, 1985–.
Demchuk, M. I. (S)	Head, Science and Educational Institutions Department, KPB, 1986.
Dragovets, V. N. (K)	Secretary, Komsomol, BSSR, 1983–5.
Evtukh, V. G. (W)	Deputy Chair, Council of Ministers, BSSR, 1986–.
Zuev, A. B. (S)	Head, Agricultural Machine-Building Department, KPB, 1980–6; Chair, BSSR, Goskom for Mining Safety, 1986–.
Karpenko, I. S. (T)	Deputy Head, Propaganda Department, Minsk Obkom, 1975–9, 1982–?
Kebich, V. F. (W)	Chair, Gosplan, BSSR, 1985–.
Kovalev, M. V. (W)	Chair, Council of Ministers, BSSR, 1986–.
Kovrigo, F. P. (S)	Director, Brest Electro-Mechanical Factory, 1982–.
Kozlov, A. P. (S)	Director, Minsk Electro-Technical Factory, 1979–.
Kononova, M. S. (E)	Minister of Light Industry, BSSR, 1972–5.
Kontus', A. K. (W)	Director, Mogilev Auto Factory, 1978–.
Korneeva, T. I. (S)	Secretary, Zavodskii Raikom, Minsk City, 1980–.
Kostikov, N. N. (W)	Director, Minsk Machine-Building Combine, 1980–.

Krinitsyn, V. (S)	Director, Minsk Factory 'Promsvyaz', 1976–?
Kritskii, V. I. (E)	Deputy Chair, Council of Ministers, BSSR, 1983–.
Kryukov, A. F. (E)	Minister of Meat and Milk Industry, BSSR, 1984–.
Kuleshov, I. I. (E)	Director, Minsk Tractor Factory, 1982–.
Lepeshkin, V. A. (T)	Secretary, KPB, 1983–.
Lopanik, G. Z. (W)	Deputy President, Supreme Soviet, BSSR, 1981–5.
Moiseevich, A. F. (E)	Deputy Minister, Industrial Construction Materials, BSSR, 1985–.
Morozov, M. A. (S)	Deputy President, Minsk Gorispolkom, 1985–.
Nerad, N. S. (K)	Secretary, Minsk Gorkom, 1979–1982; President, BSSR Society for Friendship and Cultural Ties, 1982–.
Pavlyukevich, V. L. (S)	Head, Business Office, KPB, 1986–.
Reut, A. A. (W)	Chair, Gosplan, BSSR, 1983–5; Deputy Chair, Gosplan, USSR, 1985–.
Savchenko, B. A. (W/K)	First Secretary, Moscow Raikom, Minsk City, 1977–83.
Senokosova, M. S. (S)	Director, Minsk Worsted Factory, 1976–7; Secretary, P.P.O. Minsk Textile Factory Named for Krupskaya, 1977–.
Slyun'kov, N. N. (T)	First Secretary, KPB, 1983–87; Secretary and member of Politburo, CPSU, 1987–.
Smirnov, E. P. (E)	Deputy Minister of Light Industry, 1978–?
Sukhnat, L. K. (W)	Minister of Education, 1985–.
Tarazevich, G. S. (W)	President, Prezidium of Supreme Soviet, BSSR, 1985–.
Timoshenko, B. Ya. (E)	Deputy Minister, Industrial Construction Materials, 1974–.
Tomashchuk, V. S. (E)	Head, Central Statistics Administration, BSSR, 1973–.
Khmel'nitskii, K. V. (S)	First Secretary, Frunze Raikom, Minsk City, 1977–84.
Shevchenko, E. P. (S)	First Secretary, Lenin Raikom, Minsk City, 1975–8.
Shkrebnev, I. R. (S)	Deputy President, Minsk Gorispolkom, 1971–80.

Leading Brezhnev Clients

Members	*Highest Offices Attained, BSSR and USSR*
Aksenov, A. N.,	Chair Council of Ministers, BSSR, 1978–83; Chair, Gosteleradio, USSR, 1986–.

Akulich, S. S.	First Deputy Minister, Industrial Construction Materials, BSSR, 1979–83.
Arkhipets, N. T.	Minister of Industrial Construction, BSSR, 1969–79; Deputy Chair, Gossnab, USSR, 1979–.
Bezlyudov, A. I.	Minister of Housing, BSSR, 1973–86.
Boris, V. I.	Head, Organization-Party Work Department, KPB, 1986–.
Bril', S. V.	Minister of Industrial Construction, BSSR, 1985–.
Brovikov, V. I.	Chair, Council of Ministers, BSSR, 1983–6; Ambassador to Poland, 1986–.
Verkhovets, V. L.	Chair, Goskom BSSR for Professional-Technical Education, 1980–.
Vecherko, G. N.	Head, Economics Dept., KPB, 1980–.
Gavrilenko, E. G.	Deputy President, Vitebsk Oblispolkom, 1975–85.
Goncharev, A. A.	Minister of Meat and Milk Production, BSSR, 1981–3.
Grigor'ev, V. V.	First Secretary, Vitebsk Obkom, 1986–.
Gritsuk, I. M.	Minister of Communications, BSSR, 1980–.
Danilov, I. A.	Deputy Chair, Council of Ministers, BSSR, 1975–84.
Dementei, N. I.	Secretary of KPB, 1979–.
Drobyshevskii, L. E.	Deputy Procurator, BSSR, 1979–.
Dudkovskii, P. V.	First Deputy Procurator, BSSR, 1967–83.
Zhabitskii, G. N.	Minister of Internal Affairs, BSSR, 1978–83.
Zhuk, P. S.	First Deputy Minister of Internal Affairs, BSSR, 1976–83.
Kalitko, A. Ya.	Minister of Grain Procurement, 1974–83.
Kiselev, T.Ya.	Deputy Chair, Council of Ministers, USSR, 1978–80; First Secretary, KPB, 1980–1983.
Mazai, N. N.	Deputy Chair, Council of Ministers, BSSR, 1985–.
Maidanyuk, V. F.	Deputy Minister of Internal Affairs, BSSR, 1975–83.
Makaichenko, B. D.	First Deputy Chair, Gosplan, BSSR, 1985–.
Markovskii, G. A.	Minister of the Forest Economy, BSSR, 1985–.
Metelits, V. I.	First Deputy President, Vitebsk Oblispolkom, 1973–83.
Mirochitskii, F. V.	First Deputy Chair, Gosagroprom, BSSR, 1986–.
Mogilnitskii, V. A.	Procurator, BSSR, 1973–83.
Platonov, K. M.	First Secretary, Komsomol, BSSR, 1976–9.
Prokof'eva, E. S.	Secretary, Vitebsk Obkom, 1972–8.
Radetskii, E. I.	Second Secretary, Vitebsk Obkom, 1978.
Radchenko, V. V.	First Deputy Minister of the Food Industry, BSSR, 1979–?

Rusakov, L. V.	Minister of Local Industry, BSSR, 1977–85.
Rusetskii, A. V.	First Deputy Head, Dept. of Propaganda, KPB, 1985–.
Smirnov, A. A.	Secretary, KPB, 1968–78; President, Central Union of Consumer Societies, USSR, 1978–9.
Sobolenko, V. K.	Deputy President, Vitebsk Oblispolkom, 1975–84.
Sokolov, E. E.	First Secretary, Brest Obkom, 1977–87; First Secretary, KPB, 1987–.
Stashenkov, N. A.	Permanent Representative to the Council of Ministers, USSR, 1981–4.
Timoshenko, I. O.	Deputy Minister of Internal Affairs, BSSR, 1980–3.
Firisanov, L. S.	Secretary, KPB, 1978–83.
Khitrun, L. I.	Deputy Chair, Council of Ministers, BSSR, 1971–9; First Secretary, Ryazan Obkom, RSFSR, 1987–.
Tsetsokho, V. A.	First Deputy President, Vitebsk Oblispolkom, 1985.
Chkanikov, E. A.	Minister of Justice, BSSR, 1984–.
Shevelukha, V. S.	Secretary, KPB, 1974–9; Deputy Minister of Agriculture, USSR, 1979–?
Shibeko, I. A.	President, Vitebsk Oblispolkom, 1977–84.
Yarovenko, A. G.	Deputy Chair, Narkontrol', BSSR, 1978–83.

* The letters in parentheses following members of the MCIG designate their organizational sectors of work on entering politics: 'S' stands for party secretary in an industrial firm; 'E' and 'T' for executives and trade union chairmen in same, respectively; 'K' is for Komsomol officers and 'W' for skilled workers.

Notes

1. Method, model and historical background

1 Max Weber, *Economy and Society*, Guenther Roth and Claus Wittich (eds.) (Vols. 1 and 3; New York: Bedminster Press, 1968), pp. 53–80, 130–53, 217–26, 941–83.
2 For a detailed historical account of this process, see Fernand Braudel, *The Structures of Everyday Life* (New York: Harper and Row, 1981); *The Wheels of Commerce* (New York: Harper and Row, 1982).
3 Weber, esp. p. 224–5, 1,394–5.
4 Karl Marx, *Capital* (Vol. 1; Chicago: Charles H. Kerr, 1906), esp., the section on 'the fetishism of commodities' in Chapter 1.
5 These questions are discussed in detail in: Harry Braverman, *Labor and Monopoly Capital* (New York: Monthly Review Press, 1974); Richard Edwards, *Contested Terrain* (New York: Basic Books, 1979); Graeme Salaman and Kenneth Thompson (eds.) *Control and Ideology in Organizations* (Cambridge, MA: The MIT Press, 1980); Mary Zey-Ferrell and Michael Aiken (eds.) *Complex Organizations* (Glenview, IL: Scott, Foresman, 1981).
6 Michael E. Urban, *The Ideology of Administration: American and Soviet Cases* (Albany, NY: State University of New York Press, 1982); Gerald E. Fruge, 'The Ideology of Bureaucracy in American Law', *Harvard Law Review*, Vol. 97 (April, 1984), pp. 1,276–388.
7 Weber, p. 946.
8 Jan Pakulski, 'Bureaucracy and the Soviet System', *Studies in Comparative Communism*, Vol. 19 (Spring, 1986), pp. 3–24; Don Van Atta, 'Why There Is No Taylorism in the Soviet Union', *Comparative Politics*, Vol. 18 (April, 1986), pp. 327–37; Bob Arnot, 'Soviet Labour Productivity and the Failure of the Shchekino Experiment', *Critique*, No. 15 (1981), pp. 31–56; Donald Filtzer, *Soviet Workers and Stalinist Industrialization* (Armonk, NY: M. E. Sharpe, 1986); Lewis H. Siegelbaum, 'Soviet Norm Determination in Theory and Practice, 1917–1941', *Soviet Studies*, Vol. 36 (Jan., 1984), pp. 45–68.
9 Jerry F. Hough, *The Soviet Prefects* (Cambridge, MA: Harvard University Press, 1969).
   More recently, Peter H. Soloman, Jr., has noted that rule application in the USSR over the past some 45 years has been neither 'legal' nor 'rational'.

Rather, it is the direct product of the preferences of the several organizations – police, prosecutors, party officials and judges – involved in the area. Given that none of these has a personal stake in acquitting the innocent, acquittals have all but disappeared from Soviet jurisprudence despite regular efforts by the central authorities to strengthen the legal order by ensuring that the rights of the accused are protected. See his 'The Case of the Vanishing Acquittal: Informal Norms and the Practice of Soviet Criminal Justice', *Soviet Studies*, Vol. 39 (Oct., 1987), pp. 531–55.

10 Zygmunt Bauman, 'Officialdom and Class: Bases of Inequality in Socialist Society', Frank Parkin (ed.) *The Social Analysis of Class Structure* (London: Tavistock, 1974), pp. 129–48; Ken Jowitt, 'Soviet Neotraditionalism: The Political Corruption of a Leninist Regime', *Soviet Studies*, Vol. 35 (July, 1983), pp. 275–97.

11 Michael E. Urban, 'Conceptualizing Political Power in the USSR: Patterns of Binding and Bonding', *Studies in Comparative Communism*, Vol. 18 (Winter, 1985), pp. 207–26; James R. Millar, 'The Little Deal: Brezhnev's Contribution to Acquisitive Socialism', *Slavic Review*, Vol. 44 (Winter, 1985), pp. 694–706; William DiFranceisco and Zvi Gitelman, 'Soviet Political Culture and "Covert Participation" in Policy Implementation', *American Political Science Review*, Vol. 78 (Sept., 1984), pp. 603–21.

12 Bauman; Jowitt; David E. Willer, 'Max Weber's Missing Authority Type', *Sociological Inquiry*, Vol. 37 (Spring, 1967), pp. 231–40.

13 Urban, 'Conceptualizing Political Power in the USSR . . .'

14 David Willer and Bo Anderson (eds.), *Networks, Exchange and Coercion* (New York: Elsevier, 1981); David Willer, 'Theory, Experimentation and Historical Interpretation', J. Berger and M. Zelditch (eds.) *Sociological Theories in Progress III* (Pittsburgh: University of Pittsburgh Press, 1985); Mark Granovetter, 'The Strength of Weak Ties', *American Journal of Sociology*, Vol. 78 (May, 1973), pp. 1,360–80; 'The Strength of Weak Ties: A Network Theory Revisited', Peter Marsden and Nan Lin (eds.) *Social Structure and Network Analysis* (Beverly Hills: Sage Publications, 1982), pp. 105–30; Nan Lin *et al.*, 'Analyzing the Instrumental Use of Relations in the Context of Social Structure', R. S. Burt and M. J. Minor (eds.) *Applied Network Analysis* (Beverly Hills: Sage Publications, 1983), pp. 119–32.

15 I have dealt with one such case which involved the nominal staff of one organization functioning on behalf of other bodies. See my 'Technical Assistance and Political Control: A Research Note on the Organization-Instruction Department of Local Soviets', *Comparative Politics*, Vol. 17 (April, 1985), pp. 337–50.

For a detailed analysis of this phenomenon in Soviet industry, see Vladimir Anderle, *Managerial Power in the Soviet Union* (Westmead: Saxon House, 1976).

16 Examples would include: Bohdan Harasymiw, *Political Elite Recruitment in the Soviet Union* (New York: St. Martin's Press, 1984); Ronald J. Hill, *Soviet Political Elites: The Case of Tiraspol* (New York: St. Martin's Press, 1977); T.H. Rigby, *Communist Party Membership in the USSR, 1917–1967* (Princeton: Princeton University Press, 1968); 'Soviet Communist Party Membership

under Brezhnev', *Soviet Studies*, Vol. 28 (July, 1976), pp. 317–337; Joel C. Moses, *Regional Party Leadership and Policy-Making in the USSR* (New York: Praeger, 1974); 'The Impact of *Nomenklatura* in Soviet Regional Elite Recruitment', *Soviet Union*, Vol. 8 (Part 1, 1981), pp. 62–102; Mark R. Beissinger, 'In Search of Generations in Soviet Politics', *World Politics*, Vol. 38 (Jan., 1986), pp. 288–314; Philip D. Stewart *et al.*, 'Political Mobility and the Soviet Political Process: A Partial Test of Two Models', *American Political Science Review*, Vol. 66 (Dec., 1972), pp. 1,269–94; Jerry F. Hough, *Soviet Leadership in Transition* (Washington, D.C.: Brookings Institution, 1980); *The Soviet Union and Social Science Theory* (Cambridge, MA: Harvard University Press, 1977), Chapter 3; Michael P. Gehlen, 'The Soviet Apparatchiki', R. Barry Farrell (ed.), *Political Leadership in East Europe and the Soviet Union* (Chicago: Aldine, 1970), pp. 140–56; Frederic J. Fleron, Jr., 'Representation and Career Types in the Soviet Political Leadership', ibid., pp. 108–39; 'Systems Attributes and Career Attributes: The Soviet Political Leadership System, 1952 to 1965', Carl Beck *et al.* (eds.) *Comparative Communist Political Leadership* (New York: David McKay, 1973), pp. 43–85; Robert E. Blackwell, Jr., 'Elite Recruitment and Functional Change: An Analysis of the Soviet Obkom Elite, 1950–1968', *Journal of Politics*, Vol. 34 (Feb., 1972), pp. 124–52; Robert E. Blackwell, Jr. and William E. Hulbary, 'Political Mobility Among Soviet Obkom Elites: The Effects of Regime, Social Background and Career Development', *American Journal of Political Science*, Vol. 17 (Nov., 1973), pp. 721–43; J. W. Cleary, 'Elite Career Patterns in a Soviet Republic', *British Journal of Political Science*, Vol. 4 (July, 1974), pp. 323–44; Jan Ake Dellenbrandt, 'Regional Differences in Political Recruitment in the Soviet Republics', *European Journal of Political Research*, Vol. 6 (June, 1978), pp. 181–201; B. Michael Frolic, 'Soviet Urban Political Leaders', *Comparative Political Studies*, Vol. 2 (Jan., 1970), pp. 443–64; Grey Hodnett, *Leadership in the Soviet National Republics* (Oakville, Ontario: Mosaic Press, 1978).

17 For a critique of some of these studies from the perspective of statistical analysis and its misuse, see Mary McAuley, 'Hunting the Hierarchy: RSFSR Obkom First Secretaries and the Central Committee', *Soviet Studies*, Vol. 26 (Oct., 1974), pp. 473–501, esp., pp. 473–5.

18 Harasymiw, *Political Elite Recruitment in the Soviet Union*, p. 2.

19 More or less implicit in the works cited in note 16, this research interest is discussed in some detail in William A. Welsh, 'Introduction: The Comparative Study of Political Leadership in Communist Systems', in Beck *et al.* (eds.), pp. 1–42; Frederic J. Fleron, Jr., 'Toward a Reconceptualization of Political Change in the Soviet Union: The Political Leadership System', *Comparative Politics*, Vol. 1 (Jan., 1969), pp. 228–44.

20 Although the relations set out in Figure 1.1 are my formulation of the underlying model of analysis in these studies, a similar and more elaborate representation can be found in Valerie Bunce, 'Of Power, Policy, and Paradigms: The Logic of Elite Studies', R. H. Linden and B. A. Rockman (eds.), *Elite Studies and Communist Politics: Essays in Memory of Carl Beck* (Pittsburgh: University Center for International Studies, Univesity of Pittsburgh, 1984), pp. 21–48; esp., p. 26.

21 E.g., Philip D. Stewart *et al.*, 'Soviet Regions and Economic Priorities: A Study of Politburo Perceptions', *Soviet Union*, Vol. 2 (Part 1, 1984), p. 1–30; Beissinger, 'In Search of Generations . . .'

22 Bunce, p. 22.

23 Harasymiw, for instance, sums up the bases of political mobility from this perspective as 'ambition, apprenticeship and attributes' to which he also adds 'politics'. See his 'Political Mobility in Soviet Ukraine', *Canadian Slavonic Papers*, Vol. 26 (June–Sept., 1984), p. 161.

24 See Anthony Wilden, *System and Structure* (2nd edn; London: Tavistock, 1980).

25 Harrison C. White, *Chains of Opportunity* (Cambridge, MA: Harvard University Press, 1970). See also D. J. Bartholomew, *Stochastic Models for Social Processes* (3rd edn.; New York: John Wiley and Sons, 1982), pp. 244–7.

26 For examples of the application of vacancy chain analysis in a variety of organizational settings see: Shelby Stewman, 'Two Markov Models of Open System Occupational Mobility: Underlying Conceptualizations and Empirical Tests', *American Sociological Review*, Vol. 40 (June, 1975), pp. 298–321; Suresh L. Konda and Shelby Stewman, 'An Opportunity Labor Demand Model and Markovian Labor Supply Models: Comparative Tests in an Organization', *ibid.*, Vol. 45 (April, 1980), pp. 276–301; 'Careers and Organizational Labor Markets: Demographic Models of Organizational Behavior', *American Journal of Sociology*, Vol. 88 (Jan., 1983), pp.637–85; Sam Marullo, 'Housing Opportunities and Vacancy Chains', *Urban Affairs Quarterly*, Vol. 20 (March, 1985), pp. 364–88. For another example of the use of Markov models in predicting mobility, see James E. Rosenbaum, 'Organizational Career Mobility: Promotion Chances in a Corporation During Periods of Growth and Contraction', *American Journal of Sociology*, Vol. 85 (July, 1979), pp. 21–48.

27 Although the model depicted in Figure 1.3 is my formulation, it does incorporate some of the concerns recently advanced by William A. Welsh in his 'Political Elites and Public Policy', in Linden and Rockman (eds.), pp. 49–101.

28 Nicholas P. Vakar, *Belorussia: The Making of a Nation* (Cambridge, MA: Harvard University Press, 1956), pp. 1–4.

29 Moshe Lewin, *The Making of the Soviet System* (New York: Pantheon, 1985), pp. 49–87.

30 Vakar, pp. 20–7.

31 *Ibid.*, pp. 34–5.

32 Ivan S. Lubachko, *Belorussia Under Soviet Rule, 1917–1957* (Lexington, KY: University of Kentucky Press, 1972), p. 11.

33 Thomas T. Hammond, 'Nationalism and National Minorities in Eastern Europe', *Journal of International Affairs*, Vol. 20 (No. 1, 1966), pp. 9–31.

34 Steven L. Guthier, 'The Belorussians: National Identification and Assimilation, 1897–1970' (part 1), *Soviet Studies*, Vol. 29 (Jan., 1977), p. 43.

35 Vakar, p. 34.

36 *Ibid.*, pp. 36, 219.

37 *Ibid.*, pp. 74–9.

38 *Ibid.*, pp. 84–5.

39 *Ibid.*, pp. 84–98; Lubachko, pp. 6–30; Guthier, pp. 49–52.

40 Lubachko, p. 129.

41 Vakar, pp. 139–45; Helene Carrere d'Encausse, *Decline of an Empire* (New York: Newsweek Books, 1979), pp. 24–8.

42 Geoffrey Hosking, *The First Socialist Society* (Cambridge, MA: Harvard University Press, 1985), pp. 245–6.

43 P. U. Brovka *et al.*, *Belorusskaya Sovetskaya Sotsialisticheskaya Respublika* (Minsk: Glavnaya redaktsiya Belorusskoi Sovetskoi entsiklopedii, 1978), esp. pp. 135, 264–5.

44 *Narodnoe khozyaistvo Belorusskoi SSR v 1981g.* (Minsk: Belarus', 1982), p. 3.

45 Jan Zaprudnik, 'Belorussia and the Belorussians', Zev Katz *et al.* (eds.) *Handbook of Major Soviet Nationalities* (New York: The Free Press, 1975), p. 52.

46 Vakar, pp. 180–1.

47 K. T. Mazurov, *Nezabyvaemoe* (Minsk: Belarus', 1984), Chapter 1.

48 Vakar, pp. 193–203.

49 Mazurov, *passim*; esp. p. 72.

50 I. M. Ignatenko *et al.*, *Istoriya Belorusskoi SSR* (Minsk: Nauka i tekhnika, 1977), p. 145.

51 Belorussian partisans who assumed high office in Moscow are: M. V. Zimyanin who became Editor of *Pravda* in 1965 and a Secretary of the CPSU in 1976; and V. F. Shauro who was named head of the Cultural Affairs Department of the CPSU in 1965.

52 In general, see: Amy W. Knight, 'Pyotr Masherov and the Soviet Leadership: A Study in Kremlinology', *Survey*, Vol. 26 (Winter, 1982), pp. 151–68; W. J. McGrath, 'The Politics of Soviet Federalism' (unpublished Ph.D. dissertation; Ottawa, Ontario: Carleton University, 1981).

53 The word 'myth' in this context should not be interpreted to mean make-believe or phoney. Rather, it refers to a tale told in many variants, which raises up certain events (real or not) to a supra-mundane level by investing them with, in this case, great national, social and political significance.

54 For an account of the military side of partisan activity during the Second World War, see John A. Armstrong, *Soviet Partisans in World War II* (Madison, WI: University of Wisconsin Press, 1964).

55 For some illustrations of the mythic element in Soviet communications which take up the question of how the hero of a particular narrative is marked and received by those on whose behalf he performs, see: Michael E. Urban and John McClure, 'The Folklore of State Socialism: Semiotics and the Study of the Soviet State', *Soviet Studies*, Vol. 35 (Oct., 1983), pp. 471–86; Michael E. Urban, 'From Chernenko to Gorbachev: A Repoliticization of Official Soviet Discourse?' *Soviet Union*, Vol. 13 (No. 2, 1986), pp. 131–61.

56 It is interesting to note in this respect the rather positive evaluations one is

likely to receive from Belorussian émigrés with respect to the leaders of the Partisan group. Although anti-Communist in political orientation, Belorussians in the West often regard such figures as K. T. Mazurov and P. M. Masherov as bearers, under Soviet circumstances, of Belorussian cultural nationalism. Similar sentiments are also commonly expressed by intellectuals in the BSSR who are concerned with the matter of Belorussian cultural identity. For instance during a discussion with six members of the Law Faculty of the Belorussian State University in December, 1988, Masherov's name was approbatively mentioned as soon as the issue of nationality came up. A certain sense of satisfaction, if not pride, was apparent on the face of each of these scholars as I was informed that Masherov was the first leader of the BSSR to address his countrymen in the Belorussian language.

57 Brovka *et al.*, pp. 587–8.
58 V. P. Borodina *et al.*, *Soviet Byelorussia* (Moscow: Progress, 1972), p. 85; V.P. Vorob'eva *et al.*, *Vitebsk* (Minsk: Nauka i tekhnika, 1974), pp. 196–202.
59 Brovka *et al.*, pp. 266–8; L. M. Barabanov *et al.*, *Mogilev* (Minsk: Nauka i tekhnika, 1971), pp. 203–9.
60 Borodina *et al.*, pp. 82–5; *Belarus'* (Minsk: Belarus', 1977), pp. 62–9.
61 Brovka *et al.*, p. 269.
62 Borodina *et al.*, pp. 88, 134–5.
63 Brovka *et al.*, p. 272; Barabanov *et al.*, pp. 204–7.
64 Vorob'eva *et al.*, pp. 197–8; Borodina *et al.*, pp. 93–5.
65 Brovka *et al.*, pp. 271–80; V. Ya. Naumenko, *Brest* (Minsk: Nauka i tekhnika, 1977), pp. 123–35.
66 Borodina *et al.*, p. 70.
67 *Izvestiya* (Dec. 16, 1985).
68 *Kommunisticheskaya partiya Belorussii v tsifrakh* (Minsk: Belarus', 1978), pp. 35–6, 53–4.
69 V. A. Bobkov, *Kachestvennyi rost partii i organizatsiya partinykh sil* (Minsk: Belarus', 1977), pp. 57–90.
70 Figures on recruitment to the KPB show an almost yearly linear incline, with working-class recruits amounting to 40.7 per cent of all new party members in 1965, the year in which the policy was inaugurated. See *Kommunisticheskaya partiya Belorussii v tsifrakh*, pp. 53–4.
71 Steven L. Guthier, 'The Belorussians: National Identification and Assimilation, 1897–1970' (part 2), *Soviet Studies*, Vol. 29 (Apr., 1977), pp. 272–4.
72 Brian Connolly, 'Fifty Years of Soviet Federalism in Belorussia', R. S. Clem (ed.) *The Soviet West* (New York: Praeger, 1975), pp. 114–15.
73 *Ibid.*, p. 115; Guthier (part 2), p. 281; Roman Szporluk, 'West Ukraine and West Belorussia', *Soviet Studies*, Vol. 31 (Jan., 1979), pp. 76–7.
74 See, for instance, *Letters to Gorbachev: New Documents from Soviet Byelorussia* (2nd edn; London: The Association of Byelorussians in Great Britain, 1987); 'A Letter to Gorbachev: Belorussian Intellectuals on the Language Question' (Munich: Radio Liberty, April 20, 1987). (I am indebted to Vitaut and Zora Kipel for these references.)
    See also the coverage of 'unofficial' patriotic demonstrations in Minsk in

November of 1987 in *Sovetskaya Belorussiya* (Nov. 17 and 18, 1987) and in Bohdan Nahaylo, 'Political Demonstration in Minsk Attests to Belorussian National Assertiveness', *Radio Liberty Research* 481/87 (Nov. 26, 1987).
75 Guthier (part 2), p. 275.

2. Hierarchy, mobility and a stratified model

1 Jerry F. Hough discusses numerous instances of this in his *The Soviet Prefects* (Cambridge, MA: Harvard University Press, 1969). For an illustration of same in the Belorussian case, see *Izvestiya*'s coverage (June 29, 1985) of the directives issued to the Primary Party Organization at the heavy truck-building firm, BelavtoMAZ, by the Central Committee of the CPSU.

2 This observation echoes those made by: Alfred G. Meyer, *The Soviet Political System: An Interpretation* (New York: Random House, 1965), p. 147; Philip D. Stewart *et al.*, 'Political Mobility and the Soviet Political Process: A Partial Test of Two Models', *American Political Science Review*, Vol. 66 (Dec., 1972), p. 1272; John H. Miller, 'Cadres Policy in the Nationality Areas – Recruitment of CPSU first and second secretaries in the non-Russian republics of the USSR', *Soviet Studies*, Vol. 29 (Jan., 1977), p. 33.

3 On the *nomenklatura* system in general, see: Bohdan Harasymiw, *Political Elite Recruitment in the Soviet Union* (New York: St. Martin's Press, 1984), pp. 154–73; Gerd Meyer, 'The Impact of the Political Structure on the Recruitment of the Political Elite in the USSR', in L. J. Cohen and J. J. Shapiro (eds.) *Communist Systems in Comparative Perspective* (Garden City, NY: Anchor Books, 1974), pp. 202–4; Joel C. Moses, 'The Impact of *Nomenklatura* in Soviet Regional Elite Recruitment', *Soviet Union*, Vol. 8 (Pt. 1, 1981), pp. 62–102; Michael Voslensky, *Nomenklatura: The Soviet Ruling Class* (Garden City, NY: Doubleday, 1984).

4 Ronald J. Hill, *Soviet Political Elites: The Case of Tiraspol* (New York: St. Martin's Press, 1977), pp. 114–15; Cameron Ross, *Local Government in the Soviet Union: Problems of Implementation and Control* (London: Croom Helm, 1987), pp. 40–1.

5 For an examination of this phenomenon in a department of local soviets, see Michael E. Urban, 'Technical Assistance and Political Control: A Research Note on the Organization-Instruction Department of Local Soviets', *Comparative Politics*, Vol. 17 (April, 1985), pp. 337–50.

6 Peter Solomon offers an excellent illustration of this point in the context of appointments to judicial and law enforcement bodies in his 'Soviet Politicians and Criminal Prosecutions: The Logic of Party Intervention', Soviet Interview Project, Working Paper No. 33 (University of Illinois at Urbana-Champaign, March, 1987), pp. 4–5.

7 The title of Mary McAuley's well-known and in many ways masterful article on this subject is perhaps itself an indication of the objectivist bias that has informed our approach to the problem. See her 'The Hunting of the Hierarchy: RSFSR Obkom First Secretaries and the Central Committee', *Soviet Studies*, Vol. 26 (Oct., 1974), pp. 473–501.

8 *Ibid.*; Stewart *et al.*; Peter Frank, 'Constructing a Classified Ranking of

CPSU Provincial Committees', *British Journal of Political Science*, Vol. 4 (Pt. 2, 1974), pp. 217–30.

Less explicit rankings of mobility can be found in Miller; Joel C. Moses, 'Regional Cohorts and Political Mobility in the USSR: The Case of Dnepropetrovsk', *Soviet Union*, Vol. 3 (pt. 1, 1976), pp. 63–89; George W. Breslauer, 'Provincial Party Leaders' Demand Articulation and the Nature of Center-Perifery Relations in the USSR', *Slavic Review*, Vol. 45 (Winter, 1986), pp. 650–72.

9 The main source for these data is the daily, *Sovetskaya Belorussiya*, over the period Jan., 1966–June, 1986. I also relied on the monthly, *Kommunist Belorussii* (Jan., 1966–June, 1986), selected numbers of the daily, *Zvyazda*, and on listings which appeared (far less frequently, of course) in *Sovety narodnykh deputatov* (Jan., 1976–June, 1986) and *Izvestiya* (1983–6). Some data were taken from Soviet personnel directories compiled by the CIA, from Val Ogareff's *Leaders of the Soviet Republics, 1971–1980* (Canberra: Dept. of Political Science, Australian National University, 1980), and from the short biographies in relevant editions of *Deputaty Verkhovnogo Soveta SSSR*.

10 J. W. Cleary has used a similar matrix in his analysis of the Kazakh elite. See his 'Elite Career Patterns in a Soviet Republic', *British Journal of Political Science*, Vol. 4 (July, 1974), pp. 323–44.

11 One particular difficulty in assigning jobs to strata involved five Belorussian officials who were named to Soviet diplomatic posts. Having no clear rule on which to base a decision, I assigned one of these positions (Ambassador to Poland) to the top stratum because of the putative importance of this post and because of the fact that in the careers of the individuals in question (S. A. Pilotovich, A. N. Aksenov and V. I. Brovikov) this posting followed a Stratum 1 job (Secretary of the KPB or Chairman of the Belorussian Council of Ministers) and for Aksenov, led directly to another Stratum 1 appointment (Chair of the USSR State Committee for Television and Radio) while Pilotovich returned to the BSSR to enter a Stratum 2 job (Deputy Chair of the Council of Ministers) and Brovikov remains Ambassador to Poland at the time of writing. The other ambassadorial postings (to North Korea and Pakistan) were assigned to Stratum 2. These choices are admittedly a matter of judgement.

12 In order to avoid confusing the symbols in this equation with others that appear in following chapters, I have departed from conventional notation in which i would be followed by j, k, l. As is evident in the text, i represents here initial, unstratified position, while a stands for the top stratum, and b and c for those below it.

13 *Kommunisticheskaya partiya Belorussii v tsifrakh: 1918–1978* (Minsk: Belarus', 1978), pp. 212–14.

14 Merle Fainsod was among the first to notice this feature of the Soviet system. See his 'Bureaucracy and Modernization: The Russian and Soviet Case', in J. LaPalombara (ed.), *Bureaucracy and Political Development* (Princeton: Princeton University Press, 1963), pp. 233–67.

Cleary ('Elite Career Patterns . . .') observed the same in his study of the Kazakh elite.

15 The empirical results of this study support the criticisms previously voiced in this regard by McAuley, 'The Hunting of the Hierarchy . . .'

16 *Narodnoe khozyaistvo Belorusskoi SSR v 1981g.* (Minsk: Belarus', 1982), pp. 48–53; *Belarus'* (Minsk: Belarus', 1977), pp. 86–7.

17 V. P. Borodina, *Soviet Byelorussia* (Moscow: Progress, 1972), pp. 162–3.

3. Centralization as a determinant of elite circulation

1 Charles E. Lindblom, *Politics and Markets* (New York: Basic Books, 1977), pp. 17–32, 244–60.

2 John H. Miller, 'Cadres Policy in the Nationality Areas: Recruitment of CPSU first and second secretaries in the non-Russian republics of the USSR', *Soviet Studies*, Vol. 29 (Jan., 1977), pp. 3–36; 'Nomenklatura: A Check on Localism?", T. H. Rigby and B. Harasymiw (eds.) *Leadership Selection and Patron-Client Relations in the USSR and Yugoslavia* (London: George Allen and Unwin, 1983), pp. 15–61; Gyula Jozsa, 'Political *Seilschaften* in the USSR, *ibid.*, pp. 139–73; Joel C. Moses, 'The Impact of *Nomenklatura* in Soviet Regional Recruitment', *Soviet Union*, Vol. 8 (pt. 1, 1981), pp. 62–102; 'Regionalism in Soviet Politics: Continuity as a Source of Change', *Soviet Studies*, Vol. 37 (April, 1985), pp. 184–211; Robert E. Blackwell, Jr., 'Cadres Policy in the Brezhnev Era', *Problems of Communism*, Vol. 28 (March–April, 1979), pp. 29–42.

3 For a treatment of the Markov property, see: John G. Kemeny *et al.*, *Introduction to Finite Mathematics* (2nd edn.; Englewood Cliffs, N. J.: Prentice Hall, 1966); D. J. Bartholomew, *Stochastic Models for Social Processes* (3rd edn.; New York: John Wiley and Sons, 1982).

4 For an exegesis of this approach, see Harrison C. White, *Chains of Opportunity* (Cambridge, MA: Harvard University Press, 1970), esp., pp. 23–6.

5 For a discussion of this question in the context of other settings, see *ibid.*, pp. 100–44; Sam Marullo, 'Housing Opportunities and Vacancy Chains', *Urban Affairs Quarterly*, Vol. 20 (March., 1985), pp. 364–88.

6 White, pp. 308–10.

7 *Ibid.*, p. 104.

8 W. J. Conover, *Practical Nonparametric Statistics* (New York: John Wiley and Sons, 1971), pp. 293–8.

9 Miller, 'Cadres Policy in the Nationality Areas'; J. W. Cleary, 'Elite Career Patterns in a Soviet Republic', *British Journal of Political Science*, Vol. 4 (July, 1974), pp. 323–44.

10 P. U. Brovka *et al.*, *Belorusskaya Sovetskaya Sotsialisticheskaya Respublika* (Minsk: Glavnaya redaktsiya Belorusskoi Sovetskoi entsiklopedii, 1978), p. 587.

11 I am indebted to Alexander Rahr for this observation on the leadership of delegations to congresses of the CPSU.

12 For the period 1966–76, the predicted mode in the distribution of chain lengths is one (28.6 per cent) while the observed mode is three (26.8 per cent). For the 1977–86 period, the predicted mode is, again, one (29.4 per cent) and the observed mode is two (39.6 per cent).

13 W. J. McGrath, 'The Politics of Soviet Federalism' (unpublished Ph.D. dissertation; Ottawa: Carleton University, 1981), pp. 107–87; Brovka *et al.*, p. 286–98.

4. The regional structure of elite circulation

1 T. H. Rigby, 'The Soviet Regional Leadership: The Brezhnev Generation', *Slavic Review*, Vol. 37 (March, 1978), pp. 1–24; James H. Oliver, 'Turnover and Family Circles in Soviet Administration', *Slavic Review*, Vol. 32 (Sept., 1973), pp. 527–45; Joel C. Moses, *Regional Party Leadership and Policy Making in the USSR* (New York: Praeger, 1974); 'Regionalism in Soviet Politics: Continuity as a Source of Change', *Soviet Studies*, Vol. 37 (April, 1985), pp. 184–211; 'The Impact of *Nomenklatura* in Soviet Regional Elite Recruitment', *Soviet Union*, Vol. 8 (pt. 1, 1981), pp. 62–102; John H. Miller, 'Cadres Policy in the Nationality Areas: Recruitment of CPSU first and second secretaries in the non-Russian republics of the USSR', *Soviet Studies*, Vol. 29 (January, 1977), pp. 3–36; '*Nomenklatura*: Check on Localism?', T. H. Rigby and B. Harasymiw (eds.) *Leadership Selection and Patron-Client Relations in the USSR and Yugoslavia* (London: George Allen and Unwin, 1983), pp. 64–96.

2 For the early Soviet period, see T. H. Rigby, 'Early Provincial Cliques and the Rise of Stalin', *Soviet Studies*, Vol. 33 (Jan., 1981), pp. 3–28; R. V. Daniels, 'Evaluation of Leadership Selection in the Central Committee, 1917–1927' in W. Pintner and R. Rowney (eds.) *Russian Officialdom* (Chapel Hill: University of North Carolina Press, 1980), pp. 355–68.

For the contemporary period, see Joel C. Moses, 'Regional Cohorts and Political Mobility in the USSR: The Case of Dnepropetrovsk', *Soviet Union*, Vol. 3 (pt. 1, 1976), pp. 63–89; John P. Willerton, Jr., 'Patronage Networks and Coalition Building in the Brezhnev Era', *Soviet Studies*, Vol. 39 (April, 1987), pp. 175–204.

3 See J. Arch Getty, *Origins of the Great Purges: The Soviet Communist Party Reconsidered, 1933–1938* (Cambridge University Press, 1985); Gabor Tamas Rittersporn, 'Soviet Politics in the 1930s: Rehabilitating Society', *Studies in Comparative Communism*, Vol. 19 (Summer, 1986), pp. 105–28; 'Stalin in 1938: Political Defeat Behind the Rhetorical Apotheosis', *Telos*, No. 46 (Winter, 1980–1), pp. 6–42; 'The State Against Itself: Social Tension and Political Conflict in the USSR: 1936–1938', *Telos*, No. 41 (Fall, 1979), pp. 87–104; T. H. Rigby, 'How the Obkom Secretary Was Tempered', *Problems of Communism*, Vol. 29 (March–April, 1980), pp. 57–63; Merle Fainsod, *Smolensk Under Soviet Rule* (Cambridge, MA: Harvard University Press, 1958), *passim*.

4 Michael E. Urban, 'Conceptualizing Political Power in the USSR: Patterns of Binding and Bonding', *Studies in Comparative Communism*, Vol. 18 (Winter, 1985), pp. 207–26; Robert Sharlet, 'Dissent and the Contra-System in the Soviet Union', in E. Hoffmann (ed.) *The Soviet Union in the 1980s* (New York: Academy of Political Science, 1984), pp. 135–46; Graeme Gill, 'The Single Party as an Agent of Development: Lessons from the Soviet

Experience', *World Politics*, Vol. 39 (July, 1987), pp. 566–78; 'Personality Cult, Political Culture and Party Structure', *Studies in Comparative Communism*, Vol. 17 (Summer, 1984), pp. 111–21; Jonathan R. Adelman, 'The Early Development of the Soviet Governmental Bureaucracy: Center, Localities and National Areas', *International Journal of Public Administration*, Vol. 16 (No. 1, 1984), pp. 55–95; esp. pp. 69–78.

5 To the six oblasts of the BSSR was added a seventh region, Minsk City. The decison to treat Minsk City in this way follows from the importance of positions there as noted in previous chapters and from the fact that it is the only city in the BSSR which is administratively subordinate to the Republic rather than to the oblast' in which it is located. Classifying Minsk City in this way is also consonant with the standard practices of statistical reporting in Belorussia.

6 As of January 1, 1978, Gomel' Oblast' had the largest party membership (when the figure for Minsk City is deducted from Minsk Oblast') among the oblasts (92,985), while Minsk City as of July 1 of that year, had some 102,838 party members. These figures appear in *Kommunisticheskaya partiya Belorussii v tsifrakh, 1918–1978* (Minsk: Belarus', 1978), pp. 212–14.

7 The reader will find the relevant data displayed in Michael E. Urban and Russell B. Reed, 'Regionalism in a Systems Perspective: Explaining Elite Circulation in a Soviet Republic', *Slavic Review*, Vol. 48 (Fall, 1989).

8 Harrison C. White makes the same point in a similar context in his *Chains of Opportunity* (Cambridge, MA: Harvard University Press, 1970), p. 121.

9 In addition to biographical listings in *Deputaty Verkhovnogo Soveta SSSR* and obituaries in newspapers, I have relied on the memoirs of K. T. Mazurov (former Partisan commander and Belorussia's leading political figure in the postwar years), *Nezabyvaemoe* (Minsk: Belarus', 1984), and on an article by another prominent Partisan and BSSR politician, S. O. Pritytskii, 'Kurgany slavy i bessmertiya', *Sovetskaya Belorussiya* (July 26, 1967), in order to identify members of this clique.

10 We would add three cases to Minsk City's total if these individuals were included: N. N. Slyun'kov who was First Secretary of the Minsk Gorkom (1972–4) before becoming Deputy Chair of Gosplan, USSR, and who returned to the BSSR as First Secretary of the KPB in January of 1983; A. A. Reut, Second Secretary of the Minsk Gorkom (1974–5), who became First Deputy Minister of the Radio Industry, USSR (1975–83) before returning to the BSSR to become Chair of Gosplan; and V. A. Lepeshkin, First Secretary of the Minsk Gorkom (1974–6) who became Deputy Head of the CPSU's Department of Administrative Organs (1977–83) and then returned to Belorussia as a secretary of the KPB.

11 T. H. Rigby describes a pattern in which regional or republic officials who are posted in Moscow endeavour to utilize contacts at the centre for the purpose of staffing positions back home with their own supporters. Rigby, however, confines his remarks to the first secretaries of obkoms or republic party organizations. See his, 'Khrushchev and the Rules of the Soviet Political Game', R. F. Miller and F. Feher (eds.) *Khrushchev and the Communist World* (London: Croom Helm, 1984), pp. 39–81; esp., p. 40.

12 Within this study's time frame, the First Secretary of the KPB (N. N. Slyun'kov), another KPB secretary (V. A. Lepeshkin), Deputy Chair of the BSSR's Council of Ministers (V. I. Kritskii) and First Deputy Minister of Local Industry in the BSSR (A. I. Bulgak) began their early careers as skilled workers in the Minsk Tractor Factory whose administrative, party and trade union offices represented their entries into politics. According to the available data, the primary party organizations in Minsk factories were also launching grounds for careers that include the following offices: Chair of the Council of Ministers of the BSSR, Second Secretary of the KPB, two ministers of the BSSR, the head of the Council of Ministers apparatus, two heads of departments of the KPB, head of a trade union, and a deputy president of Minsk Gorispolkom. In addition to the Minsk Tractor Factory, four other industrial managers in Minsk found their way to ministerial positions in the BSSR, another to a deputy minister's job, and a sixth to the Chair of Gosplan, BSSR.

13 Moses, 'Regional Cohorts and Political Mobility in the USSR . . .', Willerton, 'Patronage Networks . . .'; Ronald J. Hill and Alexander Rahr, 'The General Secretary, the Central Party Secretariat and the Apparat', David Lane (ed.) *Elites and Soviet Politics* (Aldershot: Edward Elgar, 1988), pp. 49–73.

14 In this respect we should not overlook the role played by V. A. Lepeshkin, mentioned in notes 10 and 12. Lepeshkin had served as head of both the trade union and the party committee at the Minsk Tractor Factory shortly before Slyun'kov was named its General Director. Lepeshkin's term as Second Secretary of the Minsk Gorkom (1968–74) overlapped Slyun'kov's tenure as the First Secretary of the Gorkom, a job that Lepeshkin then filled when Slyun'kov moved to Moscow.

15 Amy W. Knight, 'Pyotr Masherov and the Soviet Leadership: A Study in Kremlinology', *Survey*, Vol. 26 (Winter, 1982), p. 151–68; esp. p. 157.

16 The low rate of internal recruitment to leading positions in Vitebsk may be one indication of such a struggle. Another might be the fact that a Partisan, S. M. Shabashov, replaced Aksenov as First Secretary of the Vitebsk Obkom when the latter became Second Secretary of the KPB.

17 Brovikov's case is discussed in the text. What might be added is the early date at which he was coopted into the party leadership in Vitebsk. Brovikov's previous career was mainly as the editor of various local newspapers in Vitebsk Oblast' between 1955 and 1970. He also served as a raion party secretary in Vitebsk for some three years during this period. In 1970 he was named a secretary of the Vitebsk Obkom. L. S. Firisanov served as a secretary of the Vitebsk Obkom for some ten years before being named a secretary of the KPB in 1978. Some four months before Aksenov was posted to the ambassadorial position in Poland, however, Firisanov suffered a demotion to the position of Deputy Chair of the BSSR's Council of Ministers and the loss of his seat on the Buro of the KPB.

18 Luigi Graziano, 'A Conceptual Framework for the Study of Clientelistic Behavior', *European Journal of Social Research*, Vol. 4 (1976), pp. 149–74.

19 For East Europe, see Zygmunt Bauman, 'Comment on Eastern Europe', *Studies in Comparative Communism*, Vol. 12 (Summer/Autumn, 1979),

pp. 184–9; Jacek Tarkowski, 'Patrons and Clients in a Planned Economy', S. N. Eisenstadt and Rene Lemarchand (eds.) *Political Clientelism, Patronage and Development* (Beverly Hills, CA: Sage Publications, 1981), pp. 173–88; 'Symposium on *Soviet Peasants'*, *Telos*, No. 68 (Summer, 1986), pp. 109–27.

5. The structure of patronage affiliations

1 Jerry F. Hough, 'The Soviet System: Petrification or Pluralism?' *Problems of Communism*, Vol. 12 (March/April, 1972), pp. 25–45.

   Hough has revised his views on this topic, preferring 'corporatism' to 'pluralism' as a description of the Soviet system. See his 'Pluralism, Corporatism and the Soviet Union', Susan Gross Solomon (ed.) *Pluralism in the Soviet Union* (New York: St. Martin's Press, 1983), pp. 37–60; esp. p. 39.

2 This perspective is evident, for instance, in the majority of the essays included in H. Gordon Skilling and Franklyn Griffiths (eds.) *Interest Groups in Soviet Politics* (Princeton: Princeton University Press, 1971).

3 Jerry Hough has distinguished personnel decisions based on merit from those based on patronage and has argued that in industrial administration the former predominates (*The Soviet Prefects* [Cambridge, MA: Harvard University Press, 1969], pp. 174–7). William A. Welsh has reached the same conclusion regarding elites in Communist systems and has proposed that over time meritocratic criteria tend to replace patronage ties as the main determinant of elite mobility. See his 'The Comparative Study of Political Leadership in Communist Systems', Carl Beck *et al.* (eds.) *Comparative Communist Political Leadership* (New York: David McKay, 1973), pp. 1–42; esp. p. 3. Frederic J. Fleron, Jr. advances a similar view in 'Systems Attributes and Career Attributes: The Soviet Political Leadership System, 1952 to 1965', *ibid.*, pp. 43–85.

4 Gerald Mars and Yochanan Altman regard the absence of universal criteria and the ubiquity of network ties as the defining feature of career patterns in the USSR. See their 'How a Soviet economy really works', Michael Clarke (ed.) *Corruption* (New York: St. Martin's Press, 1983), pp. 259–67; esp., p. 265.

5 John H. Miller makes an obvious but nonetheless important point in calling attention to the fact that individual appointments and promotions may well reflect both meritocratic and patronage considerations. See his 'Cadres Policy in the Nationality Areas: Recruitment of CPSU first and second secretaries in the non-Russian republics of the USSR', *Soviet Studies*, Vol. 29 (Jan., 1977), p. 4, note 7.

6 *Inter alia*, T. H. Rigby, 'Khrushchev and the Rules of the Soviet Political Game', R. F. Miller and F. Feher (eds.) *Khrushchev and the Communist World* (London: Croom Helm, 1984), pp. 39–81; esp., pp. 40–1; Ronald J. Hill, *Soviet Political Elites: The Case of Tiraspol* (New York: St. Martin's Press, 1977), *passim*; George W. Breslauer, 'The Nature of Soviet Politics and the Gorbachev Leadership', Alexander Dallin and Condoleezza Rice

(eds.) *The Gorbachev Era* (Stanford, CA: Stanford Alumni Assoc., 1986), pp. 10–29; esp., pp. 16–19.

7 Mark Granovetter, 'Network Sampling: Some First Steps', *American Journal of Sociology*, Vol. 81 (May, 1976), pp. 1,287–303; esp. p. 1,300.

8 John Miller, '*Nomenklatura*: Check on Localism?', T. H. Rigby and B. Harasymiw (eds.) *Leadership Selection and Patron-Client Relations in the USSR and Yugoslavia* (London: George Allen and Unwin, 1983), p. 69.

9 On the particular attention which the KPB has paid to staffing soviet bodies with its members, see I. I. Kozlov, 'Rabota s rezervom rukovodyashchikh kadrov', *Kommunist Belorussii* (No. 9, 1974), pp. 41–6; I. F. Yakushev, 'Kommunisty v Sovetakh', *Izvestiya* (Aug. 6, 1983).

10 Miller, '*Nomenklatura*: A Check on Localism?', *loc. cit.*

11 Ronald J. Hill, 'Soviet Political Development and the Culture of the Apparatchiki', *Studies in Comparative Communism*, Vol. 19 (Spring, 1986), pp. 27–8.

12 Thane Gustafson and Dawn Mann, 'Gorbachev's Next Gamble', *Problems of Communism*, Vol. 36 (July–Aug., 1987), pp. 1–20.

13 There seems to be no particular reason to display these data in the text. Suffice to say that recruitment rates for the party, the soviets, the ministries, state committees and Komsomol over the first decade, when compared against those of the second, differ by margins of 9 percentage points or fewer and that the largest difference (9 per cent) occurred in the case of transfer rates between the ministries and the state committees. The numbers for the trade union and the judicial and cultural organizations show a wider variation but, as noted above, the incidences of transfers are too few to sustain any conclusions.

14 Gerd Meyer, 'The Impact of the Political Structure on the Recruitment of the Political Elite in the USSR', Leonard J. Cohen and Jane J. Shapiro (eds.) *Communist Systems in Comparative Perspective* (Garden City, NY: Anchor Books, 1974), pp. 195–221; esp., pp. 198, 206.

15 For a Soviet report on this matter, see G. Usmanov, 'Sovetskie kadry: podbor, rasstanovka, vospitanie', *Sovety narodnykh deputatov* (May, 1985), pp. 22–9.

16 See Yu. Feofanov's interview with O. E. Kutafin, Dean of the Law Faculty at Moscow State University, 'Deputat i apparat', *Izvestiya* (Nov. 13, 1987).

17 M. S. Gorbachev's address to Leningrad party veterans and activists, 'Partiya revolyutsii – partiya perestroiki', *Izvestiya* (Oct. 13, 1987).

18 Appropriately, this remark was made by G. Tarazevich, President of the Prezidium of the Supreme Soviet of the BSSR, in *Izvestiya* (June 23, 1988).

19 For outlines of the conventional concept of patron-client relations, see Carl H. Lande, 'Networks and Groups in Southeast Asia: Some Observations on the Group Theory of Politics', *American Political Science Review*, Vol. 67 (March, 1973), pp. 103–27; 'Introduction: The Dyadic Basis of Clientelism', Steffen W. Schmidt *et al* (eds.) *Friends, Followers and Factions* (Berkeley, CA: University of California Press, 1977), pp. xiii–xxxvii; Christopher Clapham, 'Clientelism and the State', in his *Private Patronage and Public Power* (New York: St Martin's Press, 1982), pp. 1–35.

20 *Inter alia*, Lande, 'Networks and Groups . . .'; 'Introduction . . .'; James C. Scott, 'Patron–Client Politics and Political Change in Southeast Asia', *American Political Science Review*, Vol. 66 (March, 1972), pp. 91–113.

21 Clapham, p. 19; Rene Lemarchand, 'Comparative Political Clientelism: Structure, Process and Optic', S. N. Eisenstadt and Rene Lemarchand (eds.) *Political Clientelism, Patronage and Development* (Beverly Hills, CA: Sage Publications, 1981), pp. 7–32; esp., pp. 9–16, 21.

22 On patron–client relations in pre-Soviet Russia, see Daniel T. Orlovsky, 'Political Clientelism in Russia: The Historical Perspective', Rigby and Harasymiw (eds) Chapter 5.

T. H. Rigby, who has been a leader in this field of research for the Soviet period, has demonstrated the tenacity of the patron-client pattern even under the most inhospitable conditions, viz., the Great Purge. See his 'Was Stalin a Disloyal Patron?', *Soviet Studies*, Vol. 38 (July, 1986), pp. 311–24.

23 T. H. Rigby, 'Early Provincial Cliques and the Rise of Stalin', *Soviet Studies*, Vol. 33 (Jan., 1981), p. 5.

24 *Inter alia*, Yu. A. Rozenbaum, 'Sistema roboty s kadrami v usloviyakh perestroiki', *Sovetskoe gosudarstvo i pravo* (Dec., 1986), pp. 11–20; M. Piskotin, 'Strategiya upravleniya', *Sovety narodnykh deputatov* (Dec., 1986), pp. 10–16; B. Markov, 'Byurokratizm–antipod demokratii', *Kommunist*, No. 11 (July, 1987), pp. 110–19.

The subject of political patronage has also begun to appear in the Soviet press. For a straightforward and detailed account of a particular patronage mechanism operating in one locality, see G. Ni-Li, 'Provintsial'naya istoriya', *Izvestiya* (Dec. 11, 1986).

25 E.G., Philip D. Stewart *et al.*, 'Political Mobility and the Soviet Political Process: A Partial Test of Two Models', *American Political Science Review*, Vol. 66 (Dec., 1972), pp. 1,269–90.

26 This point is made by Clapham, p. 27.

27 Gyula Jozsa, 'Political *Seilschaften* in the USSR', in Rigby and Harasymiw (eds.), pp. 139–72.

28 John P. Willerton, Jr., 'Patronage Politics in the Soviet Union' (unpublished Ph.D. dissertation; Ann Arbor, MI: University of Michigan, 1985), pp. 69–70; 'Patronage Networks and Coalition Building in the Brezhnev Era', *Soviet Studies*, Vol. 39 (April, 1987), pp. 175–204; esp., p. 177.

29 The individuals in question are V. S. Shevelukha who served as a Secretary of the KPB from 1974 to 1979, A. A. Smirnov, a member of Brezhnev's Dnepropetrovsk clique who was a KPB Secretary from 1968 to 1978, and T. Ya. Kiselev, who was Chair of the Belorussian Council of Ministers (1959–78) before becoming Deputy Chair of the Council of Ministers of the USSR (1978–80) and then returning to the BSSR in 1980 as First Secretary of the KPB (1980–2). Kiselev has been identified as a Brezhnev client by Michael Voslensky, *Nomenklatura: The Soviet Ruling Class* (Garden City, N.Y.: Doubleday and Co., 1984), p. 375; and by Baruch A. Hazan, *From Brezhnev to Gorbachev* (Boulder, CO: Westview Press, 1987), p. 58.

30 E. E. Sokolov's association with the Brezhnev network dates from his work in Kazakhstan as First Secretary of the Urlyutskii Raikom and, later, as

Secretary of the Party Committee of the Zhelezinskii Kolkhoz-Sovkhoz Administration of the Kazakh SSR. A. N. Aksenov's ties to the Brezhnev faction and the MCIG's connections to the Andropov-Gorbachev group are discussed in Chapter 7.

6. Does faction make a difference?

1 This number, 128, is greater than the number of MCIG members listed in Appendix B by virtue of the fact that membership in the latter is restricted to those who made at least one career move after having occupied one of the jobs in the data set. The figure of 128, then, includes all of those who can be identified as having occupied one of the jobs in the four organizational hierarchies in Minsk City (party, trade union, enterprise management or Komsomol) irrespective of whether or not they subsequently moved to other positions.

2 Jerry F. Hough, 'Women and Women's Issues in Soviet Political Debates', Dorothy Atkinson et al. (eds.) Women in Russia (Stanford: Stanford University Press, 1977), pp. 356–7; Genia Browning, 'Soviet Politics – Where Are the Women?', Barbara Holland (ed.) Soviet Sisterhood (Bloomington, IN: Indiana University Press, 1985), pp. 207–36.

3 Gail Warshofsky Lapidus, Women in Soviet Society (Berkeley: University of California Press, 1978), p. 200.

4 The percentage of women in the KPB rose from 18.5 per cent in 1966 to 24.2 per cent in 1978. Similarly, their representation on the raikoms and gorkoms of the KPB increased from 17.8 per cent in 1966 to 22.9 per cent in 1976. See Kommunisticheskaya partiya Belorussii v tsifrakh, 1918–1978 (Minsk: Belarus', 1978), pp. 155, 196.

5 Bohdan Harasymiw, 'Have Women's Chances for Political Recruitment in the USSR Really Improved?', Tova Yedlin (ed.) Women in Eastern Europe and the Soviet Union (New York: Praeger, 1980), pp. 159–71.

6 Kommunisticheskaya partiya Belorussii v tsifrakh, 1918–1978, p. 197.

7 Lapidus, p. 214.

8 Joel C. Moses, 'Indoctrination as a Female Political Role in the Soviet Union', Comparative Politics, Vol. 8 (July, 1976), pp. 525–47; 'Women in Political Roles' in Atkinson et al., pp. 333–53.

9 Identifications were made on the basis of either biographical data in Soviet publications or grammatical references to gender in newspaper articles. We must assume, however, that the 230 women who were identified represent only a fraction, however large or small, of the actual number of women in the sample.

10 Norton T. Dodge, 'Women in Professions' in Atkinson et al., pp. 205–24; esp., p. 215; Lapidus, p. 222.

11 Again, these figures indicate that the pattern in Belorussia is something of a microcosm of the USSR as a whole. On women in heavy industry, see Dodge, loc. cit. On women in agriculture, see Robert C. Stuart, 'Women in Soviet Rural Management', Slavic Review, Vol. 38 (Dec., 1979), pp. 603–13. On women in organizational 'housekeeping' roles, see Harasymiw, pp. 157–61.

12 Explanations for the particular patterns of political participation among women in the USSR commonly involve the idea that they are the outgrowth of traditional norms governing the role of women in the system which are in turn reflected in the educational and career choices that women are encouraged to make. For variants of this explanation, see Moses, 'Women in Political Roles'; Lapidus, *passim*; Browning, *passim*; Stuart, pp. 609–13.

A related reason for the supportive and nurturing political roles most often occupied by Soviet women has been put forward by the Soviet feminist, Alla Sariban. 'Soviet women', she writes, 'in some inner part of their beings, frequently without being aware of it, have a distinct tendency to make common cause with the Soviet system and to identify with it'. See her 'The Soviet Woman: Support and Mainstay of the Regime', Tatyana Mamonova (ed.) *Women and Russia* (Boston: Beacon, 1984), pp. 205–13; esp., p. 208.

13 See, in particular, Nicholas Lampert, *Whistleblowing in the Soviet Union: A Study of Complaints and Abuses Under State Socialism* (New York: Schocken, 1985); Constantine Simis, *USSR: The Corrupt Society* (New York: Simon and Schuster, 1982).

14 Gregory Grossman, 'Notes on the Illegal Private Economy and Corruption', in *Soviet Economy in a Time of Change* (Joint Economic Committee of the U.S. Congress; Washington, D.C.: GPO, 1979), pp. 834–54; esp., pp. 845–6.

15 'Indeterminate' here refers to those cases in which in the year following the reprimand, neither did the individual in question appear in the data sources nor did some other actor appear in the position that he held when the reprimand was issued.

16 The cases in question involve B. I. Petrov, a Partisan, who was twice reprimanded by Narkontrol' in 1976 and B. Ya. Timoshenko who was reprimanded by the KPB in 1980.

17 *Pravda* (Dec. 12, 1969).

18 The four who lost their jobs after publication of the article were: V. F. Yazykovich (First Secretary of the Gomel' Obkom), M. A. Klimenko (President of the Gomel' Oblispolkom), A. G. Kargin (Secretary of the Gomel' Obkom) and S. A. Shivakov (First Secretary of the Kalinkovich Raikom in Gomel' Oblast'). K. F. Khomyakov, Deputy President of the Gomel' Oblispolkom, was subjected to the same criticism by *Pravda* but managed to retain his job until 1975.

19 A. N. Aksenov, 'Shkola leninskoi partinosti', *Kommunist Belorussii* (No. 5, 1975), pp. 16–28.

20 *Sovetskaya Belorussiya* (Dec. 3, 1982).

21 *Sovetskaya Belorussiya* (July 9, 1985).

22 *Sovetskaya Belorussiya* (Dec. 25, 1985).

23 Slyun'kov's speech was reprinted in *Kommunist Belorussii* (No. 2, 1986), pp. 5–39.

7. Political succession

1 Werner G. Hahn, *The Politics of Soviet Agriculture, 1960–1970* (Baltimore: Johns Hopkins University Press, 1972), pp. 33–5, 80–6, 150–4.

2 Alexander Yanov, *The Drama of the Soviet 1960s: A Lost Reform* (Berkeley, CA: Institute of International Studies, University of California, 1984), p. 115.

3 Hahn, pp. 168–70; W. J. McGrath, 'The Politics of Soviet Federalism' (unpublished Ph.D. dissertation; Ottawa: Carleton University, 1981).

4 Amy Knight, 'Pyotr Masherov and the Soviet Leadership: A Study in Kremlinology', *Survey*, Vol. 26 (Winter, 1982), pp. 151–68; John P. Willerton, Jr., 'Patronage Networks and Coalition Building in the Brezhnev Era', *Soviet Studies*, Vol. 39 (April, 1987), p. 195; Yaroslav Bilinsky, 'Shcherbytskyi, Ukraine and Kremlin Politics', *Problems of Communism*, Vol. 32 (July–Aug., 1983), p. 3.

5 A number of observers have identified Kiselev as a Brezhnev client. See Michael Voslensky, *Nomenklatura: The Soviet Ruling Class* (Garden City, N.Y.: Doubleday and Co., 1984), p. 375; Baruch A. Hazan, *From Brezhnev to Gorbachev* (Boulder, CO; Westview Press, 1987), p. 58.

6 Boris Meissner, 'Transition in the Kremlin', *Problems of Communism*, Vol. 32 (Jan.–Feb., 1983), p. 10.

7 For evidence of foul play and interpretations of Masherov's death as an assassination, see Voslensky, pp. 374–6; Knight; Bilinsky, p. 19, note 105.

8 Hazan, pp. 60–1.

9 *Sovetskaya Belorussiya* (Dec. 13, 1983).

10 Archie Brown, 'Andropov: Reform *and* Discipline?', *Problems of Communism*, Vol. 32 (Jan.–Feb., 1983), pp. 18–31; esp., p. 27.

11 Jerry F. Hough, 'Gorbachev Consolidating Power', *Problems of Communism*, Vol. 36 (July–Aug., 1987), p. 35.

   Hough has also argued that Gorbachev, who appears to have had important responsibilities for cadres policy during Andropov's tenure as General Secretary, may well have been promoting a large number of supporters some two years before he became General Secretary himself. Accordingly, Slyun'kov's appointment to head the KPB in 1983 may well reflect Gorbachev's influence. See Hough's *Opening Up the Soviet Economy* (Washington, D.C.: Brookings, 1988), p. 31.

12 Thane Gustafson and Dawn Mann, 'Gorbachev's First Year: Building Power and Authority', *Problems of Communism*, Vol. 35 (May–June, 1986), pp. 2–3; Walter D. Connor, 'Social Policy Under Gorbachev', *ibid.* (July–Aug., 1986), p. 34.

13 Gustafson and Mann, p. 4.

14 Gurin's rise to this position was apparently prepared by V. I. Radomskii, one of two salaried officials of the KPB (mentioned in Chapter 5) who were posted to full-time Komsomol work in the BSSR. Having headed the Propaganda Department of the Minsk Gorkom, Radomskii became a secretary, and, eventually, the First Secretary of the Belorussian Komsomol. He left Komsomol work in 1976; Gurin was, then, likely recruited under his aegis.

15 See also the article by G. P. Razumovskii, Secretary of the CPSU for cadres, 'Sovershenstvovat' podgotovku i perepodgotovku rukovodyashchikh kadrov partii', *Kommunist*, No. 9 (June, 1987), pp. 3–13; esp., p. 5.

16 Thane Gustafson and Dawn Mann, 'Gorbachev's Next Gamble', *Problems of Communism*, Vol. 36 (July–Aug., 1987), pp. 1–20.

For a contrasting viewpoint that describes the impact of this policy in the Uzbek Republic, see I. Usmankhodzhaev, 'Rukovodstvo cherez kommunistov', *Sovety narodnykh deputatov* (Oct., 1987), pp. 17–26.

17 Although Aksenov's stock seemed to have dipped with the passing of Brezhnev, his service in Poland apparently attracted Gorbachev's favourable attention on grounds of policy orientation and political talent. See Christian Schmidt-Haver, *Gorbachev: The Path to Power* (Topsfield, MA: Salem House, 1986), p. 210.

18 See Gustafson and Mann, 'Gorbachev's Next Gamble'.

19 Hough reports that his sources in Moscow regard Slyun'kov as, if anything, a more radical economic reformer than Gorbachev. See 'Gorbachev Consolidating Power', p. 35.

20 Timothy J. Colton offers a related explanation for Gorbachev's sparing use of the traditional mechanisms of patronage, namely, a career history limited to one region of the USSR, Stavropol' Krai, and one organization, the party. See his *The Dilemma of Reform in the Soviet Union* (New York: Council on Foreign Relations, 1986), pp. 101–3.

Although Slyun'kov has held jobs in the apparatuses of both the party and state, his regional experience prior to becoming First Secretary of the KPB, was equally limited. Perhaps he then can be said to share with Gorbachev the same short 'tails' in personal matters.

With respect to the elusive issue of style, however, it appears that Slyun'kov does not measure up well to the standard set by Gorbachev. 'Slyun'kov is a technocrat', I heard many times from Moscow intellectuals in the Autumn of 1988, 'he doesn't understand politics'. Indeed, on the occasion of what seemed to have been his first important outing in the world of national politics – his sojourn in Lithuania in mid-November, 1988 – Slyun'kov failed to impart that sense of understanding and concern for which Gorbachev is so highly regarded in the USSR. The ostensible purpose of Slyun'kov's visit involved listening to, and negotiating with, the Lithuanian leadership and the Republic's popular front, Sajūdis, each of whom had expressed serious opposition to certain of the amendments to the Soviet Constitution that were under debate at the time. Slyun'kov's performance in these discussions, hours of which were carried live on Lithuanian television, was widely regarded as a heavy-handed attempt to steamroller his opponents in debate. As one of the leaders of Sajūdis told me: 'It was incredible. There we were explaining patiently to him our objections to the Constitutional project and our own plans for the future direction of the Republic. He didn't understand. He just repeated the things he had said before or just ignored the points that we had brought up. He seemed able to see things only in one way. It was at times really quite embarrassing.'

21 However, this is not to suggest that members of the MCIG have not made use of the national press in order to promote a favourable image for the group. For references to accomplishments in Minsk and, since they have

become the dominant group in the BSSR, Belorussia in which members of the MCIG lay stress on the importance of (their) leadership capabilities, see: M. Kovalev, 'K preimushchestvenno ekonomicheskim', *Sovety narodnykh deputatov* (May, 1988), pp. 19–28; V. Mikhasev, 'Minskaya Marka', *ibid*. (April, 1987), pp. 62–7; G. Tarazevich, 'Respubliki vysokaya sud'ba', *ibid*. (March, 1987), pp. 19–27; E. Gonzal'ez and N. Matukovskii, 'V dome pravitel'stva', *Izvestiya* (Oct. 27, 1987); and the interview with A. A. Reut, *ibid*. (Aug. 18, 1987).

22 See *Narodnoe khozyaistvo Belorusskoi SSR v 1982 g.* (Minsk: Belarus', 1983), pp. 79–94.

23 N. Matukovskii, '40 tsentnerov i bol'she', *Izvestiya* (Sept. 9, 1987).

24 *Kommunist Belorussii*, No. 2 (Feb., 1986), pp. 5–39.

25 By way of an afterword, we might mention in this respect a recent addition to the Belorussian leadership, Nikolai Igrunov, who has replaced MCIG member, G. G. Bartoshevich, as Second Secretary of the KPB in Oct., 1987. Igrunov's previous career has been confined to the Russian Republic and since 1974 he has been a functionary in the Organization-Party Work Department of the Central Committee of the CPSU. His transfer to the BSSR represents, then, a clear case of packing which, given both his background and his new job, indicates that Moscow intends changes in cadres policy in Belorussia. See Alexander Rahr, 'New Second Party Secretary in Belorussia', *Radio Liberty Research*, report no. 44 7–87 (Oct. 27, 1987).

Index

Soviet and East European Studies

35 WILLIAM J. CONYNGHAM
The modernization of Soviet industrial management

34 ANGELA STENT
From embargo to Ostpolitik
The political economy of West German–Soviet relations 1955–1980

32 BLAIR A. RUBLE
Soviet trade unions
Their development in the 1970s

31 R. F. LESLIE (ED.)
The history of Poland since 1863

30 JOZEF M. VAN BRABANT
Socialist economic integration
Aspects of contemporary economic problems in Eastern Europe

28 STELLA ALEXANDER
Church and state in Yugoslavia since 1945

27 SHEILA FITZPATRICK
Education and social mobility in the Soviet Union 1921–1934

23 PAUL VYSNÝ
Neo-Slavism and the Czechs 1898–1914

22 JAMES RIORDAN
Sport in Soviet society
Development of sport and physical education in Russia and the USSR

14 RUDOLF BIĆANIĆ
Economic policy in socialist Yugoslavia

The following series titles are now out of print:

1 ANDREA BOLTHO
Foreign trade criteria in socialist economies

2 SHEILA FITZPATRICK
The commissariat of enlightenment
Soviet organization of education and the arts under Lunacharsky, October 1917–1921

3 DONALD J. MALE
Russian peasant organisation before collectivisation
A study of commune and gathering 1925–1930

4 P. WILES (ED.)
The prediction of communist economic performance

5 VLADIMIR V. KUSIN
The intellectual origins of the Prague Spring
The development of reformist ideas in Czechoslovakia 1956–1967

6 GALIA GOLAN
The Czechoslovak reform movement